# Praise for Steve
# Nights in
# White Castle

"Following up on *Sting-Ray Afternoons,* about his 1970s youth, *Sports Illustrated* writer Steve Rushin explores his 1980s teen years in this humorous, lighthearted collection of anecdotes...Even with the fear of 'nuclear warheads raining down on Kansas' at any moment, Rushin describes what seems to be a safer, simpler time. For nostalgic baby boomers, this is a joyful romp down memory lane."

—*Publishers Weekly*

"In some ways, the sequel is better than the original...As *Sports Illustrated* readers know, Rushin's strength is his descriptive and playful prose."

—Casey Common, *Minneapolis Star Tribune*

"Affectionate and often funny...Rushin's account captures many slices of life in a time fast receding into the depths of nostalgia. Survivors and fans of the era will find this to be a pleasing book of meaningful touchstones."

—*Kirkus Reviews*

"Looking past the minutiae of everyday adolescent and young-adult life, *Nights in White Castle* is a story about dreams. It is the triumph of a kid from Middle America who idolized professional athletes and, as a journalist, interviewed them and covered their games. Knowing he had the maturity necessary to survive and thrive in New York and to succeed in his chosen profession was a sweet victory."

—Kevin P. McVicker, *Washington Times*

"Nobody does nostalgia like Rushin. He doesn't traffic in rose-tinted memories of golden afternoons but instead basks in the harsh lights of the White Castle parking lot and the unusual nighttime clientele those lights reveal... A fun and nuanced coming-of-age story, *Nights in White Castle* offers a rollicking ride down memory lane." —*Booklist*

# Nights in White Castle

# Nights in White Castle

## A Memoir

# Steve Rushin

BACK BAY BOOKS

Little, Brown and Company

New York  Boston  London

Back Bay Books / Little, Brown and Company
Hachette Book Group
1290 Avenue of the Americas, New York, NY 10104
littlebrown.com

Originally published in hardcover by Little, Brown and Company, August 2019
First Back Bay paperback edition, August 2020

Back Bay Books is an imprint of Little, Brown and Company, a division of Hachette Book Group, Inc. The Back Bay Books name and logo are trademarks of Hachette Book Group, Inc.

The publisher is not responsible for websites (or their content) that are not owned by the publisher.

The Hachette Speakers Bureau provides a wide range of authors for speaking events. To find out more, go to hachettespeakersbureau.com or call (866) 376-6591.

All photographs are from the collection of the author, unless otherwise noted.

ISBN 978-0-316-41943-7 (hc) / 978-0-316-41939-0 (pb)
LCCN 2019930544

10 9 8 7 6 5 4 3 2 1

LSC-C

Printed in the United States of America

*For Mike and Keith*
*and*
*my lupine saviors:*
*Alex Wolff*
*Jane Bachman Wulf*
*Rebecca Lobo*

# Contents

## PART III: STOMPIN' ON THE AVENUE BY RADIO CITY

# Nights in White Castle

# Introduction

# The Game of Life

On a bright spring day in his senior year of high school, my brother Jim and his buddy Fluff persuaded the manager of our local White Castle to lend them two steel-blue smocks and paper hats of the kind worn by Whitey's kitchen personnel everywhere. Jim put on matching pants, and Dad's white belt and loafers, and arrived that evening in period resplendence at Shultzy's house for the costume party that would live in lore among the Lincoln Class of 1979.

They left the party early, at eleven o'clock. Their night ended—as nights often did in Bloomington, Minnesota—at White Castle on Lyndale Avenue, where Jim and Fluff introduced themselves to the night manager as his newest employees, hired that very afternoon. They were assigned to the stainless-steel steam grill where the restaurant's famous five-holed hamburgers were loaded onto square buns. "It didn't bother anyone," Jim would say later, "that we were completely hammered."

Thirty minutes after Jim and Fluff punched in, Shultzy and the rest of the party turned up at the Castle, a hundred Lincoln Bears ravenous for gut bombs and roach burgers. White Castle hamburgers are known by two dozen other pejoratives, but my brother refused to serve anyone who used them. He insisted on decorum and brandished a stainless-steel burger-flipping implement at any patron who—literally or metaphorically—stepped out of line.

As that line grew, Jim frantically filled paper sacks with cheeseburgers and fries and handed them over the counter to his friends and classmates, bypassing the White Castle cashiers. When the night manager realized what he was witnessing—a meticulously planned hamburger heist, an inside job—he shouted at Barney, the Castle rent-a-cop, to chase Jim, Fluff, Shultzy, and the rest of the Lincoln seniors off the premises.

At the time, Charley Pride had a hit on the radio that went, "Burgers and fries and cherry pies, it was simple and good back then." And while Pride was singing of a vanished 1950s drive-in culture, our White Castle remained—as the 1970s turned into the '80s—a backdrop for our burgeoning dreams.

White Castle was a halfway house for adolescents as they moved from child to teen to young adult, in that brief period when life resembles a classroom evolution poster: the child rising from his Schwinn Sting-Ray; now walking upright with his car keys in hand; now striding away from home holding a suitcase.

The question I got most often as a child in the 1970s was "What do you want to be when you grow up?" My answers varied along the usual lines of fantasy—fireman, Vikings wide receiver, author—but the question also could be taken at face value: what do you want to *be,* as in how do you want to live, *where* do you want to live, what kind of person will you *become*?

For me, that becoming happened in the 1980s between the ages of thirteen and twenty-two. For forty-five minutes on that spring night in 1979—with an endless string of nights laid out before them like runway lights—Jim and Fluff play-acted as workers at White Castle. But their complementary futures had already taken shape: Jim would play ice hockey in college while Fluff would study dentistry—the symbiotic pursuits of best friends.

I was in seventh grade in 1979, and what *I* wanted to become was Jim: high school athlete, unflappable prankster, cinematic tough guy. For many years, without provocation, Jim made a highly specific threat to his three brothers: "I will rip your lips off." It wasn't until he left home for good—and I was in high school myself, frequenting the Castle on weekend nights—that I could pass his former bedroom door without clamping my lips together in self-protection.

When the five Rushin children were still under one roof, we gathered on rare occasions at the kitchen table and played Milton Bradley's The Game of Life. As in actual life, The Game of Life encouraged participants to attend college, get a job, fall in love, amass a fortune, and have children in the form of pink or blue plastic pegs that plugged into little plastic cars. Those cars sometimes crashed, triggering hospital bills and higher insurance premiums. Luckier players got stock dividends or identical twins. Life—and for all I knew, life—was a zero-sum game. It could only end at one of two places: Millionaire Acres or the Poor Farm.

At the center of the board was a wheel of fortune. I would sometimes spin it as a solitary pursuit, just to see what number came up. The following pages are set during that quicksilver time—high school, college, and leaving home forever—when the great wheel is still spinning and, for a moment at least, everything in life remains possible.

# PART I

# In the High School Halls, in the Shopping Malls

# 1.

# Nights in White Castle

There are two masterworks called *1984* that the Class of 1984 has to reckon with. The first is required reading for seniors at John F. Kennedy High School, whose address is stamped all over the Signet Classics in our hands. Those addresses are a theft deterrent, the exploding dye in a bank robber's bag of cash, meant to shame and identify a would-be thief, though who would want to steal a copy is an open question in room 101. "As *if*," says a girl in front of me. Her friend replies: "I know, right?"

On page 9, deeper than most of my classmates will make it into Orwell's dystopia, Winston Smith sees a book in the window of a London junk shop and is "stricken immediately by an overwhelming desire to possess it." I know the feeling. Fanning the pages of the paperback, I see a stick figure drawn in blue ballpoint by a previous student spring to life in flip animation. He runs across the upper-right corner of every right-hand page of the book in a futile effort to escape. It's what many of us here want to do.

This isn't the *1984* that any of us cares about in 1984. The new album by Van Halen—also called *1984,* rendered in Roman numerals as *MCMLXXXIV*—better reflects our senior year, yielding "Hot for Teacher," "Panama," and the unavoidable "Jump." In the video looping on MTV, David Lee Roth leaps about in yellow spandex pants worn *under* a red Speedo—what my big brother Jim would call, when mocking Speedo wearers at Bush Lake Beach, a "marble bag." As in: "Look at the squid in the purple marble bag."

Last week, before basketball practice, some fry tried to persuade our team that David Lee Roth could beat every one of us in basketball. "Diamond Dave," he said in a voice honey-cured by Marlboros. "There's a *real* athlete."

This brought howls from my teammates, some of whom had just seen Van Halen in concert at the Saint Paul Civic Center, where Roth dressed exactly as he does on MTV. "Roth came on like Charo in a codpiece," went the withering review in the next morning's paper, "a crimson jockstrap worn over his tie-dyed pants." And now, for the first time, this startling image is available for home delivery, piped directly into my family room. For I arrive home on this day to find that a remarkable change of fortune has occurred at 2809 West 96th Street. While I was in Reading Comprehension, cable TV arrived at the Rushin house, in January of 1984. The coaxial cable buried beneath South Brook finally snaked its way into our family room like a long, lit fuse. I can practically hear it hissing.

A wood-paneled cable box sits on top of our wood-paneled TV, trying and failing to camouflage itself. There are twelve buttons on the front of the box and, next to them, a plastic lever with three settings. That lever, like the gearshift on my old Schwinn three-speed, turns those twelve buttons into thirty-six channels, where this morning there were seven. Each of the buttons makes a satisfying *chunk* when I press it, the same sound the cigarette machine at the Bloomington Ice Garden makes when I idly pull its knobs.

"Pull *this* knob," Tom would say if he were here, except that he's no longer sharing our bedroom, as he did for all of my seventeen years. Tom is two hundred miles away, a freshman at Iowa State, where his genius for pyrotechnical mayhem is already playing out on a grander stage, in and around the fraternity houses and emergency rooms of Ames, Iowa.

My own room. At long last there is no shadowy figure five feet away in the dark, whispering to me over a midnight soundtrack of Steely Dan cassettes. I still watch the tape deck's wheels turn when I can't sleep, like little spoked ship's wheels forever steering to the right. But now there is no brother bursting through the door to breathe in my face on a Friday night and say, "Smell anything?"

"Peanut butter and Grain Belt?" I'd ask, sending him down the stairs to spoon more Skippy onto his tongue, or bite into a raw onion as if it were an apple, anything to disguise the beer on his breath.

In Tom's place, there is only an empty twin bed, forever made. His high school mementoes—graduation tassel, prom photo, pin-backed homecoming button—have turned our room into half a museum. On his side, in the wall-to-wall blue carpet, Mom's vacuum tracks remain untrammeled. I half wish Tom had left a set of footprints in them, as at

Mann's Chinese Theatre in Hollywood, to prove he'd ever been here at all.

I drop my book bag. In it is the copy of *1984* that I've just stolen from room 101 at JOHN F. KENNEDY HIGH SCHOOL, NICOLLET AT OLD SHAKOPEE ROAD, BLOOMINGTON, MINNESOTA 55420 (as the cover stamp reminds me). I add it to a small library of paperbacks I've stolen elsewhere—including Roger Kahn's *The Boys of Summer* and Jim Bouton's *Ball Four*—fruits of my budding career in biblio-kleptomania.

Downstairs, the new cable box sits like so many boxes of fable before it. Pandora's box, the presents under the Christmas tree, the wrapped prizes on the TV game show *Treasure Hunt*. Except that I already know what's in the cable box, disguised to look like wood. This Trojan horse is smuggling into our house Bananarama's "Cruel Summer" and Atlanta Braves telecasts and scrambled soft-core movies on premium channels that Mom and Dad scarcely know exist.

Two houses down, a different wood-paneled box has arrived in the Nelsons' driveway: a brand-new Plymouth Voyager, a whole new kind of automobile for the model year 1984. While it looks like a bloated Ford Country Squire and calls itself a wagon—the "Magic Wagon," in ads—the Voyager is really the death knell for the station wagon, the fixture of every South Brook driveway only a few years ago. The Voyager is a kind of van—also sold as a Dodge Caravan, the name a double entendre suggesting it's part car, part van. But really, it's a smaller version of the van I wanted in the '70s, the kind that had wall-to-wall carpeting, a tinted bubble window, and a mural painted on the side—a wolf howling at the moon. The Voyager is a miniature van. A minivan.

All these wood-paneled boxes—television, cable box, minivan—designed to transport, to take us away from our humdrum present, to move us from where we are now to a place less ordinary. I want to leave home, I suppose—run off the pages of *1984,* like that stick figure whose physique I share—but mostly I want to stay, and I've heard very few pop songs about teenagers wanting to stay. "She's *Not* Leaving Home"? "We *Don't* Gotta Get Outta This Place"? I feel myself, with every passing week, walking the plank into adulthood, nudged at sword point another foot closer to the drop.

Jim, the oldest of the five Rushin children, graduated last spring from Providence College. In the final hockey game of his career, the Friars lost 2–0 to Wisconsin in the NCAA semifinals in Grand Forks, North Dakota. Weeks later, at Jim's graduation, Dad gave him the Golden Handshake, officially absolving Don Rushin of any future financial responsibility for his firstborn. With that, Jim vanished from sight. He shares a house in the city of my birth, Elmhurst, Illinois, and works in the business office of the Sheraton Hotel near O'Hare Airport. Where once he gave me the 99 Bump—99 shots to my sternum with a raised knuckle on his right fist—he now gives me unsolicited presents: most recently, from the accounting office of the Sheraton, the autograph of hotel guest Ivan Lendl. The dour tennis champion from Czechoslovakia signed the translucent onionskin imprint of his American Express card, unaware that it would be sent to a seventeen-year-old boy in Minnesota, who keeps it in a Tretorn shoebox in his closet. It is a small comfort to have access, should I ever need it, to the vast fortune of a four-time Grand Slam runner-up.

My two younger siblings remain under our roof, a roof still spangled with sporting goods—the dry-docked Frisbees and guttered tennis balls that are already becoming a relic of a rapidly fading era in the Rushin yard and driveway.

In a few months, Amy will complete her nine-year stretch at Nativity—a.k.a. Captivity—the Catholic K through 8 whose desktops bear the scratched initials of three previous Rushin children. She already has one foot in Holy Angels, the Catholic high school, where she'll be a cheerleader, performing on ice skates between periods of boys' hockey games. One night, doing the splits at the blue line, she'll remain there, adhered to the freshly Zambonied ice, crotch frozen to the rink like a tongue to a lamppost. Her complicated removal will involve hot water and a putty knife.

John is in fifth grade at Nativity. In one more year, Mom and Dad will allow him to bail and become the first Rushin to attend public junior high school, whose girls will routinely phone our house late at night, asking for "Johnny." Dad will wake from a blubbering coma to answer his bedside phone and hear a giggling high-pitched voice purr: "Is Johnny there?" A comic-strip stream of ampersands and exclamation marks will issue from Dad's mouth before he slams down the receiver of his Band Aid–colored Ma Bell telephone. Its blunt handset weighs three pounds. That phone, an instrument of authority, is already antiquated next to the push-button, plastic models of modernity. On New Year's Day, Ma Bell was "broken up," smashed to pieces like a false idol.

It isn't just Jim, Tom, Amy, John, Ma Bell, and me—everyone is moving on, matriculating in one way or another. When Mom asked me last year where I wanted to go to college

I said, "The U," as the University of Minnesota is known here. It's a few miles away and as far from home as I care to imagine living. If the biggest rock star on the planet—bigger even than Diamond Dave—has stayed in Minnesota, why shouldn't I? Some girls from Kennedy claim they'll be *in* the movie Prince filmed here last summer, dancing in front of the stage down at First Avenue. They're waiting for this summer's release of *Purple Rain* to see if they made the cut.

"I like Hollywood," Prince said on TV, "but I like Minnesota better." Nobody in Minnesota has any desire to live anywhere else. But my inertia is particularly acute, for while I like Minnesota, I like my particular corner of it—the maroon love seat in our family room—even better. *Maroon* is right. I am marooned here, as on a desert island.

Dad comes home from work one evening and announces some news he heard on Sid Hartman's WCCO sports update. Tom Copa, the football and basketball star at Coon Rapids High School, has decided to play college basketball at Marquette University in Milwaukee.

"Okay," I reply.

*"Marquette,"* Dad says, as if I didn't quite hear him, "is a Jesuit school with a journalism department. It's close to home but not too close."

"How close?"

"Three hundred miles."

"That's close?"

Journalism would help me transition from stealing books to writing them. Mom and Dad would love to see me back in Catholic school, where the stealing was always done by public school kids who used my desk for CCD on Sundays, helping themselves to BIC pens and Pink Pearl erasers. So I apply to Marquette and am accepted and resolve to attend school there for the next four years, despite never having visited the campus or even Milwaukee or any other colleges.

But I do go to the Penn Lake Library, warm and snug on a winter's day, snow drifting at the window, to research my future home. Milwaukee has the second most bars per capita of any city in the United States, after New Orleans, and is the birthplace of Miller and all the beers that sound like blunt-force blows in a Batman comic. Pabst! Blatz! Schlitz!

Schlitz is "The beer that made Milwaukee famous," not to be confused with Schlitz's secondary brand, Old Milwaukee, the beer that "tastes as great as its name." I know these beer slogans like I know the back of my baseball cards, for I have been steeped in beer without ever having drunk one thanks to TV and radio.

Minnesota's own Hamm's commercials had an Indian tom-tom drumbeat backing their jingle: "From the land of sky-blue waters (wa-a-ters), from the land of pines, lofty balsams, comes the beer refreshing, Hamm's the beer refreshing, Haaaammm's."

These songs are every bit as ubiquitous as the Top 40 hits on Casey Kasem's countdown, and occupy the same permanent place in my memory. "When you say *BUD*-weis-er! You've said it all."

There was no inoculating even the nine-year-old me against Budweiser's insidious jingles. Like marketing a power company, Budweiser's advertising seems unnecessary, promoting a product that is all but compulsory in American homes. "Here comes the king, here comes the big number one. Budweiser beer the king is second to none..." is locked in a clinch for my affection with "The king is coming, let's hear the call. When you say Bud, you've said it all..."

Budweiser is a behemoth. Its label is full of filigrees and fancy script and even a kind of Anheuser-Busch coat of arms. Schlitz has a globe on its can, connoting a kind of alcoholic megalomania. Pabst has its famous blue ribbon for being—as it says right there on the can—"Selected as America's Best in 1893." This is a sad boast, as when nearby towns leave up faded signs at the city limits: WELCOME TO DRIVELTON, CLASS A SOFTBALL CHAMPIONS, 1967.

I can't think of Marquette without thinking of Milwaukee, and I can't think of Milwaukee without thinking of beer, a key component of a happy existence. "Life's too short to settle for less," Schlitz says. "Go for the gusto or don't go at all."

Miller Lite has a stable of ex-jocks and showbiz personalities, among them Bob Uecker and Dick Butkus, who are always having a good time in a bar.

Miller's non-Lite beer has the best commercials, invariably about manly themes, narrated in a manly baritone. "Thirty years ago on a hot summer's day your father taught you how to dig for clams," goes one. "Now that it's a job, the sun seems hotter and the day seems longer. But the clams taste just as sweet. And now comes Miller time." The men in these commercials are always deep-sea fishing or chopping down trees or engaged in violent logrolling contests or manning oil rigs or steadfastly refusing to be thrown from a bucking bull. The Miller bottle is clear, see-through, its golden contents visible behind a label that calls it "The Champagne of Beers." The mellow-gold, soft-rock jingle at the end of every ad goes: "If you've got the time, we've got the beer—Miller beer."

Miller is more or less what I know about Milwaukee. Detroit means cars, San Francisco means Rice-A-Roni, and Milwaukee means Miller. I don't know what my future holds, but I know that it lies abroad, in Milwaukee, across an ocean of beer.

Mom and Dad know I'm inert. Six months after my sixteenth birthday, Mom asked me, "Don't you want to get a driver's license?"

"I guess."

"You *guess*? I can't chauffeur you for the rest of your life."

When the Driver's Ed instructor picked me up in a car for my first lesson, he asked me how many times I'd driven before. "A rough estimate," he said. "A round number. Ballpark it for me."

I told him I had never driven in my life. Tom, by contrast, had logged at least a hundred illicit miles before he was sixteen. At fourteen, his buddy Dwight would take his father's station wagon—the Chuckwagon—and mow down garbage cans. Their steel lids would crash like cymbals. Tom and Dwight knew the garbage pickup days in various neighborhoods like other kids knew their baseball statistics. When John is fourteen, Mom and Dad will go to the movies one night while their youngest child plows over a neighbor's mailbox after taking Dad's car for a spin in a snowstorm. But not me. I reminded the instructor that driving without a license is illegal and would likely go down on my Permanent Record.

He looked me in the face to see if I was serious, then

gripped his clipboard with both hands and gently slapped it against his forehead in our driveway.

And so began my six required hours of behind-the-wheel instruction, driving fifteen miles an hour below the speed limit, popping the trunk when trying to activate the windshield wipers, activating the windshield wipers when trying to signal a turn, and signaling every turn a quarter of a mile in advance.

My teacher didn't care for the way I ignored his instructions to merge onto I-35W while building slowly to fifty-five miles an hour, choosing instead to lock up the brakes at the end of the on-ramp, in a panicky homage to Mom, who often does the same, necessitating a zero-to-sixty-five merge ahead of an onrushing semi. My death grip on the ten-and-two positions of the steering wheel was often supplemented by the instructor's hands on the same wheel, so that we made our way around Bloomington wrestling for control in the ten-and-two and nine-and-one positions.

After 360 harrowing minutes parceled out over many weeks, I was awarded my diploma from the Esse School of Driving. After more weeks watching Mom or Dad pump invisible brakes in the shotgun seat of the Honda while I squired them about town with my paper learner's permit, I took my road test on a closed course and got an early insight into DMV inefficiency. Despite failing to parallel park ("If those cones were real cars, you'd have two separate insurance claims") and blowing one stop sign ("That's what is known as a 'rolling stop'"), I was awarded a Minnesota driver's license. It becomes the third thing—along with my Hennepin County library card and a YMCA membership card that identifies me as Hernando Gomez—to go in my blue nylon wallet with the Velcro seal. ("Velcro, wonder fabric of the eighties," declares David Letterman, who devotes an entire show to the hook-and-loop sensation.)

A month after I received my license, Mom and Dad flew to Monte Carlo on a sales-incentive trip for 3M and, on returning, asked me to pick them up at the airport. But when I approached the curb outside arrivals, where Mom and Dad stood tanned and smiling, suitcases at their sides, I also saw a traffic cop instructing the idling cars to move along. In preemptive obedience to the law, I passed Mom and Dad by and made another ten-minute loop of the Lindbergh Terminal. When I approached a second time, I saw the same cop, and the same parents. This time Mom and Dad weren't smiling. Dad was gesturing wildly for me to pull over, but I powered past him in a panic, beginning another ten-minute circum-navigation of the airport. The third time I approached, Dad was standing in traffic with both suitcases, defying me to run him over. "What in the hell is the matter with you?" he said by way of greeting.

It was a rhetorical question, but I answered honestly. "I don't know."

The driver's license is one more object on a scavenger hunt. Contact lenses, braces, deodorant, confirmation certificate, eighth-grade diploma, driver's license...the prize at the end of all this is adulthood. In eight months I'll turn eighteen and by law go to the post office to register for Selective Service, in case the army reinstates the draft, which is Dad's dream. "Uncle Sam straightened me out," he says. "Taught me discipline, the importance of a made bed, how to shine my shoes..." Six weeks after my eighteenth birthday, I'll vote in the presidential election. Reagan will win every state but my own, further proof of Minnesota exceptionalism.

Shaving is another rite of passage. In eighth grade, Jim said to me: "Nice 'stache. You gonna shave or let the cat lick it off?"

One Saturday morning Dad turned on the hot tap in the upstairs bathroom, showed me how to cup my hands like a supplicant, fill them with hot water, and dip my face into my raised palms as if bobbing for apples. He dispensed a dollop of Foamy on my fingertips, I swiped it across my upper lip, and—after seven downward scrapes with a single-blade disposable Schick—I had shaved. At Dad's instruction, I applied bits of toilet paper to staunch the bleeding where I'd cut myself. A stinging splash of Skin Bracer numbed my upper lip. It felt rubberized. I could still feel the burn at the bus stop. Like the Party spokesman on the two-way telescreen in *1984,* I now had "skin roughened by coarse soap and blunt razor blades and the cold of winter."

There's enough hair on the back of my hands that my friend Dan Olson greets me the way Paul Lynde once greeted Herman Munster. Instead of shaking my hand, he pets it and says, "Oh, you brought your doggie." We have a hundred similar inside rituals, my friends and I—many of them dating to kindergarten—but this one is literally a secret handshake. Every time I see Oly, I extend my hand for petting. Likewise, we retract our hands into our sleeves before shaking hands with Danny Keane, universally known as Gator. At lunch,

Oly will put his right hand in a ziplock sandwich bag before offering his hand for shaking. In eighth grade, at Nativity, we removed a ski glove from a coat pocket at the handshake of peace during Mass. Gator's skin is no longer excessively dry, if it ever was, but our nicknames are built from the smallest physical traits and tics. Some are an obvious corruption of the person's name. There's a kid in our grade named Bill Folz whom we inevitably call The Wallet. But most of our nicknames are subtler. I have difficulty remembering names and call most people "man" as a stand-in.

"Hey, Rush."

"Hey, man."

As a result, my grade school handle of "Rush" has given way to my high school nickname of "Man." Even Dad has picked up on my propensity for the word and will sometimes use it against me in a kind of parental jujitsu: "Hey, *man,*" he'll say, in a beatnik voice twenty-five years out of date. "Get your shoes off the ottoman, *man,* and bring me the Schedule, *man,* because I'm not watching this guy play guitar in a leotard. *Man.*"

In their effort to get me eventually to move out, my parents do not have an ally in cable TV, which is urging me to stay in. By 1984, cable is in 40.5 percent of the 83.8 million "U.S. television households." It only seems we're the last to get it. In fact we're right on time. *TV Week* magazine—the Sunday newspaper supplement known in our house as the Schedule (as in Dad's exhaled question to himself: "Where in the *hell* is the Schedule?")—has just been redesigned to accommodate the new universe of channels. Readers of the

*Star and Tribune,* accustomed to their seven-channel world, open the paper to find a full-page grid crosshatched with obscure networks (ARTS) and even more obscure programs. The Saturday lineup for SPN includes *Crafts 'n' Things, Sewing with Nancy,* and *Personal Computer,* which is odd, as SPN—a truncation of ESPN—is billed as an all-sports network.

All of this is confusing to a great many readers of the *Star and Tribune.* In weeks to come, the paper's Letters to the Editor will make for hilarious out-loud reading by Dad, declaiming from his Archie Bunker chair.

"Here's a good one," he says. "Henry A. Carson of Excelsior writes, 'After two weeks trying to decipher the new *TV Week,* I have decided to return to Princeton to pursue my master's degree.'"

Dad finds these rubes hilarious. We picture them gazing in openmouthed wonder at the new TV schedule.

We've just gotten our first-ever channel changer and suddenly it is obsolete. The "flipper," we call it, though others insist it is a "clicker." A single silver button on top of a black barrel activates a steel bolt that somehow, miraculously, makes the dial turn on the television from across the room. And now, with the arrival of a cable box that requires the manual pushing of buttons, the clicker is useless.

I walk across the room, turn on MTV, and there it is, in all its crimson glory: Diamond Dave's Marble Bag.

More happily, in the back of *TV Week* is an alphabetical listing of every movie on cable for the next seven days. It's a treasure map directing me to "adult situations," florid profanity, and "nudity."

**The Beach Girls** / Freewheeling girls cruise and carouse at Malibu Beach. Debra Blee, Val Kline. 1983. Adult situations, nudity. 91 m. TMC / Thu. 3:30 p.m.

**Black Emanuelle** / Photographer neglects her job to explore other areas. Laura Gemser, Karin Schubert, Angelo Infanti. 1975. Adult situations, nudity. 91 m. MAX / Wed. 1:15 a.m.

**American Desire** / Lovers search elsewhere for fulfillment. Veronica Hart, Robert Kerman. 1981. Adult situations, language, nudity. 79 m. SPC / Mon. 10:00 p.m.

Retreating to the basement—for there is a new cable box down there as well—I switch between two unsubscribed-to channels at lightning speed. Back and forth, back and forth, back and forth. Doing so reveals, for a split second, a wavy image in the static "snow." It is a bare breast, possibly—though it could well be an elbow. Checking the Schedule, I realize what's playing is *Herbie, the Love Bug,* and what I thought might be a breast is in fact a sentient cream-colored Volkswagen Beetle. Only one thing is verifiably indecent, and that is the hour. It's 4:30 in the afternoon.

As I flip between premium channels, the snow briefly clears and a squiggly image emerges for a beat, possibly of two Swedes in a hayloft, more likely of pay-per-view professional boxing. And then the channel reverts to its scrambled state of snow and squiggles, so that sex, in my mind, becomes something that happens sporadically in a snowstorm, while reflected in a fun-house mirror. In a January blizzard, perhaps, on the barren State Fairgrounds. In Minnesota, on a night-dark

January afternoon in my basement, the scenario is not entirely out of the question.

Indeed, the actresses all seem to be Scandinavian. A costar of *She's 19 and Ready* is Gina Janssen. The costars of *The Silence* ("A free-loving young woman and her lesbian sister try to go their separate ways") are Ingrid Thulin and Gunnel Lindblom. The credits for all these movies read like the Minneapolis White Pages. Even Prince's last name is Nelson.

Within five minutes, I stop the futile button punching and just read the *TV Week* movie listings. They are soft-core erotic literature—very short stories serialized every Sunday in the *Star and Tribune*. The plot descriptions are so vague as to be titillating: "Visitors are entertained by an estate owner and her nieces" or "Two young people stranded in the desert discover secrets about each other."

Television's new wonders do not stop here. As an executive at 3M—Mickey Mouse Mining, as it's known at our dinner table—Dad is charged with selling as much audio and video recording tape as he possibly can. In that role, he receives a letter from a Los Angeles inventor who has a secret product that he promises will revolutionize home entertainment, turning every home into a home theater. Enormous profits could accrue to Mickey Mining, makers of blank VHS cassettes for home VCRs, should 3M acquire this wondrous new technology. Dad is dispatched to Los Angeles for an exclusive first look at this modern-day Edison in his laboratory.

When he returns from L.A., Dad tells Mom that his map of Los Angeles—he has a hundred other maps in the basement, for New York, Vienna, Tokyo, Buenos Aires—led him from the Hertz lot at LAX straight to a little bungalow beneath a freeway flyover. A little man answered the door, and his little wife bade Dad to sit in an overstuffed armchair with a floral print. It was the seat of honor in their house. As Dad removed a pillow from his lumbar, the lady disappeared to the kitchen and returned through the swinging door with a glass of milk. The little man asked Dad to sign a multipage nondisclosure agreement in triplicate, after which curtains were drawn, lights extinguished, TV tuned to an afternoon soap. The man asked if Dad was ready to experience the twenty-first century. Dad assured him, with growing impatience, that he was. At which time the man withdrew from a drawer...

"A pair of glasses," Dad says, sighing heavily. "Eyeglasses. With a big magnifying glass bolted onto the front."

The man solemnly placed the glasses on Dad's face and made minute adjustments to the fit. For a few moments, the three of them—inventor, wife, and Mickey Mining executive—sat in reverential silence, watching the soap. After a respectable interval, during which he drained his glass of milk, Dad complimented the inventor on his remarkable achievement, assured him that the 3M Company would soon be in touch, politely excused himself, got into his rental car at the curb, and waved goodbye to Mr. and Mrs. Magoo, who waved gratefully back from their doorstep.

If Dad couldn't see the future of home entertainment through those glasses, at least the phrase "home entertainment" is no longer an oxymoron. My friend Kevin got Pong when it came out nearly ten years ago, but already that black-and-white pioneer has been consigned to the curbside trash barrel of history. Every other kid in South Brook now has Atari or Intellivision, eight bits of spellbinding joy in primary colors and with synthesized sound effects. Intellivision was the family present last Christmas. Like Atari—and the cable box and the TV itself—Intellivision's inner workings are concealed in a box veneered in simulated wood paneling. We no longer have to pump quarters into machines in the lobby of the Southtown Theatre, or the smoke-shrouded cavern of Beanie's Arcade. Our short stack of Intellivision game cartridges—Pitfall, Dig Dug, Donkey Kong—beckons me to stay in the basement under self-imposed house arrest.

More change arrived on our doorstep. Where once there were two newspapers—the morning *Tribune* and the afternoon *Star*—Minneapolis now has just one: the *Star and Tribune,* conjoined by a conjunction in a marriage of economic convenience, pregnant with ad pages and thumped on our stoop every day by 7 a.m.

In it this morning is an ad for Sound of Music (slogan: "The Best Buy Company"). Once the place to buy your turntable, tape deck, and speakers, Sound of Music now offers touch-tone phones for fourteen bucks. These new phones are lightweight, plastic, push-button beauties with squared-off ear- and mouthpieces. Space-age. Our banana-yellow wall-mounted rotary-dial phone in the kitchen, with its round ear- and mouthpieces, is, by contrast, a reminder to Mom that her kitchen is outdated. Sound of Music still sells rotary-dial phones from ITT and Western Electric, but they are used, cut-rate, and "refurbished."

Mom has plans to refurbish the kitchen, change its harvest-gold palette to all white. White tile will show every speck of dirt, but Mom considers this a benefit, the better to root out the filth. I've seen it said, in the journalism books I've begun to hoard, that "sunlight is the best disinfectant." But Mom knows better. When she has finished her daily ministrations—a chemical cocktail of Pine-Sol, Formula 409, and Wisk—those white tiles will gleam like the teeth of TV's Wink Martindale.

The journalism book I most recently read is *The News Business,* by John Chancellor and Walter R. Mears, bought with my own money at B. Dalton Bookseller in the Southdale mall. B. Dalton is another Minnesota invention, and this is its flagship store, its first ever, founded by Bruce Dayton, whose Dayton's department store anchors Southdale. B. Dayton changed one letter of his own name when christening B. Dalton, which now has more than seven hundred branches nationwide.

In the weeks to come, I will notice Sound of Music's name becoming less prominent in their ubiquitous display ads in the newspaper, while the store's slogan—"The Best Buy Company"—is printed in an ever-larger font. Soon the name Sound of Music will disappear entirely, leaving only the slogan as the chain's new name: The Best Buy Company, operating out of Sound of Music's modest outlets, but also from a Burnsville "superstore."

The superstore will come to be known as a "big box." Like the Voyager minivan, or the cable box, or the VCR, or Mattel's miraculous Intellivision, a big box can hold everything a seventeen-year-old boy could want and fear. Like Winston Smith, I am stricken with an overwhelming desire to possess it. "It" being everything: books, cars, games, the company of girls, life itself. American Desire indeed.

*   *   *

Even better than Staying In is Going Out, which usually means Friday night, after a basketball game, freshly showered, feet still sore, cruising triumphantly in my navy-blue Kennedy letter jacket with the terry-cloth "84" limned in gold on the leather sleeve. I wear a terry-cloth shirt under the jacket as we aimlessly cruise the Strip.

There are strips marginally more famous than ours. But the Vegas Strip, the Sunset Strip, even the Gaza Strip—whose name is frequently uttered on WCCO radio, the AM news giant and only station that plays in Dad's car—all confirm what we already suspect: that the 494 Strip in Bloomington is a place of endless excitement and bottomless interest to the outside world. Bloomington, like Hollywood, is strip-worthy. My best friend, Mike McCollow, and I cruise this wide river of asphalt in Dr. Terry McCollow's Bonneville Brougham, charting a course for No Place in Particular, occasionally stopping for gas, which Mike charges to his dad's Mobil credit card, to which we also bill tins of smokeless tobacco and cans of pop.

"Won't Terry be pissed?" I ask Mike, referring to his dad by his first name. We all do this now, even with our own parents, though never within their earshot. "He can't be happy that six tins of Copenhagen and a twelve-pack of Mountain Dew are billed to him." But Terry McCollow, DDS, has to be tired by now—Mike is the youngest of four—and never says anything about the charges.

I-494 is the southern section of the freeway that encircles the Twin Cities. But it's the ten-mile stretch running east and west through Bloomington—the 494 Strip—that is world famous to Minnesotans. On its banks are the bars and restaurants and hotels and nightclubs patronized by our local athletes and anchormen, to say nothing of the B-list entertainers who croon or crack wise at the Carlton Celebrity Room dinner theater, which has brought "Vegas-style entertainment" to the prairie.

Tomorrow morning, we'll pile into the Bonnie again—Mike and I and Gator and our buddy Martin—and hit another hotspot on the Strip: Wally McCarthy's Lindahl Olds, the world's largest Oldsmobile dealership, with its yellow-and-white-striped circus tent, red pennant flags aflutter, and an annual advertising budget that must exceed Coca-Cola's. Every Saturday morning, WCCO radio broadcasts live from Wally's, offering free hot dogs, popcorn, and pop to anyone who walks in, which is what we do most weekends, pretending to be any group of kids in the market for an Oldsmobile Cutlass Supreme. We sword-swallow several hot dogs and self-consciously kick a few tires, then leave with popcorn and persuade ourselves that once again we've made fools of gullible grown-ups.

But the Strip, like us, is most alive at night, when the lighted signs reflect off the windows of passing cars and rinse my cheeks in neon pastels. The Rusty Scupper is known to us as the Crusty Supper, a multilevel bar and restaurant whose nautical theme demands ropes and fishing nets and stenciled life rings. None of us has ever set foot in the place, but we have a vague idea that its sunken bar is a thriving pickup joint, where men who wear hats like Captain Stubing from *The Love Boat* buy Harvey Wallbangers for women who resemble Heather Locklear.

Vikings quarterback Tommy Kramer—renowned as Two-

Minute Tommy for his last-second heroics on the football field—is the unofficial mayor of the Strip, where his late nights have earned him a supplementary nickname: Too-Many Tommy.

From the shotgun seat of the Bonnie the bars and restaurants go by in a blur: Mother Tucker's, Chi-Chi's, the Ground Round, all these places our parents go when they Go Out, their names on the matchbooks Mom keeps in an ashtray above the range in our kitchen. Eddie Webster's, Steak and Ale, the Decathlon Club—the places they smelled of when they came home to dismiss the babysitter.

The Bonneville's seats are upholstered in a synthetic crushed velvet. And so am I, practically, in my plush terry-cloth V-neck. (I've come to think of it as Terry Cloth, named for Dr. Terry McCollow and his Bonneville Brougham.) We are rolling in deep velour, and the tape deck is playing its equivalent—the soft textures, the sonic velour, of George Benson, Al Jarreau, Grover Washington Jr., and the Crusaders.

Near the eastern terminus of the Strip, past Airport Bowl but before the airport itself, is the Airport Inn. The building is forlorn, and at seventeen, I am already nostalgic for what it once was. The Airport Inn is the former Airport Holiday Inn, where, as an eight-year-old, I procured my Vikings hero Alan Page's autograph, and so many other souvenirs, which I know from Madame Wicklund's French class means "memories."

The Holiday Inn was two stories and L-shaped, each room overlooking either the parking lot or the outdoor swimming pool. The hotel sold pool memberships to locals in the summer, and the McCollows always had one. Mike often brought me as his guest to what we called Airport Beach, directly under the flight path of MSP. But in 1981, during the final season of nearby Metropolitan Stadium—now a Roman ruin, a cyclone-fenced rubble heap and testament to a happier time, before the Twins and Vikings moved to the Metrodome in downtown Minneapolis—the Holiday Inn was rebranded as the sad-sack Airport Inn. Down came its iconic green-and-gold Holiday Inn sign, its pathway of lights leading to an arrow, the whole gorgeous structure topped by a star like the star of Bethlehem. And at the bottom was a marquee that hinted at its buzzing and fizzing interior life: CONGRATULATIONS BARRY AND LUANNE or WELCOME AMERICAN FEDERATION OF QUILTERS.

"Check out Airport Beach." Mike sighs as we speed by, surveying the faded majesty of its courtyard: the swimming pool, whirlpool, shuffleboard court, and rectangle of grass where we threw a football on childhood's hottest summer days. Those days were once innumerable, but now—college and my eighteenth birthday looming in September—they are scarcely more than a couple of hundred.

There follows a litany of memories: getting out of the pool and lying on towels on the baking shuffleboard deck, which was always 20 degrees warmer than the pool; ordering malts from the lobby coffee shop, delivered poolside in a 30-ounce cup that preserved our fingerprints in the frost on its stainless-steel surface. You might see anything on any given day: Vikings backup quarterback Bob Lee—The General—throwing a Nerf football pass to Mike, who tried to catch it while jumping into the pool; a group of girls from Saint Paul wearing what appeared to be homemade, crocheted bikinis that gave each of them a crosshatched tan, covering them in grid marks like one of Mom's string-bagged pork roasts from Red Owl.

And once, for one brief shining moment, a flock—a gaggle? a flight?—of Swedish stewardesses sunning themselves topless on the pool deck. (It sounds now like the description of a movie in *TV Week:* "**Air Strip** / Stockholm stews have fun on the 494 Strip. Adult content, mature themes, *very* brief nudity.") On that day, in less than a minute, the Holiday Inn's "innkeeper," Mr. Chaika—father of our friend and classmate Troy Chaika—sprinted from the lobby with a floral bedspread and threw it across the stewardesses as if putting out a fire. Which is exactly what he had done, as far as Mike and I were concerned.

The Strip was built on stewardesses and professional athletes, in endless supply on an artery flanked by the airport and the arena.

The Rolling Stones even stayed at Airport Beach in 1964, when they played at Danceland in Excelsior, and Brian Jones threw a chair into the pool from the second-floor balcony, as if marshaling his strength for the heavier ordnance—TVs and Rolls-Royces—to be heaved poolward in future visits to future, more luxurious hotels.

It's all now just a memory, preserved by one of the postcards filched from a spinning rack in the glory days of the gift shop. On the card, the "Holiday Inn Minneapolis Airport" is forever in its golden age, a Boeing 747 sharking in just feet above the rooftop.

We cruise the Strip, past Airport Beach, and follow one of 494's off-ramp tributaries—Lyndale Avenue—south to the

White Castle, its unspeakable lighting visible from the many passing planes.

A block north of the Castle, we pass the brand-new McDonald's, with its tantalizing novelty menu item the Chicken McNugget. But we resist its siren song and continue on to the Castle.

Viewed from outside, from its barf-and-bottle-riddled parking lot, the White Castle is a Hopper painting. The light fluoresces the pavement and everyone on it, a glare intended to sober up the customers in line. It's the kind of light that prepares those patrons for an interrogation lamp, or possibly for a surgical theater. As in prison or an operating room, the tables are stainless steel and bolted to the floor. The very décor warns that jail or open-heart surgery is in our future.

"On a typical Friday night," wrote columnist Jim Klobuchar in the *Star and Tribune,* of his most recent experience at White Castle, "the customers included a runty old man with a scowl who claimed to be Adolf Hitler and two women who ordered two cheeseburgers apiece and tried to pay with Monopoly money. Neither gave a destination but all three appeared to have originated in the bar across the street."

Every White Castle, a.k.a. Whitey's, a.k.a. the Castle, is alike. Almost from the chain's beginning, in Wichita in 1921, every Castle has been built identically, interchangeably—the white porcelain exterior hinting at the lavatorial exertions to come, the whole place designed to be hosed down at the end of the day, except that there is no end of the day, for the Castle is open twenty-four hours.

The one in Bloomington looks like the one in Bay Ridge, Brooklyn, where Tony, Joey, Double J, Bobby C, and Stephanie go in *Saturday Night Fever*. The workers there wear the same V-neck smocks the color of the light-blue Bonneville, identical to those Jim and Fluff wore to Shultzy's costume party five years ago. The ketchup and mustard are combined in a single squeeze bottle in every Castle. In *Saturday Night Fever,* as in our own Friday night visits, Bobby C stands on a table barking like a dog and no other customers take much notice at all.

When it's our turn to order, Mike tells the middle-aged manager in a paper hat, "Ten disgustings and a box of nails."

"Ten *what*?" says the manager, who knows perfectly well what Mike wants but is in no mood for this shit tonight.

"Disgustings," Mike says, as casual as can be. "And a box of nails."

In grade school, when the playground at recess became a bazaar of baseball cards and marbles and other items that were contraband in class, no object was more esteemed than Wacky Packages stickers. And among the Wacky Packages parodies I remember most vividly is "Fright Castle," in that famous Gothic type. "Greaseburgers. Horrific Taste. 6 Culinary Monstrosities." A fly has alighted on the burger on the box as various creatures of the night—Frankenstein, Dracula, the Wolfman—chow down on sliders, gut bombs, and greaseburgers, reinforcing the Castle's image as a nocturnal haven for freaks who disparage the very product they're about to ingest.

Even among White Castle management there are any number of acceptable euphemisms for White Castle hamburgers—sliders, gut bombs, Castles, Whiteys—and the crinkle-cut french fries are almost universally referred to as nails. A cheeseburger is always a "slider with vinyl." The turkey sandwich with cheese—a favorite of Tom's—is a "gobbler with glue." High schoolers working the counter will accept any synonym, no matter how unflattering. Ask for "ten pieces of shit," as we once heard another customer in line demand, and they'll respond: "With vinyl?" But the manager on this night will not countenance our favored euphemism. He will not make ten disgustings unless Mike calls the burger by one of its proper names. There is a brief standoff until Mike finally downgrades his order to ten sliders. I want to intervene, to defuse the tension and explain to the manager, "If we're paying for something that we think is repulsive, then perhaps the joke is on *us*."

But something about his expression, sweat condensing on his mustache, his eyeglasses fogging from the burger steam, tells me that his dignity has not been compromised by a group of seventeen-year-olds, that perhaps the reverse is happening.

My unease is compounded by the knowledge that he isn't the only adult we talk to this way. Or not *we,* exactly, for I don't lip off to adults. But I do smirk along with my friends when they're being smart-asses. It's no different from the way I move my lips without singing in Mass. Our mockery is all an act. Mock mockery, like our mock bravado around girls, though I'm incapable even of faking that. I'm still struck dumb around "chicks," hoping my silence will be mistaken for mystery. This hasn't happened yet, but college, like the federal witness protection program, will offer a new life in a new setting with all new people oblivious to my high school identity.

Come fall, everyone seated at this table—many of us

friends since kindergarten—will scatter. We'll still see each other on occasion, but never in the same way, despite our adamant yearbook inscriptions to remain best buds forever. (I recognize in the word "adamant" the name of "Goody Two Shoes" singer Adam Ant.)

An individual slider costs 28 cents, $2.80 for ten, but a coupon in *TV Week* usually cuts that price in half. Each of us always orders ten or more sliders at a single feeding. I am blessed with the appetite of a Tasmanian devil and the metabolism of a hummingbird and have every reason to believe that that will never change. In my hands, a "family size" bag of Doritos is abruptly reduced to a cloud of orange dust. Two Hostess apple pies are often bought and ingested on impulse at the checkout counter of a SuperAmerica gas station. Life has become a Coneheads sketch. "Consume mass quantities." My driver's license says I'm six foot four inches and weigh 169 pounds.

Gluttony is not without consequence. Our labors in the lavatory often eclipse the competitive eating spectacles that precede them. Junior year, our friend Ronnie was at a house party, using the bathroom, a line of girls accruing in the hallway, when he discovered to his horror that his turd was too large to flush. After several failed attempts, and the water threatening to breach the bowl, he removed it by hand and placed it in the bathtub, discreetly drawing the shower curtain before vacating first the bathroom and then the premises.

These stories are solemnly related over sliders the way some dads talk about fish they've caught. Z from our basketball team was so proud of one epic bowel movement in the locker room at Normandale golf course that he summoned

Oly from the first tee box to verify it for posterity. "A python," Oly now confirms at the Castle. "Three coils."

Outside, Barney the rent-a-cop stands watch over the White Castle parking lot. He has a Yorkshire terrier named Jet that he strokes while often reciting long extracts of poetry, lovely stuff that none of us recognizes. He has a pickup truck with a camper top, where we assume he sleeps in the daytime, after a long night shift spent taking abuse from high school kids and whoever crawls off the bloodred barstools of David Fong's at closing time. It's said that the Plantation Punch at Fong's should be registered as a lethal weapon at City Hall.

I look at Barney, in his white uniform shirt with the vague badge, standing sentry in the parking lot. My friends and I are reflected in the window as a faint overlay, so that I can almost literally see myself in him. Already I have shared some of his uniformed indignities, with many more to come—as convenience store clerk, dishwasher at Bennigan's, and maintenance boy at the New Orleans Court apartment complex, where I will sit in the toolshed and read baseball books by Roger Angell and Roger Kahn and dream of being a New Yorker named Roger so that I too can write about baseball. I'm in that limbo state, not quite a kid, not yet an adult. Childhood dreams, in which anything can still happen, are running up against the foreclosed possibilities of having to *choose*. Choose a college, choose a major, choosy mothers choose Jif.

Gator was a short, red-haired force of nature who Dad said, even when we were eight years old, was the toughest kid on our Bloomington Athletic Association football team. "Little Danny," as Dad still calls him, has become a muscled, indomitable wrestler, tops in his weight class in the state. Eating our sliders at Whitey's, we speculate on Gator's weight-lifting limits and wonder who the strongest kid at Kennedy might be. And then it happens. Gator lifts his butt from his seat and grimaces as if preparing to stage-fart. But no, his hands are gripping the edges of the table. After a weight lifter's grunt, he stands and rips the table from its moorings. There's a clatter of floor tile where the table has been uprooted like a tree. The manager shouts at us to stay where we are while he summons Barney. We sprint for the powder-blue sanctuary of the Bonneville Brougham, careful to grab our food, as Barney fast-walks after us with a slider in one hand and a walkie-talkie in the other, shouting at Gator that he's "banned for life!" Whether the ban applies to this Whitey's only or every turreted castle in the realm remains unclear, but Barney is now squinting at the Bonnie, attempting to memorize Dr. Terry McCollow's license plate.

In the parking lot, the muscle bikes of my grade school years—the Schwinn Sting-Rays and CCM Mustangs and Huffy Rail Dragsters—have morphed into muscle cars: Firebirds and Thunderturds and Trans Ams.

The lettering on the lit-up White Castle sign—an Old English font—is the same as that on the many heavy-metal concert T-shirts inside the Castle itself: Motörhead or Mötley Crüe. I've come to think of sliders as heavy-metal hamburgers.

We sprint through the parking lot, beneath that beacon of a White Castle sign. My heart is hammering. For a moment, I think Barney might throw himself on the hood before we can drive away. I picture him sprawled there, spread-eagled, like the Screaming Chicken on a Trans Am.

But Barney doesn't have the speed or agility of a Starsky or Hutch. He's approaching at a stately pace as we dive into the Bonnie.

"He's calling for backup!" I yell at Mike, as Barney says something into his radio.

"He's calling for ketchup." Mike laughs, turning the key as the Bonneville purrs to life. We lurch onto Lyndale Avenue, squealing along with the tires, as the Crusaders resume singing "Street Life" on the Pioneer tape deck, and I alone cower beneath the window line, hoping not to be ID'd.

One block from the Castle, the Bonnie is filled with laughter and adrenaline. It smells of fear and diced onions. In thirty minutes I'll be snug in bed, every nerve end still buzzing. None of us will say it out loud, but we all wish this moment could continue indefinitely. Nights in White Castle, never reaching the end.

## 2.

# We're the Kids in America

Tucked up in my twin bed, the satin cuff of the Sears blanket soft on my skin like a mother's touch, I can see—through the uprights of my size 12 feet—my little homework desk beyond the foot of the shrinking bed.

The Gettysburg Address, in Jim's unmistakable printing, is still Scotch-taped to the woodlike veneer of the bookshelf overhanging the desk, the notebook paper having yellowed in the five years since Jim had to memorize it at Lincoln High School. Jim repeatedly rendered those three words—"Lincoln High School"—in bubble letters in the margins of the famous speech. These doodles are a souvenir of his days as a high school hockey star, idling away the hours in American History. Jim is left-handed so all his writing leans backward instead of forward, each letter looking like the guy in the leather chair in the Maxell tape ad being blown back by his own speakers—hair, tie, lampshade, martini glass, all in retreat against some powerful sonic wind. Dad hates that ad because it's famous and Maxell is a competitor. He issues a long sigh whenever he finds in my room a mix tape, borrowed from a friend, recorded on Maxell or Sony or TDK. He makes it clear that Scotch brand recording tape would have rendered, in far higher fidelity, these "Sweet Toons of Summer '83."

Why the Gettysburg Address is still on display on my desk I cannot say, except that it used to be Jim's desk, and anything on it remains there with the approval of Mom, whose otherwise fanatical cleaning sometimes sees cash, baseball cards, and other valuables dispatched to the wastebasket in her daily rounds, like innocent bystanders swept up in a police raid. She likes having the Gettysburg Address around, a reminder of our once-full house.

On the two bookshelves above the desk, where Mom's Royal typewriter is on permanent display, resides my growing collection of stolen books, some permanently borrowed from Mike McCollow's brother's basement bedroom while Tim McCollow is off at college.

I'm not amassing stolen goods so much as assembling a stage set. This small collection of books, just enough to fill a single shelf, is really a backdrop for the kind of author photo I've seen on the dust jackets of some of the other books on the shelf—guy jauntily leaning on typewriter, book spines displayed behind him—just in case I write one someday.

In the back of these paperbacks are checklists of still more books that I want. All I have to do is cut out the coupon at the bottom of the page, stick it in an envelope with $1.50 in cash for *The Bad News Bears* by Richard Woodley, add 35 cents for postage and handling, and mail it to Dell Books, PO Box

1000, Pine Brook, NJ 07058. In eight short weeks, the book will appear in my mailbox as if by magic.

Not every one of my books is stolen. My friend Ope—Keith Opatz—has discovered a dumpster behind B. Dalton Bookseller at the Southdale mall into which the manager tosses unwanted books. Each of their covers has been torn off and returned to the publisher as evidence of the book's unsellability. And so Ope has dumpster-dived for the annual editions of *The Complete Handbook of Pro Basketball,* with its pithy put-downs of lumbering white guys, including disheveled Rich Kelley of the Phoenix Suns, whose scouting report includes the burn "Hair by Weedeater."

The books are edited by Zander Hollander, whose name I can't see without thinking of Xaviera Hollander, author of *The Happy Hooker,* whose 1975 film adaptation has yet to appear in *TV Week,* though I know from Johnny Carson's monologue that the memoir got her kicked out of the United States.

I can now stay up to see Carson whenever I like, though I still have to pretend not to understand certain jokes, as when his turbaned alter ego, Carnac the Magnificent, divines the contents of an envelope by holding it to his forehead:

Carnac says, "Lassie, King Tutankhamen, and the Happy Hooker."

He tears open the envelope, removes a card, and reads, "Name a mutt, a Tut, and a slut."

Uproarious laughter from the studio audience in Burbank. Dad gazing into the distance as if he hasn't heard what Johnny just said, father and son sharing an unspoken pact to pretend we're oblivious to something—the word "slut," but also the word "hooker"—the kind of thing that might be said at school or on scrambled cable but never in your own family room on "free TV." It's a construction that would have been entirely redundant just last week: "free TV."

"Free" is our guiding ethos. When *Return of the Jedi* came out and kids openly skipped school to line up outside the Southtown Theatre under the baleful gaze of God and TV news crews, Ope and I regarded them as fools. We walked right into the opulent lobby, stacked our quarters on adjacent arcade games, and pretended to play Frogger and Gorf for a plausible fifteen minutes before asking the ancient ticket taker for permission to use the bathroom just beyond the velvet ropes.

Ope and I occupied adjoining stalls for thirty minutes, until the rabble were allowed in, after which we melted into the crowd filing into the darkened theater and sat at the back, mesmerized.

Other days we spring for one three-dollar ticket and open the fire door inside the theater to let five friends in, briefly piercing the theater with a rectangle of light. Or we duct-tape the door latch, a trick we learned from *The Rockford Files,* so we can pull it open from the outside, our fingertips grappling for purchase in the gaps at the bottom of the door. At theater 4 at the Southdale multiplex, our piece of duct tape remains in place for weeks, allowing us to see whatever is playing there. This week that means Michael Caine in *Blame It on Rio,* Dudley Moore in *Unfaithfully Yours,* and a movie called *Angel,* whose poster tagline gives away the plot: "High school honor student by day, Hollywood hooker by night."

The suspense on the screen competes with the suspense in our seats. Will another patron narc on us? Will an usher's flashlight beam fall on me, like the searchlight in a prison yard in the very escape movie I'm watching?

We even play free basketball at the Y, approaching the front desk one by one and telling them we lost our membership card, at which time we're allowed to rummage around in a basket full of lost membership cards and choose one with the most distant expiration date.

The Y is full of red-faced forty-year-old men on their lunch breaks, bald middle managers in headbands, aging athletes in knee sleeves, glasses secured to their scalps by neoprene Croakies. Ope wears three pairs of socks, two wristbands, and Curtis Js, sweatpants jaggedly cut off at the knees in the style of Curtis Jackson in *The White Shadow*. Mike plays in a knit beanie. He hits a three in the face of a middle-aged defender and then Benny-Hills the man, patting him on his bald head, as Benny does to an old geezer in every episode of *The Benny Hill Show*.

But we also find a full basketball court in the rafters of a barn on the campus of Bethany College of Missions, a private Christian school on Auto Club Road, and let ourselves in late at night. We usually stride with confidence through the open front door—there's a poolroom and lounge on the main floor—but when it's locked we climb a ladder to the upper barn door, the former hayloft, and climb in like burglars.

In the stifling heat of that airless space, we play for hours, for free basketball is our God-given right. The barn roof slopes so low in the corners that a baseline jumper is impossible. The baselines themselves are flush with the walls on which the baskets are mounted, so we can use the wall as a vertical ramp and run up it for monster dunks. The ball and my boom box provide a double bass line. "They're playin' basss-ket-ballll," Kurtis Blow's background singers wail. "We love that basss-ket-ballll."

We speak in urban playground slang that is out of place in a barn on a campus of missionaries. We shoot the J. We dish the rock and call for the pill. We throw down sweet jams. We don't jump, we *sky*. We don't block shots, we *erase* that shit. Most of the slang we've picked up from books: Rick Telander's *Heaven Is a Playground,* checked out from the Penn Lake Library and never returned, and something called *The In-Your-Face Basketball Book,* by two white guys named Alexander Wolff and Chuck Wielgus Jr. I ordered it from B. Dalton in eighth grade. Ten agonizing days later, the store called to say it was in. Mom drove me there, $7.95 in birthday money burning a hole in my pocket. I read half the book's 187 pages on the car ride home. It contains everything a suburban white kid needs to act and speak and dress like a black teenager from what after-school specials always call the "inner city," including a glossary of slang and street fashion tips, not to mention intricate shoelace-tying patterns, which I immediately emulate.

"That's it?" Mom said when I finished the book an hour after purchasing it. "That didn't last long."

"I'll read it again," I promised. And I have, over and over.

My appetite for basketball and books is exceeded only by my appetite for food. At the Shakey's Bunch of Lunch buffet, we stack tottering towers of pizza slices *and* chicken wings on our plates. Whenever a Shakey's employee delivers a fresh pizza to the buffet, we are waiting for her, fogging the sneeze guard with our heavy breathing, ready to denude the silver pan of every slice. Our bottomless cups of soda are never emptied. We drain their Pepsi reserves. And we do all of this for $3.37.

We never dine and dash. We eschew the chew and screw. Still, at the twenty-four-hour diner inside Byerly's grocery store, where we sometimes go late on a Friday night while the heat cools off at White Castle, we order bacon and eggs and sausage and toast and always—always—"twelve grape jellies" on the side. The waitress complies, and we eat the jelly packets as a free side order, using the toast as a jelly-delivery system.

Every meal is a banquet. There's a Burger King across from JFK, and a girl who works there has a crush on Mike, so she hands us, through the drive-through window, a contraband stack of one hundred trivia scratch-off cards. We hit on almost all of them, scoring thirty Whoppers, two dozen large fries, and nine chocolate shakes. We deplete the cards in two weekends. By myself, I can put away twenty White Castles in a single sitting, whole frozen pizzas, and an almost limitless number of Steak-umm sandwiches, thin translucent layers of meatlike product that I lay out on paper towels, top with sliced Velveeta, press between two halves of a roll, and nuke until the microwave dings like my typewriter, the whole thing tasting of salt and moist paper towel.

"You're eating me out of house and home" has always been Mom's redundant phrase. "Where are you putting it all?" A year after getting my driver's license, I'm six foot five and weigh 175 pounds.

\*       \*       \*

I'm now working during the school year at Met Center arena, popcorn vending during Minnesota North Stars hockey games and occasional concerts. My reticence to shout in public makes me a good boy but a terrible vendor. I walk up and down the steeply staired aisles in a green polyester smock and matching visor with a pin on its crown that says "$1.25." There is literally a price on my head, but I also feel as if there's a metaphorical one, for I wander the arena trying to go unnoticed.

I look for raised hands without ever shouting "Popcorn!" until one night I'm told by a supervisor that I have to hawk the goods. I am still looking, in the manner of an auctioneer, for the smallest twitch from a fan—a woman stretching her arms, perhaps—as a demand for my popcorn.

I need a patter, a rap, and decide to shout "Pop-CORN," with the emphasis on the second syllable, "corn," to distinguish me from guys who are selling pop—Coke and Sprite. Except that I'm hawking popcorn in Bugs Bunny Brooklynese circa 1940: "Pop-CAWN! Getcha pop-CAWN HEAH!"

It is unfortunate that my maiden call of "Pop-CAWN" comes just as Kenny Rogers—bestriding the Met Center stage like a rhinestoned colossus—begins singing his hit ballad "Lady."

*"Lay-deee,"* Kenny begins.

"Pop-CAWN!"

*"I'm your knight in shining armor..."*

"Getcha pop-CAWN heah!"

*"And I love youuuuu..."*

"Pop-CAWN!"

The catcalls that rain down on me do little for my self-confidence: "Be quiet!" "We can't hear *Kenny*!" "Hey, Orville Redenbacher, shut the hell *up*!"

I'm shamed by the Gambler's middle-aged groupies, and warned by one man that if I do not desist I will need a surgeon to remove his pointy-toed lizard-skin cowboy boot from my rectum. At North Stars games, I receive similar abuse when blocking the sight lines during a Norris Division donnybrook, so I return to wandering the stands in silence, simultaneously hoping to be noticed while trying to disappear, the way I am around girls and other strangers.

North Stars rookie defenseman Randy Velischek was a teammate of Jim's at Providence. Twenty-two years old and far from his hometown of Montreal, he comes to dinner at our house in Bloomington, even though he plays in the National goddamn Hockey League, where his job is to prevent Wayne Gretzky and Bernie Federko and Michel Goulet from scoring on Stars goalie Donny Beaupre. My God, the names in the National Hockey League! The North Stars have Dino Ciccarelli and Willi Plett. Willi, without the *e,* the way some girls at school have gone from Sandy to Sandi or Nancy to Nanci. I wonder if Willi dots the *i*'s with smiley faces, the way girls do when signing yearbooks. Other people's yearbooks, obviously, for I solicit yearbook signatures the way I solicit popcorn sales: in silence, hoping in vain they will come to me.

There's a real NHL referee whose magnificent name— Swede Knox—has become a euphemism among my friends for a lady's bosom. In the kind of Navajo code talk that we often employ, "Swede Knox" is a thinly disguised stand-in for "sweet knockers," which derives from a memorable comment that a barber made when I was ten years old. Poised above my scalp with comb and shears, he paused to gaze through the shop window at a woman walking across the parking lot at Penn Lake Plaza. With a wistful tone in his voice, he said to no one in particular: "Would ya look at the knockers on that gal." After a reverential moment of silence, he returned to snipping at my scalp.

The mention of Swede Knox on an NHL telecast always brings an illicit thrill, but so do other sports names, including Börje Salming, the great defenseman for the Toronto Maple Leafs. Hearing his name, I think of Gutzon Borglum, designer of Mount Rushmore, as I learned in a baseball book by Roger Kahn. "Gutzon Borglum," went one line I can quote by heart, "sounds like a fart in a bathtub."

I didn't know you could write like this. Roger Angell, in a baseball book I bought with my own money at B. Dalton— *Late Innings,* $3.95 for the paperback, or two shines of Dad's wingtips—likens Reggie Jackson swapping the orange tops of the Baltimore Orioles for Yankee pinstripes to "Clark Gable no longer in the Klondike or on the China seas but entering a drawing room in a dinner jacket." Royals rookie Joe Zdeb has a surname that is "the last draw in a Scrabble game."

I love how the surname of Twins rookie Tim Teufel is German for "devil," and the surname of Blue Jays pitcher Jim Gott is German for "God," so that Gott pitching to Teufel is a Teutonic battle of good and evil. Perhaps I'm overthinking it, but all of baseball—the names, statistics, ballparks, uniforms, logos, and objects—are a self-contained universe, with a language that sings: Dubble Bubble bubble gum, twi-nite doubleheaders, Rawlings gloves with the Edge-U-Cated Heel. I stopped playing organized baseball after ninth grade, after taking a one-hopper to the eye while playing third base, having already given my front teeth to the game. I no longer want to play major-league baseball; I want to write about it, use its names and characters as modeling clay.

A kid on the bus builds model cars. I quietly envy him, his head bent toward his father's workbench, assembling a 1:25 scale replica of a 1964 Ford Fairlane Thunderbolt beneath a clamp-on lamp that illuminates his collection of tools, laid out as for a surgeon in an operating theater: hobby knife, sanding sticks, tweezers, toothpicks, masking tape, modeling cement. Is the contact high from the glue or from having a diversion of one's own—a world to withdraw into?

Some kids at school play D&D. I see them in the hall, each holding a blue *Dungeons & Dragons Expert Rulebook*. They hold it close the way I clutch *Sports Illustrated* after its Thursday arrival in our mailbox. They talk of Regdar and Tordek the way I talk of Redfern and Hrbek, so that it's difficult to tell which ones are characters in D&D and which ones are characters on the Minnesota Twins. Major-league baseball—MLB—is no less a fantasy role-playing game than D&D.

One Christmas I received, unasked for, a stamp-collecting kit. Opening the vinyl-covered album, I fell into its pages as if into a canyon, lost myself in the cancelled stamps from West Germany and the Dutch Antilles and the Republic of Zaire. They came in a glassine envelope. I mounted them in the album on gummed hinges whose adhesive was activated by my own tongue: twice-licked stamps bearing, in their perforated frames, queens' heads and raised fists and exotic animals.

When the stamp album was complete, I returned to the hobby shop and bought a blue coin folder for Washington quarters, and pressed into its rows of round beds every quarter in my piggy bank—a slotted Twins batting helmet. The quarters fitted in with a satisfying snap, from the year of my birth in 1966 all the way up to 1983. I did the same for Lincoln pennies and Eisenhower dimes, using the little plastic magnifying glass that came with the stamp album to identify which U.S. mint issued each coin. They're all empty now. I punched out the quarters to buy baseball cards. Even among my private obsessions, the world of baseball trumps all.

I have my own dice-and-tabletop role-playing game called Strat-O-Matic baseball, which reduces every player in the big leagues to a coded index card. I select two teams and lay the cards on the table in the basement, where I'm a baseball Dungeon Master, playing out nine-inning baseball games with cards, dice, and fully annotated scorecards that I three-hole-punch and clip into a three-ring binder until there are 162 sheets in there, a full season of games. I've played the entire Kansas City Royals schedule, embellishing each score sheet with imaginary tales of life on the road, of autographs signed in big-league hotel lobbies, of raucous pranks played on flights to Anaheim. Every index card is a living, breathing ballplayer with an envelope full of per diem meal money. The completist zeal I once brought to philately I now channel into Strat-O, as the game is known to its devotees, none of whom I know. This is my private obsession.

There's a poster in the basement, another Christmas present unvetted by Mom or Dad, featuring a kid my age. The headline says ARE YOU A NERD? and lists the symptoms, including a "fascination with word problems," "reads too much," and prefers "Farah, Sta-Prest, Dads and Lads, or other fine brands" of slacks to blue jeans. I've had my balls busted at school for never wearing jeans, with the glorious exception, sophomore year, of bib overalls. I wear what Mom buys me: khakis that come with a striped fabric belt or—my favorite—Dickies gas-station-attendant pants in navy blue. Forbidden to wear jeans from kindergarten through eighth grade, most of my friends wear *only* jeans now. Not me. Like the Vietnam veterans who have returned to Bloomington but still sport their army jackets, I've continued wearing the navy-blue pants of the Catholic schoolboy.

In dressing me, Mom relies on her style bible. *The Official Preppy Handbook* was published as a parodic celebration of an East Coast sailing set far removed from our lives in landlocked Bloomington, but I see that these people are distantly related to Mom through her love of the Kennedys. This is why my closet is full of Izod alligator shirts, wide-wale corduroys, oxford-cloth button-downs, and *two* kinds of "dress" shoes: penny loafers and Top-Siders, a.k.a. docksiders, a.k.a. boat or deck shoes.

A year from now, as a freshman at the Academy of the Holy Angels, Amy will be photographed for the yearbook as the quintessential preppy in Weejuns, knee-high socks, a tartan skirt, and a white oxford worn under a green Izod sweater.

"Is Amy Rushin the last of a dying trend of preppies?" the yearbook wonders. "Maybe at other schools, but at AHA, lurking behind new-wave skirts and punky haircuts are self-confident people clad in plaid Bermudas and argyle socks. If you knock these preppies, the alligators might bite you!"

The very first sentence of the *Preppy Handbook* declares: "It is the inalienable right of every man, woman, and child to wear khaki." In my khakis, playing Strat-O in the basement, with only the rattle of dice to keep me company, I contemplate the accusing poster. Am I a nerd? More telltale signs: "undue respect for authority" (check), "using big words" (check), "passivity" (check), and "sexual ignorance" (checkmate).

One day after school, standing on the grass, holding a stray football I've idly picked up from the practice field, I see a group of girls huddle, confer, nod in agreement, and then chase me as a pack, shrieking and giggling. Instinctively, I run like Eric Dickerson, the football held the way Dad always told me to carry it: tucked snug against my rib cage as a safeguard against fumbling. "It's not a loaf of bread," he always said, so I protect the ball, elude the girls' shoddy attempts at tackling, stiff-arm one of them, execute a spin move, and break free, sprinting up the sideline until I stand alone—chest heaving, lungs burning—in the end zone instead of lying at the bottom of a pile of girls. And only then does it occur to me that I might have missed the point of this whole exercise.

To be in high school in the 1980s is to see yourself depicted in countless movies, in *Fast Times at Ridgemont High*, in *The Breakfast Club* and *Sixteen Candles* and *Ferris Bueller's Day Off*, in *Risky Business, Weird Science, Better Off Dead, Teen Wolf, Footloose*, and the Porky's trilogy, confirming your place at the center of the culture. To be seventeen is to be the subject of song. Stray Cats: "She's sexy and seventeen." Kool & the Gang: "At seventeen we fell in love." The Cars: "She won't give up 'cause she's seventeen." Tom listens to an English new-wave band called Heaven 17, which sounds like a multiplex in the afterlife. (Even the majestic Southtown Theatre has become a duplex. The vast screen on which I saw *The Poseidon Adventure* and *Rocky* and *The Empire Strikes Back* is now two smaller screens, divided by a wall, showing *Return of the Jedi* and *Mr. Mom*.)

"We're the kids in America, whoa-oh," sings a woman from England, on the radio, and you can tell she's not from here when she says, "New York to East California, there's a new wave comin', I warn ya." And that nonexistent place—"East California"—annoys me the way Sadé will when she sings, "Coast to coast, L.A. to Chicago…" It occurs to me that the kids in America aren't always being written about by the kids in America.

In none of these songs—in no movies or TV shows—are any seventeen-year-olds listening to Grover Washington Jr., scavenging for books in dumpsters, living in fear of Kenny Rogers's female fans, playing Strat-O-Matic baseball, or longing for not a black Trans Am but an olive-green IBM Selectric II, the kind I use in Mr. Cavanaugh's typing class, where twenty of them are arrayed in a row, all of them going off like guns, a metal golf ball with eighty-eight characters on it punching letters onto a page. Writing as an act of violence. The Pavlovian *ding* at the end of a line, the RETURN button so responsive to touch, all that power in your right pinkie. The way the whole thirty-five-pound beast hums to life when I turn it on also turns me on. It might as well be a car. I have no interest in cars but would love to be behind the wheel of an IBM Selectric II for the rest of my days, pulling out pages of prose and handing them to a copyboy, who then races them to a chain-smoking editor in an office overlooking the newsroom, as in *All the President's Men*.

A weird commercial aired during the third quarter of this year's Super Bowl. The game was already a blowout—the Raiders beat the Redskins 38–9—and the only thing I remembered the next day, apart from Barry Manilow singing the national anthem in a bomber jacket, was the Olivia Newton-John look-alike who jogged into a room full of gray totalitarian worker drones and threw a sledgehammer through a giant telescreen with the image of Big Brother on it. "On January 24th Apple Computer will introduce Macintosh," the voice-over went. "And you'll see why 1984 won't be like *1984*." I still don't know what that's supposed to mean, but I do know that the Apple Macintosh, with its off-white keyboard hooked up to an off-white monitor, puts me in mind of hospital equipment, like something you'd see in a patient's room on *St. Elsewhere*. The Selectric hums and dings—it is, in every sense of the phrase, a real humdinger—while the Macintosh is clinical, antiseptic, and silent. The commercial aired only once, but its meaning has been debated on the news and in the papers ever since. Apple was saying it would save the world from the future tyranny of staring slack-jawed at a screen all day, while offering a screen of its own at which to stare.

Contrast that with the beautiful Selectric. It was designed for IBM in 1961 by architect Eliot Noyes. His son Eliot (Eli) Noyes Jr. is an animator who made a series of short films for *Sesame Street* called the Mad Painter, in which a bearded man in a Chaplinesque bowler and black Chuck Taylors paints numbers on other people's property: a 4 on a woman's umbrella (she is Stockard Channing, Rizzo from *Grease*); an

8 on a bald man's scalp; a 10 on a barstool that a maintenance man in a boilersuit promptly sits on, transferring the number to his bottom. I loved these sixty-second silent movies as a little kid. Truth be told, I love them now. If I'm alone in the room and *Sesame Street* is on, I'll happily watch it. The Mad Painter—actor Paul Benedict—has grown up to be Mr. Bentley, George and Weezy's British next-door neighbor in that dee-luxe apartment in the sky on *The Jeffersons,* but I still think of him painting a 5 on a yellow bouncy ball inside the gorilla enclosure at the zoo. Like Stockard Channing and Paul Benedict, even the ape would go on to greater fame—as Paul the Gorilla on *The Electric Company.*

But Eli Noyes also made for *Sesame Street* a memorable stop-motion series in which sand shaped itself into letters of the alphabet. With the Selectric and the Sand Alphabet animated shorts, respectively, Eliot Sr. and Eliot Jr. played with letters in a way that appealed to me, forming and re-forming them with sand or an electric typewriter.

By contrast, many computers are now advertised in the paper as "word processors." Like the "food processors" that serve as prizes on *The Price Is Right,* they reduce diverse ingredients of varied textures to a pabulum the color of the Macintosh itself.

Three percent of American households have a telephone answering machine. I don't know anybody who has one besides Jim Rockford. Ten percent of American homes have a videocassette recorder, and because Dad sells videocassettes, ours is among the lucky few. Twenty-one percent own video-game consoles, and ninety percent own color TVs. But only seven percent of American homes have a home computer.

Commodore has sold the most, followed by Texas Instruments, Atari, Timex Sinclair, Radio Shack, and Apple. But I don't want a Macintosh. I want a Selectric.

Dad wants a Cadillac so he buys an Olds. I want an IBM so, at a garage sale in South Brook, I buy a Brother electric typewriter with brown keys and a yellow body, a color scheme inspired by the coffee-and-cigarette-stained teeth of every reporter I have ever seen in any movie that requires journalists. It's louder than an idling bus and of course has no golf ball embossed with letters, but it has regular typewriter keys that rise up and occasionally entangle themselves when I'm typing too fast. I love everything about it.

At my desk, at the kitchen table, on my own thighs on the bus to school, I put my fingers on imaginary keys in ready position—left fingers on A, S, D, F; right fingers on J, K, L, semicolon—and type out entire paragraphs, my right thumb striking an invisible space bar between every word, the way some kids air-drum Alex van Halen's intro to "Hot for Teacher" on their thighs.

I can properly type my first name using only my left hand. But I can also type longer words—"afterward," "reverberated," "desegregated"—using only my left hand. The guy two desks down finds he can type "unhook bra" this way—"unhook" right-handed, "bra" left-handed—and we are impressed. I type two other words with just my left hand—"Abracadabra, stewardesses"—and think of the magical appearance of Swedish air hostesses poolside at the Airport Holiday Inn.

I'm afflicted by shyness and wordplay, both of them crippling, both of them battling each other in my Business Law class, taught by my typing teacher, Mr. Cavanaugh. When he asked us to read a passage in the textbook about disputed rights to a causeway, a classmate asked, "What's a causeway?"

Mr. Cavanaugh turned the question back on the class and said, "Anyone know the answer? Mr. Rushin, what's a causeway?"

"About eight pounds," I said.

There was a long silence before he said, "What's ... a cause ... weigh?" Mr. C suppressed the tiniest smile and looked over his glasses and said, "Very funny, Mr. Rushin. Anyone else?"

He didn't get mad—or, worse, groan; he just explained it to the rest of the class without them knowing he was explaining it and then moved on. Likewise, my Contemporary Issues teacher, Roger House—whose name appears as "R. House" on class rolls and report cards—doesn't mind, or possibly understand, when kids sing Madness within earshot: "R. House, in the middle of our street..."

In this style of wordplay as comedy, we're guided by Benny Hill, whose reruns air every night after the local news. "This is the dumbest show in the world," Dad says, half rising from his Archie Bunker chair to go to bed. "Who watches this?" Thirty minutes later, still poised on the edge of his chair, as the closing credits roll, and Benny chases a woman around a field to "Yakety Sax," Dad snaps off the TV, tears in his eyes: "Why am I still up? This show is for imbeciles..."

"I fell in love with an opera singer named Maria," Benny says wistfully one night. "Was *that* a woman." He waits a beat before adding, "That's what everyone kept asking—'Was that a woman?'"

The only show that can compete with Carson as an influence on our sense of humor is *M*A*S*H,* which reruns every night at 10:30 on channel 11, preceding Carson by half an hour. In delaying Johnny's monologue, Trapper and Hawkeye get an extended afterlife following the show's demise the previous year.

"I loved a girl in San Francisco once," Hawkeye says. "Or was it twice?"

Last February, on the day the final new episode of *M\*A\*S\*H* aired, Mike and I went to school dressed as Hawkeye and Trapper John. I wore Dad's paisley bathrobe and carried a plastic martini glass and walked the halls of Kennedy High on a Monday morning doing dialogue from the show.

Me as Frank Burns: "You disgust me!"

Me as Hawkeye: "That's right, Frank. I discussed you with everyone I know, and we all find you disgusting."

I watched the finale that night along with 122 million other Americans, 52 percent of the country, the most watched television program in history, though given the weeks-long buildup to the episode, the more startling figure is the 112 million U.S. citizens who somehow failed to watch it. And though the two-and-a-half-hour episode was melodramatic and disappointing, I took comfort in one last exchange of army humor written by men who had served in World War II and then used the Korean War as a vehicle to comment on Vietnam.

"Just a minute, you handle our food *and* dig latrines?"

"Don't worry, sir. I always wash my hands before I dig the latrines."

In the year since *M\*A\*S\*H* went off the air, I've found a new comedy hero on nights I can stay awake to watch him. David Letterman also wears khakis and polo shirts, and he broadcasts his show from Rockefeller Center, which is at the center of Manhattan, which is at the center of New York, which puts it at the center of the world. "Dave" is a smart-ass who loves Johnny Carson and has a gap between his front teeth like the one I had closed by orthodontia, then blown wide open by a baseball. He occasionally does sketches from a bar downstairs called Hurley's, and when I switch his show off at midnight and put on Steely Dan's *Katy Lied* cassette, I fall asleep by the second track, "Bad Sneakers," which contains the line "Stompin' on the avenue by Radio City, baby." By the time the fourth song on side one is playing, "Daddy Don't Live in That New York City No More," I've incorporated the lyrics into my dreams: "He can't get tight every night pass out on the barroom floor." I think of Rockefeller Center, Radio City, Hurley's bar, David Letterman, and Steely Dan, and though I've never been to New York City, I decide—in my sleep—that I'd very much like to go someday.

*Young Doctors in Love* is showing at the Southdale multiplex, where we've duct-taped the fire-door latch to theater 4. Martin picks me up, with our friend Miles riding shotgun. Miles went to Nativity with us but now goes to Holy Angels. Ope is next to me in the back seat. On a sunny spring Saturday afternoon we're cruising up France Avenue, three lanes running north and south divided by a landscaped median. There's nothing French about France Avenue except that, like the Champs-Élysées, it's broad and well trafficked and full of diversions.

Principal among these diversions is the Mann France Avenue Drive-In theater, ringed by a solid corrugated metal fence twelve feet tall, so that the parking lot inside is like a prison yard in reverse. For eighteen years, since it opened in the summer of 1966—billed as "The world's most beautiful and distinctive drive-in theater"—young men and women have been trying to break *in,* smuggled inside the trunks of cars, four kids popping out like spring snakes.

Some guests at the adjacent Ramada Inn have a view of the gigantic screen and—if we're to believe the rumors, and we always believe the rumors—so do some houses in the neighborhood behind the theater, where a boy roused from sleep at 11 p.m. might idly part his bedroom curtains to find, outside his window, a naked woman looming over his house in 70-millimeter Cinerama.

As we drive north on France, into ritzy Edina, past the condos and glass office buildings, a police car cruises south, on the other side of the median. The driver looks at us as we pass, and then makes a U-turn at a break in the median, so that he's two hundred yards behind us. We're going the speed limit, forty-five, but now Martin, his eyes in the rearview mirror, accelerates and changes lanes. The cop behind us does the same.

Martin has prior moving violations and would like to avoid another. "Cops" is all he says.

"Cops," "heat," "fuzz." These are our names for officers of the law. Most of what we know about them comes from TV: the pressed uniforms and gleaming badges of *T. J. Hooker,* the hood rolls executed by Starsky and Hutch, the fat, indolent Murray the Cop in reruns of *The Odd Couple,* still one of my favorite shows because Oscar Madison is a sportswriter living in a sprawling Park Avenue apartment, and as far as I know that's something that can happen in real life.

Seeing the cops in the wing mirror, I fear an imminent besmirching of my Permanent Record.

"It will go down on your Permanent Record," Mom is fond of warning me even now, to preempt any indiscretion I might be contemplating. A Permanent Record is the list—recorded on parchment or stone, something venerable and timeless—enumerating a child's many sins, sins that may not be expiated even by Catholic confession, sins that even God can't fix.

Martin accelerates to fifty-five and turns right, hangs a Rodney off of France, heading over to York, which can take us into Southdale the back way. The police car, which has maintained pace with us, also hangs a Rodney, and when Martin accelerates again to put distance between us, the cop turns on his red and blue lights—his cherries and berries, as I've heard them called on TV—and I am frightened and relieved in equal measure, for while we're being pulled over at least this police pursuit will end with a speeding ticket.

Except that it doesn't end. Martin hangs another Rodney while running a red light, and Miles shouts, "What is happening?"

"I'm gonna lose my license!" Martin says.

"Pull over!"

"I can't!"

Everything I know about police chases I know from TV and the movies, and this one is going remarkably to script. The cop car's siren is wailing. A second car is now in pursuit. On our way to the Southdale mall, we've stumbled into a high-speed police chase, for no reason that we can think of, though I'm privately wondering in the back seat if the police have discovered the duct tape on the door latch of theater 4 at the multiplex.

"Pull over," I plead, while Martin hangs a Rodney, then a Louie, and pulls into the parking lot of the Embassy Suites hotel on the western end of the Strip, only to find there is no exit. He stops the car with a screech, so that the only sound is the buzzing in our ears and "Karma Chameleon" on WLOL and an angry voice on a bullhorn saying, "Raise your hands to the ceiling and remain in the vehicle."

I notice he said "Raise your hands to the ceiling," not "Put your hands up" or "Reach for the sky" or any number of phrases we used playing cops and robbers or cowboys and Indians when we were kids, not all that long ago.

We press our sweaty palms to the fabric of the ceiling.

"Remain in the vehicle," the bullhorn orders. It doesn't say, "Freeze!" We were playing it wrong all those years with our cap guns and cowboy hats. I want to be that little boy again, or even the boy I was a half hour ago, at home with my Strat-O-Matic.

The four officers from two cars surround us. They open all four doors and pull each of us out, instructing us to place our hands behind our heads. Each one of us gets our own cop. We're paired off like dance partners. Miles gets a woman; he'll never hear the end of it. Martin surrenders his keys and invites them to inspect the trunk. They pop it open. I half expect five more of our friends to pop out and make a run for the Mann France Avenue Drive-In. The cops, likewise, expect to see something illicit, bundled drugs, perhaps, or bricks of cash. But all they see is a jack, jumper cables, a snow brush, and a spare tire, the usual cargo of the Minnesota sedan.

Inspecting the interior of the car also reveals nothing, save for eight moist palm-print stains in the soft fabric of the ceiling.

"Why were you fleeing us if you had nothing to hide?" the driver of the first cop car asks Martin.

"Why were you chasing us?" Martin reasonably asks, in what rapidly becomes a chicken-or-the-egg conundrum.

"You were rubbernecking me," the officer says.

Martin explains his fear that he would lose his license if he was caught driving one mile over the speed limit, a fear that now appears to have been well-founded and self-fulfilling.

The police radio squawks. Our faces are bathed in the blue and red lights, revolving, at two o'clock on a Saturday afternoon. Guests are gathered at the hotel entrance and peering through upper-floor windows to rubberneck us, the alleged rubberneckers. My hands are still raised behind my head, though at least this position allows me to air out my equatorial armpits.

I keep waiting for them to say they're taking us "downtown," while wondering where exactly downtown Bloomington is. In the '70s, when Dad bought a famously unreliable wood-paneled Ford LTD Country Squire station wagon at Freeway Ford, it came with a complimentary pop record, a 45 called "Downtown Bloomington," whose protagonist was told to meet a girl in the center of our suburb: "She said, 'Go to downtown Bloomington, that's a great place to go.' / But where is Downtown Bloomington, nobody seems to know…"

But we won't be "booked" downtown. After fifteen minutes,

a cop asks Miles, Ope, and me if we have someplace nearby we can walk to. Or failing that, he says with a straight face, would we prefer a ride home?

I see Mom, devastated, as the squad car pulls into the driveway. I type it out on my left thigh: D-E-V-A-S-T-A-T-E-D. Another left-handed word.

"We'll walk," the three of us say in unison.

Martin is being "detained." With a backward glance—relief masquerading as sympathy—the rest of us set out for Ope's house, a mile away. They never read us our Miranda rights. We don't get fingerprinted. A rogue cop like Animal on *Hill Street Blues* doesn't threaten to bite off my nose while calling me a "hair bag." The only TV police trope we've encountered is the female officer who frisked Miles.

"Was that Cagney or Lacey?" I ask him as we jog south through the Target parking lot toward Ope's house.

"It wasn't Heather Locklear," Miles says, of T. J. Hooker's rookie colleague. "Officer Stacy Sheridan can frisk me any day."

To make light of the terror we all just felt but cannot acknowledge, we imagine being frisked by various fictional policewomen: Sergeant Pepper Anderson from *Police Woman*. Any one of Charlie's angels. Officer Bonnie Clark on *CHiPs*.

From Ope's house, I walk the three miles back to South Brook, emerging from the park across the street into my own driveway like Shackleton returning to base from his Antarctic misadventure. All told, I've been gone three hours, or about how long it takes to see a matinee. When I finally walk through the front door, wearing a look of practiced ennui, Dad is dozing in front of the TV and Mom is watering the houseplants. I'm relieved that she doesn't ask why I've walked home from a place to which I had been driven. But more than that, I'm relieved to be arriving home by any means other than a squad car, with nothing whatsoever on my Permanent Record.

"How was the movie?" Mom says, tending to her spider plants and philodendrons.

"Okay."

"Just okay?"

"Funny, I guess."

Taking them four at a time, it's three strides up the stairs, then three more to my room, where I lie on my bed. It's still too small but suddenly feels just right.

# 3

# Simply Waste the Day Away

In these moments, I think of John, eleven years old, sleeping in my old room, and I envy him his trivial pursuits, among them Trivial Pursuit and the other board games that fill our basement cabinet, with fewer takers each year, as the required participants on the box ("4 to 6 Players") exceed the number of kids in our house.

*Our house.* It's no longer the house in "Our House," where "there's always something happening and it's usually quite loud."

Some days I'm home from school before John and Amy and can hear a clock ticking on a basement shelf. The clock is an executive award presented to Dad, with a brass plate on it engraved with his name and the acronym of some trade organization. If Mom is out running errands and isn't playing her *Cats* original-cast recording cassette in the kitchen, or listening to Steve Cannon on *The Cannon Mess* on WCCO, then all I hear is the clock ticking, and the compressor of the basement fridge kicking on and off.

On those days, it's a relief to hear the Nativity bus go by, and thirty seconds later John's footsteps on the kitchen linoleum upstairs. In some ways, he is who I was, in thrall to whatever sport is in season. John plays baseball all summer in two Franklin batting gloves—they have to be Franklin—and real eye black. Mom used to burn a cork and smear it on my cheeks for eye black. She used the same technique to give me a dirty face and five-o'clock shadow when I dressed as a "bum" for Halloween. But John has some authentic, professional-grade eye black bought at Kokesh, probably during Kokesh Krazy Days, when "Prices at Kokesh go kompletely krazy" and everything is deeply discounted, and we ransack the bins on the sidewalk for shirts with subtly botched sponsor names. You can get a sweet basketball jersey for a couple of bucks if you don't mind that the back says MURPHY'S PUBIC HOUSE.

John's a good athlete. He plays football in the fall, too big to carry the ball so he's on the offensive and defensive lines. Right now, he's still playing hockey in mid-spring. The kids wear the colors of their high school district, so John has the Kennedy jacket. Mom dutifully sews on his tournament patches: SQUIRT CLASSIC. PEEWEE SHOWDOWN. SILVER STICK. Youth hockey players look like decorated soldiers. "John" is stitched in script on the front of the jacket, though Tom and I and all our friends call him Junie, short for Junior.

At Nativity recess, John plays Smear the Queer, in which you kill the guy with the ball until he coughs it up. It's always best in winter and spring, when the snow and padded snow clothes soften the impact of getting tackled. John's pal Mike Broiles has his pants and shirt ripped so frequently by the baying mob that his mom has to drive on a near-daily basis to Nativity all the way from PWB—Prestigious West Bloomington, as they say in the real-estate ads on the radio—to deliver spare uniform pants and shirts.

I picture Broiles sitting in the office shirtless and bloody but uncomplaining, waiting for Mrs. Broiles to resupply him with a fresh uniform. Nothing has changed at Nativity. The ladies in the office, the nurses and the secretary and the principal, take it all in their stride. John still goes in on Monday mornings to find the CCD kids have stolen pens and erasers from his desk.

On Saturday afternoons, when we go to four o'clock Mass at Nativity, the school across the parking lot looks shrunken. I imagine the eyes of the parish are on me as I walk up for communion, head bowed, in my Kennedy letter jacket, purchased with great ceremony at Westwood Skate and Bike: The navy wool body with the navy leather sleeves, and the letter *B*—navy, trimmed in gold—on the right breast. Made of felt and chenille. "Kennedy" in script on the middle bar of the *B*. A gold basketball pinned to the letter. And sewn to the right sleeve, just below the shoulder, that navy-and-gold "84."

I do the math. John will be in the Class of '91, a decade so distant—the nineties—as to be science fiction. He'll essentially be a kid forever, and I envy him. John spends his summer days playing ping-pong and box hockey at Parks and Rec, my old summer hangout in the otherwise-empty Hillcrest Elementary School across the street. But he's also a frequent visitor of the high dive at Valley View, the municipal pool on 90th Street. I never had the balls to climb the ladder to the top of the high dive, much less jump off it, ten meters down into a pool that must look from the platform like a footbath. But John doesn't just jump off; he *dives*. "So the water doesn't go up my nose and drown my brain," he explains, a persistent fear of his that I do nothing to dispel.

My irrational fears of age eleven (quicksand, killer bees, lake sharks) have grown into the rational fears of seventeen: girls, military draft, nuclear annihilation. On a Sunday night a few months ago, I sat in the basement and watched *The Day After* on ABC while Mom, upstairs, watched part one of the seven-part NBC blockbuster miniseries *Kennedy,* starring Martin Sheen as JFK, assassinated twenty years ago to the week. *The Day After* was terrifying from the get-go, the dread building from its opening disclaimer: "Because the graphic depiction of the effects of a nuclear war may not be suitable for younger children, parental discretion is advised."

The paper suggested no one under twelve should watch, so John was exonerated while Amy and I cowered beneath two afghans knitted by Grandma Boyle and watched Jason Robards try in vain to save his fellow citizens from the nuclear warheads raining down on Kansas. Cows grazed and bees flitted in a final tableau of life-on-earth-as-we-knew-it. The Emergency Broadcast System sounded its shrill alarm, but this was not a test. The ensuing horror of locals getting liquefied by the Russkies was so terrifying that I feared I would need Mike Broiles's mom to bring me a clean pair of pants. The prime-time hellscape of charred bodies and irradiated skin would have been unbearable if not for the North Stars–Black Hawks game on channel 9, and my pressing need to check that score from time to time.

After two hours of unremitting bleakness on channel 5,

Robards returned to the ruin of his family home, fired up his homemade radio—I was reminded of the Professor from *Gilligan's Island,* and the jerry-rigged radio's central role in survival—and pleaded over a black screen: "Hello? Is there anybody there? Anybody at all?" The only answer was a slow scroll, white on black: "The catastrophic events you have just witnessed are, in all likelihood, less severe than the destruction that would actually occur in the event of a full nuclear strike against the United States. It is hoped that the images of this film will inspire the nations of the earth, their people and leaders, to find the means to avert the fateful day."

One hundred million Americans watched *The Day After.* It left me utterly bereft, though there was some consolation when Neal Broten notched the game winner for the North Stars with two minutes and twenty-three seconds left at Chicago Stadium. By the time *The Bud Grant Show* came on channel 4 at 10:30 to break down the Vikings' win in Pittsburgh that afternoon, enough was still right and true and familiar in the world that I could face the night alone, or at the very least in the company of Steely Dan on the boom box. But not Prince: "Everybody's got a bomb, we could all die any day..."

John doesn't listen to music on the other side of the wall. His dreams are untroubled by *The Day After.* On nights he does watch TV, he basks in the cathode-ray glow of *Happy Days* and *Diff'rent Strokes* and Mrs. Garrett's other show, *The Facts of Life,* and, on Saturday nights when he can stay up later, *The Love Boat* and *Fantasy Island* back-to-back on channel 5. I still love these shows too.

John has no desire to be "out" on a weekend night, nor any anxiety that he is the only one among his friends who is home, watching TV with Mom and Dad. This is precisely where and with whom he wants to be, without embarrassment for now.

I've spent my whole life wanting to be older, and now that I'm on the cusp of adulthood, I envy my little brother.

There are parties most weekend nights at Kwai Chang's house. Kwai Chang was David Carradine's character on *Kung Fu,* a show that's been off the air for nine years. I don't know how our Kwai Chang got his nickname, or what his real name is. But I'm exceedingly uncomfortable at these or any other parties. I've never drunk a beer and I have no intention of starting now, pounding Hamm's beneath a bare bulb in Kwai Chang's garage, not because I'm morally abstemious but because I'm underage and don't want to get in trouble. "Stay out of trouble" are Mom and Dad's parting words when Tom goes out, but not when I do. On the contrary, they're surprised and delighted when I go out, and their expressions seem to say: *Get into trouble.*

Kwai Chang was thrown through the picture window of his house while playing poker—his defenestrator thought he was dealing from the bottom of the deck—and now the window is boarded up. I don't have the sangfroid to get into that kind of trouble and brush it off, like shattered glass from my shoulders.

Adam Ant—*adamant*—is singing about me: "Don't drink, don't smoke—what do you do?"

What I do is bowl. To give it an ironic cool, Mike and Oly and Z and I say we're "rolling the rock," as in "Man, wanna roll the rock?" The best nights out are when I get that call, to go to Airport Bowl, on the Strip by Airport Beach, for there will be laughter, semi-athletic competition, and the chance to witness criminal damage to property—from some patron comically heaving a fifteen-pound bowling ball into an adjacent lane or through a drop-ceiling panel. At least once a night Z will chase Oly across the parking lot while swinging a sixteen-pound Ebonite at him like a wrecking ball as the manager meekly implores both of them to remove their rented shoes before taking their dispute outside. The manager would likewise prefer we not write our names on the score-card, visible for everyone to see on the overhead display, as "Hugh Jass" or "Ben Dover." But a quick scan of the adjacent scoreboards reveals an unbroken line of Mike Hunts, Phil McCrackens, and Seymour Buttses.

I'll return home via the Castle with secondhand smoke deeply embedded in my letter jacket, and the scent of bowling-shoe disinfectant lingering in my nostrils.

Some nights we go to Lyn-Del Lanes, on Lyndale Avenue next to White Castle, which is flanked on the south side by Beanie's Arcade, making it a mini Strip for Kennedy students who can play Punch-Out!! or Galaxian for two hours, cleanse their palate with a sack of sliders, then roll the rock to the thunderous clatter of bowling pins and Journey.

We bowl in teams, for money. It's always Mike and Oly against Z and me. Z and I are the starting forwards on the bas-ketball team. We're the same height, but he outweighs me by twenty-five pounds of muscle, intensity, and bottled anger. Z is cocaptain of the basketball team and captain of the football team, in which he plays middle linebacker in a neck roll and comically large shoulder pads, though he's terrifying enough without them. In basketball practice the other day, Mike threw a pass when Z wasn't looking. The ball hit Z in the face and knocked out a false tooth that none of us knew he had. There was a long interval of silence when everyone—coaches included—paused to see if Z would rip Mike's head off.

A student manager retrieved the tooth and, with a bow of deference, handed it back to Z. Enraged and embarrassed, Z reared back and threw the tooth like a skipping stone across the gym floor. It skittered under the accordion bleachers, never to be found.

And then, with a single bleat of Coach Strommen's whistle, practice resumed as if nothing had happened.

One day after an evening of rolling the rock, Z overhears me talking to one of the juniors before practice about Strat-O-Matic basketball. Like Strat-O baseball, it's a cards-and-dice game. It simulates real NBA games between real NBA teams of real NBA players, with one significant difference. If the NBA is jazz—improvisation within a group dynamic—Strat-O is double-entry bookkeeping. Every move of every play requires rolling dice, reading charts, cross-consulting with other charts, ordering double-teams, calling time-outs, addressing player injuries, and—best of all—keeping a detailed and elaborate score sheet replete with arcane statistics. I love it. As with writing, Strat-O-Matic is a game played on paper, where I can bend it to my will. The NBA is aerial; Strat-O-Matic is actuarial.

"What are you talking about?"

It's Z, who I fear knows exactly what I'm talking about, this nerd game in which I pretend to be Michael Jordan and Magic Johnson.

"Nothing."

"You were talking about... Strat-O-Matic?"

"Yeah, but only because—"

"I *love* Strat-O-Matic," Z says. "We should play sometime."

And so begin my visits to Z's house after practices to play Strat-O-Matic in his basement. Our Strat-O games are intensely contested—I'm the Celtics, Z's the Sixers—but the tension of them is undercut by the pure joy of our temporary return to prelapsarian boyhood. Sitting in the basement, playing a board game after school, we could be nine again, if not for Z's tin of Copenhagen, the complicated nature of the game itself, and the knowledge that he can, if required, bench-press Mom's Honda Accord.

His own mom supplies us with chips and pop, a service moms still provide, regardless of our age. Our moms are sacrosanct. We've grown taller than them but remain afraid of them. As a species, dads are less universally revered. Some dads are absent, some dads are dicks, some dads let their kids drink beer in the house, some dads drink beer in the house themselves at noon on Wednesday. If some moms do these things as well, I've never heard of it. On the contrary, moms are the ones supplying us with pretzels and lemonade, laundry service, livery service, a maddeningly cheerful reveille every morning at 6:30, the aggravating discipline of household chores, and the domestic bedrock of rigorously balanced meals and checkbooks. My own mom keeps a household budget in a spiral notebook, every single expenditure—every postage stamp and bottle of Prell—logged with ballpoint pen in the impeccable script of an eyeshaded scrivener out of Dickens.

A year ago, when reminded that I had promised to mow

the lawn for three consecutive days, I told Mom to get off my back, and then yelled, "Damn it!" while storming down the hall. Swearing in front of my parents was a novelty. I was trying it on, seeing how it looked, like I used to do in the three-way mirror at Dayton's when Mom would take me back-to-school shopping.

In ordering me back to the kitchen to apologize, Dad addressed me as "buster," a poker tell that he was livid. I returned to the kitchen with the confidence of the morally righteous and declined to apologize, adding, in front of Mom, "I'm not kissing her ass." The words hung in the air, as visible as in a cartoon balloon. They had a physical weight. We all stood around for a second and regarded them from various angles. I wanted to snatch them from the air and stuff them back into my mouth like Lucy Ricardo on the haywire assembly line, stuffing the chocolates into her cheeks.

My shame was instant. In not sending me through the kitchen wall, Dad summoned every subatomic particle of his patience. I stormed upstairs to my room and paced it like a caged animal, trying and failing to justify my actions. I didn't face Mom again until morning, when she declined to acknowledge me at breakfast. After an hour of a blanketing silence, as thick as fog, I found the strength to issue a wildly inarticulate apology, an unintentional homage to Fonzie, who couldn't say the words "sorry" or "wrong" and instead always apologized with "I'm suh-suh-suh..." and "I was wruh-wruh-wruh..." Mom returned me to her good graces after an overnight defrosting.

This twenty-four-hour thaw is customary. With Jim and Tom out of the house, I'm the next man up: big brother, protector, and counselor, charged with handing down the secrets, customs, and knowledge that they passed along to me. There's a spot in his sock drawer, for instance, where Dad keeps a drum-shaped box filled with dimes. He'll never miss three or four of them when you need spare change for candy at Pik-Quik. Likewise, any contraband you keep in your bedroom—ancient Halloween candy, racier *Mad* magazines, typewritten essays aping the newspaper columns of Mike Royko or Art Buchwald or Erma Bombeck that would cause you to die if anyone read them—all of that is best hidden in plain sight inside your shoeboxes of baseball cards. As long as those boxes are stacked neatly in your closet, Mom will never look inside them.

All of this I tell John, but not Amy, whose skepticism of her brothers is well earned.

Amy is finishing eighth grade, its own rite of passage: confirmation and graduation and her first slow dance, to "Time After Time."

She's taller than the boys in her class. Jim and Tom have told her that her feet are big. "Look at these boats," they say, picking up one of her Tretorns. Her butt, they've told her, is enormous.

And yet, to the evident horror of her brothers, Amy is becoming—in Dad's words—a "young lady," a phrase Mom usually employs as an admonishing form of address: "Don't talk to me that way, young lady."

She has shed her braces, has traded her glasses for contact lenses, and was recently granted permission to grow her hair longer—out of the Dorothy Hamill haircut that all moms, including ours, still love eight years after Dorothy Hamill became America's sweetheart at the 1976 Winter Olympics in Innsbruck, Austria. Many of those moms still wear over-sized Dorothy Hamill glasses, their last connection to the figure skater, now that their daughters have achieved tonsorial autonomy.

No longer will Amy sustain tinfoil burns in the backyard while Mom and Mrs. O'Brien give her a perm. Mom still won't let her wear ripped jeans, but Mom has also instituted a new Secret Santa program to promote sibling bonhomie. We draw one another's names from a hat and buy that brother or sister a Christmas present. Last year Jim drew Amy and got her a pair of Calvin Klein jeans with white stitching and a velour V-neck sweater. It's her favorite ensemble, but like Twins pitcher Frank Viola, it is only allowed to appear every five days or so.

John already has his own pair of designer jeans, whose red triangle has replaced the red tag of Levi's as the hood ornament of choice among Bloomington eleven-year-olds. "Check out my Guess jeans," he says. "Sweet." My friends will impersonate this line for years, replete with John's slur, for which he gets speech therapy: *Guessh jeansh. Shweet.*

It only occurs to me now, several weeks after the fact, that Mom rigged the Christmas lottery so that Jim, the only one with money, drew Amy, the only one of us cruelly bereft of designer jeans. (I don't have them because I don't want them.) The notion of Jim shopping for Amy's clothes—holding up the V-neck on its hanger, checking the jeans tag for Amy's waist size—is suddenly absurd. Mom bought Amy the jeans she'd forbidden her to wear, using Jim for plausible deniability.

Jim and Tom and I now openly laugh at some of the good-faith presents we get from well-meaning relatives, specifically our Uncle Pat and Aunt Sandy in Reno. This past Christmas, they sent five Rubik's Cube key chains, each in individual boxes. Two of the boxes were empty.

Mom laughed so hard she was in tears. We still don't know why two of the boxes arrived empty, but it was clear from Pat and Sandy's enclosed note that it wasn't a practical joke.

"When you write the thank-you card," Mom said, "don't say that your box was empty."

"I'll send them an envelope with no card inside," I suggested.

Like most American families, ours was already in possession of a roughly used Rubik's Cube, the white-hot pop-culture artifact of 1981. Thirty million had been sold by 1982, at which time ours had been frequently thrown against walls or trod upon in the dark by Dad in his stocking feet, eliciting a burst of stifled profanity.

The colors of the Cube itself—decals in red, white, blue, orange, yellow, and green—are all turned up at the corners, after being peeled off and rearranged countless times as a shortcut solution. We also became adept at popping off the corners of the Cube and replacing them to our advantage, often to win a bet. "I bet I can solve this in three minutes," Tom might boast, before disappearing and returning with a solved Cube. Erno Rubik taught the Rushins nothing about algebraic principles—his original purpose for inventing the Cube as a teacher in Budapest—but he inadvertently taught us quite a bit about grifting and cutting corners.

Two Christmases ago, Pat and Sandy sent us audiocassettes. I got Billy Squier's *Don't Say No,* containing the hit single

"The Stroke," whose chorus was an endlessly repeated two-word phrase. "Stroke me, stroke me..."

"Perfect for you," Tom said.

"Isn't your sister pretty?" Dad often says to the Boys. "Pretty *ugly*," we reply. Why Dad keeps offering up this straight line is anybody's guess, but she is unquestionably Dad's favorite. We know because he says so. If John and I are laying waste to the refrigerator at noon on a Sunday, devouring great stacks of lunch meat and drinking orange juice straight from its Tupperware decanter, Dad will walk through the kitchen and sing, "All the monkeys aren't in the zoo, every day you meet quite a few."

Mom doesn't coddle Amy the way Dad does. "Why don't you fix a sandwich for your brothers," Mom tells her as we play hockey in the basement. When John is old enough to drive and has cause to run an errand with Amy, Mom will ask, "Why don't you let your big brother drive," even though Amy is three years older than her "big brother." Dad tells Amy she's going to be a doctor, but Mom suggests she aim higher and become a nurse.

Jim has told Amy she should only play a sport whose uniform is a skirt. Golf, perhaps, or field hockey. She chooses tennis, but all the matches are right after school, so Dad never gets to see her compete. She nurses a persecution complex, often expressed with righteous indignation. I'll think of Amy this summer when I hear a line on the radio that goes "It's obvious you hate me though I've done nothing wrong..." The song is by Depeche Mode, in keeping with the current vogue for pretentious and ridiculous band names. Orchestral Manoeuvres in the Dark. Kajagoogoo. Echo and the Bunnymen. Haircut One Hundred.

Fun Boy Three. Psychedelic Furs. There are three Thompson Twins and none of them is named Thompson.

I've grown up on bands named for great flying beasts— Eagles, Zeppelin, Wings—and the familiar places they soar to and over: Boston, Chicago, Kansas...*America*. New wave's great flying beast is A Flock of Seagulls. Its one band named for a city is Berlin. I can't metabolize the music or even the haircuts. The new music I listen to is almost exclusively by black artists. I turn to the R&B chart first whenever Dad purges his briefcase of his unread *Billboard* magazines, complimentary copies of which pile up on his desk, for he is a titan of magnetic tape, the lifeblood of the recording industry.

So I listen to Cameo, the Gap Band, the Whispers, the S.O.S. Band, and the Jonzun Crew. In a couple of months, Prince is going to release his "long-anticipated" album and "major motion picture" of the same name, its title borrowed from "Ventura Highway," by America. That song always puts me in mind of the previous decade and our family trip down the California coast in a rented wood-paneled station wagon during the glorious summer of '77: "Sorry, boy, but I've been hit by purple rain..."

Before I leave for college, those last two words will forever belong to Prince, who has already mined Orwell in a similar way. On New Year's Day of 1984, while eating my Cheerios and reading the *Star and Tribune,* I paused over this line in an op-ed column by Anthony Burgess: "Orwell, writing his novel in 1948, set its events in 1984 because that year seemed remote enough to be mythical." With *1999,* Prince set the apocalypse for 2000, still safely sixteen years in the distance, no matter what *The Day After* would have me believe.

# 4

# Dancing with Myself

In the backyard of a house on West 98½ Street, there's a basket-ball half-court in a spot where most people have their patios. I gaze at this concrete square through the window of the school bus every morning. It's roughly equidistant between my house and Mike's and right next door to our friend Tony's, whose dad we call the Fly, because that's what the Fly calls all of us: "Tony, who are these *flies* you brought into the house?"

One afternoon, Tony walks into his family room to tell the Fly that we're all going to grab a Quarter Pounder with Cheese at the new McDonald's on Lyndale. "Dad," Tony says, "we're going to Mac and Don's."

The Fly never breaks eye contact with the TV as he replies: "Who's Mac, who's Don, and you ain't goin'."

The Fly has a genius for inserting swear words into already existing words to create something greater than the sum of its parts, the way Mom likes to stuff rice into hollowed-out red peppers. "Unbe-fucking-lievable," he might say as Ron Davis gives up another bomb in the bottom of the ninth for the Twins. Sometimes the Fly will double down on the profanity and declare something "Bull-fucking-shit," and I like the way he's cracked open one swear word and inserted another inside it, the way some baseball players wrap Bazooka around a chaw of Red Man to get the double rush of sugar and tobacco.

From Tony's house, the train tracks run all the way out to Prestigious West Bloomington. Tony and his best friend, Flynn, have become adept at hopping on a boxcar *while holding on to their bikes* and riding the train out to the Valley West mall before riding their bikes back home.

So Mike and I go to Tony's to listen to the Fly, and to see Tony hop a train, or to drag him to the softball field behind John Deere and take turns hitting towering home runs with a tennis ball. But in the course of visiting Tony's house we hear a rumor: the guy next door with the half basketball court in the backyard is Flip Saunders, former captain of the University of Minnesota basketball team that sent three of its other starters—Ray Williams, Mychal Thompson, and Kevin McHale—to stardom in the NBA. Only Flip's size—he's five foot ten—prevented him from making the Celtics. He's now an assistant coach with the Golden Gophers after four seasons as head coach at Golden Valley Lutheran College, where his team went 56–0 at home behind a captivating forward with a supreme Minnesota name: Nelson Johnson.

Mike and I start to mill around outside that house, in the street, hoping to see Flip go in or out. After many days of fruitless loitering, Mike has an idea. He opens that mailbox on West 98½ Street and examines the contents while I stand a hundred feet away, knowing that tampering with the United

States mail is a felony. With a suppressed shriek, Mike stuffs
the mail back into the box, but not before briefly brandishing
a smoking gun—the homeowner's Minnegasco bill, in whose
cellophane window appears the name Philip D. Saunders.

As I stand at the foot of the driveway, Mike walks up
to the door and knocks. A twenty-five-year-old blond former
Gophers cheerleader answers.

"Yes?" she says, looking for the candy bars Mike is almost
certainly selling for his Little League fund-raiser.

"Is this Flip Saunders's house?"

"Yes," she replies. "I'm his wife, Debbie. Can I help you?"

"Can he, uh…"

"Can he what?"

"Come out to play?"

There is a moment of stifled laughter as Debbie says something into the void behind her. Then she turns back to Mike.

The answer, to our everlasting astonishment, is yes. Yes,
Flip can come out to play. Or rather, we can come in, to the
backyard, and shoot hoops on his half-court. He has a coach's
easy banter with younger people. Flip suggests minute adjustments to our jump shots and expresses his admiration for our
wooden attempts to impress him with spin moves and finger
rolls. Then he disappears into the house to let two strangers
play one-on-one in his backyard. If he and Debbie saw us
rifling their mail through a gap in the blinds, they are kind
enough not to say so. The balls on Mike, to open up their
mailbox, knock on their door, and talk to the grown woman
who answers, when I can't talk to a girl much less ask one to
the prom, despite Mom's frequent suggestions that I do so.

"If you don't go to your prom," she says, "you'll regret it

for the rest of your life." She still has matchbooks, supper-club menus, and carnations from her own prom in Cincinnati pressed into a scrapbook in her bedroom closet.

We both know that I will forever regret not going to the prom. We also both know that I won't be going.

On the night of the winter formal dance, Mike, Ope, and I are seeing Kool & the Gang at the Carlton Celebrity Room. We've purchased tickets this time, though previously we've only ever snuck into the Carlton, a Las Vegas–style dinner theater in East Bloomington, which means grown-ups in blazers and dresses dining at tables with cutlery and china while watching Tom Jones sing "Delilah."

Sneaking in isn't hard. Half the people we know work at the Carlton, including Oly and Gator.

The trouble is, once our friends have spirited us in through the kitchen—Oly is a busboy—we spend the night walking to or from our nonexistent table to the men's room, never reaching either destination. I'm often content to hang out near the can, in the carpeted lobby outside the doors to the auditorium, where all I really get is the bass line and the cocktail-buzzed patrons leaving or entering the men's room.

Occasionally, though, one of us finds a dropped ticket stub on the lobby floor and will pass it back and forth like the letters of transit in *Casablanca,* allowing us—one at a time—to occupy a folding seat and thus hear a snippet of a set from the Commodores or the Little River Band. Behind the booths and tables are theater seats occupied by the majority of the 2,200 patrons who fill the pie-shaped theater to hear synth-pop gods Spandau Ballet play "True."

The singer Mel Tillis, whose stutter evaporates in song, headlined the Carlton Celebrity Room when it opened five years ago, in 1979. Putting the word "Celebrity" in its name was an effort to speak something into existence: call it a "Celebrity" room, the celebrities will come. And they did. I'd seen Tillis on *The Tonight Show*—and there has followed a parade of men and women onto the Carlton stage who previously appeared on that show: Charo, Wayne Newton, and the insuperable Engelbert Humperdinck.

Rodney Dangerfield once killed in a three-minute stand-up set on *Carson,* then moved over to the couch to plug his upcoming gigs. "I'm gonna be in a place I've never been before in my life," he told Johnny. "Minnesota."

An audience member whooped.

"Minnesota?" Johnny said.

"Minnesota," said Rodney. "Bloomington, Minnesota."

I nearly fell off the love seat.

"Land of a thousand lakes," Johnny said.

"That's right," Rodney said. "There'll be a lotta lakes over there."

"A thousand!" Johnny said.

"That's right," Rodney replied, rolling his eyes. "A thousand lakes'll be there. And I'll be at the Carlton Celebrity Club."

"The Carlton Celebrity Club," Johnny echoed.

"In Bloomington, Minnesota," Rodney repeated.

"Bloomington, Minnesota," Johnny said, to titters from the audience.

"This place is so far out in the woods," Rodney said, "my act'll be reviewed by *Field & Stream.*"

It was unbelievable to witness. Rodney Dangerfield from

the Miller Lite commercials and Johnny Carson himself, the king of late-night TV, were talking about my hometown on the set of *The Tonight Show*. And it almost didn't matter that they called the Carlton Celebrity Room the Carlton Celebrity *Club* or that Johnny said "a thousand lakes" when "10,000 Lakes" is the phrase on our license plates. The point was Johnny Carson had seen our license plates. He spoke the words "Bloomington, Minnesota."

Mike and Ope and I also snuck in to hear David Brenner, another comic who appeared on *Carson*. But for Kool & the Gang, we've not only purchased the best seats in the house — a red-leather banquette front and center — we're properly dressed for the occasion.

Mike picks me up in the Bonneville. He's wearing a pair of Stacy Adams shoes that I can only surmise he has gently removed from an unconscious pimp. Mike's also wearing a white tuxedo shirt and a red clip-on bow tie purchased at the Valley West Marshalls. He's gone deep into his well of Dippity-Do, gelling his hair into a style that we've called — on other people — a Dippity-Don't.

I'm wearing a blue blazer with gold buttons embossed with anchors, and a maroon argyle V-neck sweater over a blue button-down oxford shirt. My khakis break just above my cordovan penny loafers as I duck into Dr. Terry McCollow's sky-blue land yacht. Ope is wearing his dad's sport coat over a puffy pirate shirt from Marshalls. We roll into the Carlton parking lot, pass the entrance to its Backstage disco, moor the Bonnie in a space, and walk three abreast into the Carlton Celebrity Room with the bravado of Frank, Dean, and Sammy strolling into the Sands Hotel and Casino.

At the edge of the stage, we brandish our tickets at the skeptical ushers, who show us to our sumptuous booth, where we order three Cokes. "On the rocks."

In the next booth is a Jefferson hockey player Mike knows, and he's brought a date. By the time the house lights go down and Kool & the Gang materialize onstage in matching white marching-band pants and silver lamé shirts, our mouths are too busy chewing prime rib to sing along to "Get Down on It." As the show carries on, the Jefferson hockey player, whose name I now know is Kyle, slides into our booth with his date, and the five of us bask in the warm glow of the footlights, our cavity fillings gently vibrating to Robert "Kool" Bell's bass.

I'm too self-conscious to dance, but I'm already throwing caution to the wind tonight, rolling the dice in this mini Las Vegas, by exposing myself to the stage's strobe lighting, which Mom often reminds me could trigger a recurrence of the grand mal seizure I had as a three-year-old.

The music critic for the *Star and Tribune,* Jon Bream, has called the Carlton "mediocrity for Middle America," but you wouldn't know it on this night, when the Backstage disco seems to have moved into the main room. A small crowd of Minnesotans—generally loath to show emotion in public—have turned the narrow moat between our booth and the stage into a dance floor.

Mike and Ope are up dancing solo, both of them displaying symptoms of White Man's Overbite, while the other three of us—Kyle, his date, and I—listen to the slow jam of "Too Hot" and gaze up at the stage, where James "J.T." Taylor is purring, "At seventeen we fell in love, high school sweethearts, love was so brand new..."

And yet I somehow feel less awkward here, as the third wheel at my own table, than I would at the winter formal. Prom theme this spring will be "Dancing in Heaven," named for last year's smash by the British one-hit wonders Q-Feel. "Dancing in Heaven" is about getting down in outer space. If the future prophesied in books, songs, and movies is even remotely punctual—Orwell's *1984*, Prince's *1999*, Kubrick's *2001*—we'll be among the celestial bodies by the time we're thirty, consigned there by rocket ship, or reduced to carbon by nuclear oblivion. On this night, I can't yet imagine turning eighteen, never mind thirty, not as Kool & the Gang kick into their finale and every repressed Minnesotan in the Celebrity Room dances in the aisles. In the darkness of the booth, I bite down on my lower lip and gyrate in my seat, making a motion like I have to pee. Across town, other kids are attending the winter formal: the boys in suits, banding their dates with wrist corsages like the banded ducks tracked by the Minnesota Department of Natural Resources. Like all of them, I'm dancing. Not in heaven, but close enough—in Bloomington, shining the seat of my red banquette with my pleated khakis.

A familiar pang of longing descends as we leave the Carlton and gaze next door at the abandoned rust-hulk of Metropolitan Stadium—former home of the Twins and Vikings—whose magnetic pull I still feel, three years after it closed. The Met is derelict. Bereft but not yet bulldozed. The field on which Rodney Cline Carew won seven batting titles in the 1970s, where the Purple People Eaters ruled the National Football Conference in the same decade, is often infiltrated by kids my age leaving behind beer cans. Bloomington still feels done wrong by the teams that abandoned us for a dome in downtown Minneapolis, so we trespass upon those who trespassed against us.

The decaying molar of the Met recedes in the rearview. Mike and Ope and I are still high from the concert and six Coca-Colas. It's not "Celebrate" that we're singing in the Bonneville on the way to White Castle, where we appear to be regular winter formal attendees who released their banded dates back into the wild. As Ope's Hush Puppies hit the white-tiled floor, and our pupils contract in the Hopper light of the "dining room," and Barney the rent-a-cop fails to recognize us in our dress-up clothes, my two best friends and I are still singing our favorite Kool & the Gang song. All together, and without irony: "Oh yes, it's Ladies' Night, oh what a night…"

Every night ends at the Castle. After Tom's friend Nelly got ejected from the Saint Paul Civic Center for hocking a loogie at Jerry Blackwell as the beer-gutted villain made his bombastic entry into the ring at all-star wrestling, Tom and Nelly went to the Castle. After prom, after keggers, even after gorging oneself at a different fast-food franchise, the night ends at the Castle.

In high school, Tom and his friend Digger teamed up in a competitive eating contest against two other friends, Timmy C and Shootsy, who earned his nickname for saying "shoot" instead of "shit." Shootsy arrived at Pizza Hut having fasted, armed with a powerful appetite and a grim determination to vanquish Tom and Digger. The pizza-eating contest that followed would live in legend as The Sow-Down.

Pizza Hut is cheap. Somewhere, in what I imagine is

the chain's hut-shaped headquarters, their bean counters have calculated how much even the most ravenous person is likely to choke down at an all-you-can-eat buffet and set their price accordingly. Tom, Digger, Timmy C, and Shootsy are not those average people. They're fueled by petty rivalries that date back to grade school, the kind of grudges—over marbles, Little League, musical tastes, hairstyles, and cruel nicknames—that only good friends can nurture.

As each new steaming pie was delivered to the Pizza Hut buffet, Tom, Digger, Timmy C, or Shootsy was there to collect it. They kept a strict accounting of how many slices each participant devoured, and as that number crept, per capita, into the double digits, the four of them eyed each other above the tops of their bottomless pop glasses and wondered whose gastrointestinal tract would blink first.

One by one they cried uncle, first Timmy C and then Digger, until it was just Tom vs. Shootsy for the Pyrrhic victory. As Tom continued to eat like Pac-Man—with a relentless, almost robotic joy—Shootsy retreated to the bathroom, via the buffet. When Tom and Digger followed soon after, to make sure nothing fishy was going on—"Trust, but verify" as President Reagan put it—they found Shootsy in a stall, on the toilet, with his pants around his ankles and a whole pizza on his lap.

He was trying to eat it while trying to make room for it. Exposed in this way, Shootsy knew it was over. He summoned what remained of his dignity and waved the white paper napkin of surrender.

And even then, having just won The Sow-Down, Tom insisted they all go to the Castle. This was partly to prove he could eat more—a few sliders with vinyl, a few gobblers with glue—but also as a kind of valedictory, the victory cigar after a fine evening. Every night ends at the Castle.

Turning up there after Kool & the Gang, we see the usual suspects: freaks, jocks, dirts, dorks, lops, fries, and gearheads—the entire taxonomy of Bloomington's high schools.

Any kid who smokes, wears an Iron Maiden shirt, has a leather wallet chained to a belt loop, or clomps around in Frye boots is a "freak" or a "dirt." "Dirt" is short for "dirtball." Frye brand motorcycle and hiking boots are also known as shitkickers, freak boots, and wafflestompers. So ubiquitous are the Frye boots that the freaks are also called "fries," partly for the footwear, partly because their brains are presumed to have been fried by the many controlled substances they presumably ingest.

It will be another three years before the Partnership for a Drug-Free America airs its public-service announcement with an egg popping and hissing in a cast-iron skillet: "This is your brain on drugs." But fries and Fryes and frying metaphors are already coupled with drugs in Bloomington high schools.

At Jefferson, the fries smoke in the Pit, and the jocks hang out on the sundeck directly outside Jock Hall, where passing girls are rated. Or so I've heard from Jefferson exiles. The boys hastily scrawl a number—anything from 1 through 10—in BIC pen on a sheet of notebook paper and hold it up as if they're Olympic judges watching the figure skating at Sarajevo.

I never talk about girls. I don't tell anyone that I'm secretly enamored of Mallory from *Family Ties,* Bailey from *WKRP in Cincinnati,* Jo from *The Facts of Life,* Jayne Kennedy from *The NFL Today,* the brunette from Bananarama, Sadé, Fawn Liebowitz's roommate in *Animal House,* Phoebe Cates, Valerie Bertinelli, Daphne from *Scooby-Doo,* Rachel Ward in *Dead Men Don't Wear Plaid,* Mrs. Kotter, Jennifer Beals, Julie the cruise director on *The Love Boat,* Daphne Zuniga from *The Sure Thing,* and—with an ardor undimmed since elementary school—Clarice, the doe-eyed caribou love interest of the title character in the stop-motion animated Rankin/Bass production that airs once a year in December, *Rudolph the Red-Nosed Reindeer.*

In a bit of architecture that John Hughes might have dreamed up, the sundeck at Jefferson, purview of jocks, overlooks the Pit, purview of fries. Inevitably, the jocks once poured a pot of ink from Art class onto the fries below, touching off a free-for-all, the news of which made its way to Kennedy, where we hate the Jefferson jocks because they're our basketball (and hockey, football, and wrestling) archrivals—the Jefferson Jaguars, a.k.a. Jag-offs.

"Dickie Turner had a sweet pair of wafflestompers at Olson," says Oly, who attended Olson Junior High. "But then he set a girl's hair on fire in Music class and got sent to juvie."

Dirts, freaks, and fries go to juvie. Some of us who went to Lincoln High School before it closed still call fries "gumbies." We could fill a dictionary with our slang. Farting is "creasing." Money is "skins," "jing," or "bones." Our classmates resort to "kiping" or "gripping"—petty theft—when they have no jing, or merely for laughs. Laughing is "rolling." Fun is "yuks." Some kids—jocks and fries alike—get their yuks at the expense of nerds, who are known variously as lops, doofs, dinks, dorks, and spazzes. If jocks, fries, and dorks are the three circles of a Venn diagram, many of us fall into at least two of the overlaps. There are smoking jocks, dorky fries, and—if I'm being honest, under the baleful gaze of the ARE YOU A NERD? poster—at least one jockish dork who collects coins, simulates baseball games with pencil and dice, and writes stories about those games in his bedroom on his mom's typewriter. The only thing that marks him out as a jock are his hoop shoes.

As it was at Nativity, when we wore a school uniform, our sneakers are the only things that set us apart. Shoes contain multitudes. They're the one article of clothing I care about, and therefore the only real variable in my wardrobe. There's a line from "Moving in Stereo" by the Cars, the song Phoebe Cates gets out of the pool to in *Fast Times at Ridgemont High:* "Life's the same, except for my shoes."

The closest thing a non-fry has to Frye boots are Hush Puppies, which we also call "desert highs" or "wallabees." They're high-topped, lace-up, brushed-suede, crepe-soled, sand-colored "desert shoes" that make no sound. Like the cornmeal balls of the same name—once fed to hounds to keep them quiet—Hush Puppies stop your dogs from barking. Hoop shoes announce themselves with a squeak on the polished corridors of Kennedy High. Hush Puppies, like nursing shoes, are silent—something a meek assassin might wear with his cardigan sweater. I have a cardigan sweater, kelly green, with the alligator on the breast, love child of Mister Rogers and Jack Nicklaus, but I'll never wear Hush Puppies.

"Hoop shoes and sandals are all I'll ever need," Mike says, dreaming of a life shuttling between the basketball court and the shuffleboard court at some Airport Beach of the future. "They'll call my biography *High-Tops and Flip-Flops*."

Our high-tops are Converse Dr. Js or Adidas Top Tens or Adidas Pro Models, the high-top version of the shell-toed Superstars worn by rap group Run-DMC on the back of their self-titled album that just came out. We also like Nike Blazers and Bruins, Pro-Keds, Ponys, Batas, and Chuck Taylors. With his Chucks, Ope often wears four or five pairs of socks, in homage to Pistol Pete Maravich; I prefer a single pair of three-striped tube socks with a pair of baseball "sanitary socks" worn over them, preferably gold, to offset the blue-and-gold uniforms we wear as members of the Kennedy Eagles basketball team.

There's a growing appetite in Bloomington for Doc Martens, army boots, and other signifiers of the punk aesthetic. A secondhand clothing store has opened in Bloomington and attracts high school students like flies. Or rather: in addition to flies. Ragstock specializes in army jackets with someone else's surname stamped on the breast; gas-station-attendant shirts with someone else's first name stitched in cursive inside an oval patch ("Buster"); and bowling shirts with a jaunty team name emblazoned on the back ("Pin Pricks").

I come home one day in the spring wearing a wool navy pea coat purchased for nine dollars at Ragstock. Mom has complicated feelings about it, torn between her love of a bargain and her fear of anything that reeks of "hillbilly." And this coat literally reeks of hillbilly.

"Pea coat?" Tom says, on a rare weekend home from Iowa State. "You mean a smells-like-pee coat."

Tom looks slightly different. His Brillo-pad hair can never be teased into the full Flock of Seagulls, so he's settled for something more staidly new wave, a tonsorial tribute to Echo, perhaps, or one of the Bunnymen. He wears boxers now, like Dad, and laughs at my tighty-whities. The wire arms of his John Lennon glasses loop around his ears, but it's the ears themselves that have been most radically transformed. His eardrums were punctured in a cataclysmic explosion and are just now mending.

I don't know what he's told Mom and Dad, but he tells me that the freshmen were required to dig a mock grave in the front yard of their frat house and bury an effigy of a fictitious alumnus in an annual rite of freshman passage. Tom thought there must be a more efficient way to make a six-foot hole than with a spade and a wheelbarrow, and so he and a colleague mixed oxygen and acetylene in a trash bag, which blew the yard, and themselves, to smithereens.

The explosion was heard several blocks away at the ER, to which Tom was taken posthaste. The concussive wave he touched off blew his pants into tatters. "The first thing I did was look in my boxers," Tom confesses, as the *Katy Lied* cassette plays between us at 1 a.m., "to see if I'd blown my balls off."

He hadn't. Like the Roadrunner, Tom always emerges from these situations with his extremities intact and his Permanent Record pristine. This time is no exception, apart from his ruptured eardrums and absent eyebrows.

He returns from Iowa as if from a five-year circumnavigation of the globe. He's into bands I've never heard of that open for bigger acts I've still never heard of. "I saw this awesome band called 10,000 Maniacs open for R.E.M.," he tells me. "I hung out with R.E.M. at a bar after the gig, then we all went to some random house after that.

"At the Violent Femmes show in Iowa City," Tom says, "my buddy Shithead, who never wears underwear, had a hole in the thigh of his jeans. One of us ripped his pant leg *off,* leaving him partially naked. He got onstage to dance and got booted out by security. But he snuck back into the balcony and sprayed the crowd with a fire extinguisher..."

The stories go on like this, all of them involving college bands and buddies named Shithead being escorted out of bars, houses, or concert halls while wearing a T-shirt as a fig leaf.

Back in January, Mike and I drove down to Ames to visit Tom, two teetotalers staying overnight in the communal guest room of a fraternity house whose subtropical heating required us to sleep with the windows open on a 20-degree night. Not that we slept. The house throbbed and thrummed with music and mayhem until 3 a.m. We had left the hothouse party downstairs and ascended to the guest room, wall-to-wall and floor-to-ceiling bunk beds, stacked three-high, so that we very nearly had to be slid into them on long-handled peels of the sort that pizza makers use to slide pies into brick ovens. That we were the only sober people being warehoused in that room—quite likely the only sober occupants in the long and checkered history of that room—only heightened our discomfort. In this context, *we* were the debauched ones, wantonly undrunk.

Back in Bloomington, Mike sometimes carries a half-gallon carton of milk with him, swigging from it at parties to advertise his fealty to athletic good health, and our basketball team's wholesome determination to follow wrestling and hockey to the mountaintop of high school jock experience: "going to State," which is to say the high school state tournament.

# 5

# Hold On to Sixteen as Long as You Can

Basketball is our outlet and our altar, our vocation and avocation. We play it in driveways and suburban parks, in cutoff sweats, in red Chucks with blue laces, in striped socks, terry-cloth wristbands, Rambis glasses, Kareem goggles, and careworn T-shirts from the Mychal Thompson Basketball Camp, where Dr. J signed a piece of notebook paper that I held out to him like a trembling leaf on a sapling branch. The magnificent orb of his Afro remained bowed over the card table as he signed with long tapered fingers that made the BIC pen in his hand look the way the scorecard pencils at Putt-Putt mini golf look in mine. When those fingers slid the notebook paper back to me, the signature on it—"Julius Dr. J Erving"—had the healing power of a real doctor signing a scrip for some powerful euphoric.

Thompson and Doc and all the other NBA players at camp carried leather briefcases that turned out to be backgammon sets. So strong was our desire to *be* these men that Mike and I asked for and received backgammon sets for Christmas, preparing ourselves for our future lives as Rolls-Royce-driving, fur-coat-wearing, prodigiously gifted professional basketball players exempted from gravity's law.

That was years ago, in eighth grade. There has since emerged an even higher power, a basketball god greater than Doc. Larry Bird—Larry to us, shorn of surname—is why I wear white athletic tape on my fingers and black Converse Weapons whose soles I wipe with the sweaty palm of either hand before I shoot a free throw. Larry is the reason Mike and Ope and I watch every televised Celtics game as if we have a hundred grand riding on the outcome. "You are looking liiive..." Brent Musburger intones on CBS, stirring our blood as the lacquered crazy quilt of Boston Garden's parquet floor fills the screen.

If we see something of ourselves in slow, white, earthbound Larry, we never say so out loud. All our other favorite players are black: Doc, Iceman, Gus Williams, Bernard King, and World B. Free, whose name I've written in ballpoint pen on the rubber ball I dribble and spin and shoot at home. That ball is attached to me like a goiter, its pebble-grained surface worn bald and smooth over the years.

We watch the Celtics in Mike's basement, on the TV we call Richie the C, because it looks like Richie Cunningham's 1950s console set on *Happy Days,* a great walnut casket, eternal and immovable by fewer than six men. Dad returns from his biennial trips to Japan to tell us of the consumer-electronic wonders that await us in our adulthood—that mythical space-age future—including slim high-resolution TVs that will hang above fireplaces like oil paintings. These TVs are already in the works in Tokyo, whose Akihabara neighborhood Dad describes as an electronic wonderland, where he first saw the Sony Walkman that is now part of any self-respecting basketball player's pregame wardrobe.

Gazing into Richie the C, a TV that could never be hung above a fireplace without the aid of a crane, the only future we can see is the future of basketball, as Larry whips a no-look pass to Kevin McHale, Flip Saunders's former teammate with the Gophers and a demigod himself, Orpheus to Larry's Apollo. We have watched McHale play in person at Williams Arena on the campus of the U. Sitting up in the bleeders, with a box of popcorn and Cokes, engulfed by noise.

Woe unto Mrs. McCollow whenever she descends to the basement with 7 Ups and cheesy popcorn while Larry's on a cold streak or the Celtics are suddenly trailing. "I thought you boys might like some popcorn," says the woman we call Dory (though never within earshot) while standing in front of Richie the C with a butler's tray.

"Jesus, Mom, can you just leave it on the table? We can't see the *game,* for Chrissake!"

Dory shakes her head in quiet dismay but remains unbowed. "I'll leave it here, boys. Oh dear. I've forgotten napkins. I'll just nip back upstairs and—"

"Mom! *Please!* Nobody cares about napkins!"

Dory smoothes her apron with both hands as Ope and I sit on the couch in silent mortification. "Michael!" she mutters, disappearing up the stairs. "I never!"

In the absence of girlfriends, wives, children, or careers, Larry is our source of pride, our object of adoration, vessel of our hopes and frustrations. His achievements are our own, as are his failures. We defend him against charges of being inferior to Magic Johnson, of dunking lamely and cultivating a dubious mustache.

Our dream as basketball players is no longer to play for the Celtics or even for the Gophers. At seventeen, those dreams—of being Rod Carew or Evel Knievel or Rocky Balboa—have burst like soap bubbles, leaving only the faintest residue as evidence that they ever existed. Our dream now is to play one game on the famous raised court at Williams Arena, televised throughout Minnesota on channel 11, covered by the *Minneapolis Star and Tribune* and the *St. Paul Pioneer Press* and the *Bloomington Sun*. And this dream is only marginally more achievable than playing for the Celtics.

The dream is to play in the Minnesota state basketball tournament, which is always reduced to a single word: "State," like "Oz" or "Mecca."

Because for all the basketball we play—on playgrounds, driveways, and the court at the Y, with Nerf hoops and Strat-O-Matic boards—we play above all else for John F. Kennedy High School. We play in navy-piped double-knit polyester gold shorts and jerseys that fit us like sausage casings. In class, before practice, we doodle in our notebooks, redesigning our ridiculous warm-up suits, purchased in the early '70s and never modified, so that the bell-bottom pants feature vertical stripes in navy and gold and white. They're the kind of pants a color-blind Uncle Sam would wear to conceal his stilts in a Fourth of July parade.

We breezed through the regular season with 18 wins and 2 losses, both of them to Jefferson, the first time at our place on a half-court shot at the buzzer, leading me to the unspoken conclusion that those bastards from Prestigious West Bloomington might be unbeatable. It is inevitable that we face them again in the regional final of the playoffs: the Jefferson Jag-offs, denizens of Jock Hall, resplendent in their classic uniforms of Columbia blue and silver, in their blue Adidas Top Ten high-tops and shooting shirts with their names emblazoned on the back. Winner goes to State.

The game is in Minneapolis, on the neutral court at Augsburg College. I've never been as nervous or excited about anything in my life, even though I know instinctively that Jefferson will win, because winning is what they do, and pessimism is what *I* do. But I also feel—after playing basketball almost daily for the last five years—a serenity in surrendering to whatever happens.

Mom and Dad won't witness it. They're on a Mickey Mining sales-incentive trip to the Caribbean that was booked ages ago, when they assumed I wouldn't be playing in the regional final for the right to go to State. Amy and John are old enough to be home alone. Tom and Jim are in Iowa and Illinois, respectively. No member of my family is there to witness the Kennedy Eagles—from the opening tap—beat the ever-living snot out of the Jefferson Jaguars.

Everything is easy. I feel like a precision component in a Swiss ass-kicking machine. I'm reminded of the moment in our driveway a few years ago when I finally beat Dad at one-on-one, despite his fifty-pound weight advantage and disinclination to play by the rules. In the waning moments of the game, the Kennedy student section chants, "Wrestling, hockey, basketball!" Our wrestling and hockey teams have already gone to State—wrestling won it all—and the growing chant serves as a taunt to the Jefferson players, parents, coaches, and student section. By the time the crowd counts down the final ten seconds, my own skin is pebble grained, like the basketball's.

At the apocalyptic horn, I run around mazily before getting swallowed by court-storming students, a photo that will run on the front of the *Bloomington Sun* Sports section. Borne off my feet on a human tide. Jefferson cheerleaders are in tears.

I just want to get home, put Amy and John in Mom's Accord, and drive us to Bridgeman's ice-cream parlor, home of the La La Palooza Sundae, where Mom and Dad have taken us to celebrate good report cards and Dad treated Tom and me after taking us to see *Jaws* when I was eight.

I tell John and Amy to order anything they want. "On me." It could hardly be otherwise. This feels like the first grown-up act of my life. It's the first check I've ever reached for. Three marble sundaes. I calculate the 15 percent tip in my head and leave $1.78 on the table instead of grandly stuffing it into the waiter's breast pocket, which is what I feel like doing.

Some of my teammates are partying or out with girlfriends or even celebrating at the Castle right now. Amy, John, and I are experiencing the instant hangover of the ice-cream brain freeze. For perhaps the last time in many years to come, I'm marking a milestone not with beer or champagne or cigar or shot glass but with vanilla ice cream, chocolate syrup, and sprinkles. The cherry on top is an actual cherry on top. Hold on to sixteen as long as you can—at least until you're seventeen or eighteen.

\*     \*     \*

When Mom phones from their Caribbean hotel to ask how the game went, I know she has prepared some maternal words of consolation. "We're going to State," I say casually. "They're going to State!" Mom says, for the benefit of Dad, somewhere in the hotel room. There is disbelief, and joy, and a touch of melancholy when she speaks to me: "Oh, honey, I wish we were there." A week later, Mom and Dad are back home and we are set to play the state quarterfinals in the home of the Golden Gophers. If we win there, we're on to the final four at the Saint Paul Civic Center.

We skipped school yesterday for a banquet at the Saint Paul Athletic Club. Mom placed a matchbook with the SPAC logo into the maroon pages of a scrapbook she bought for me, along with the sign that had been taped to our mailbox this morning by the cheerleaders: YOU CAN DO IT...WE KNOW YOU CAN. GO STEVE!! SHOW 'EM WHO'S #1. It's the first note I have ever gotten from a girl. Mom will place that in my scrapbook too. In her mind, this is my prom.

It always snows at state tournament time, what the rest of the country calls March. One and a half inches today and 88.6 inches for the winter, the third highest total in Twin Cities history. Inside Williams Arena, as the snow falls, we change out of ski jackets and into tiny shorts and tank tops. Bare thighs on cold metal folding chairs: the bane of every Minnesota basketball benchwarmer.

Dad leaves work on a Thursday to be at our afternoon game, against North Branch, who has a six-foot-ten-inch center. The raised floor at Williams Arena is springy. For the first and last time in my life, I easily dunk in the layup line. Our band is here, and I think of all the times I've sat in this building, singing along to the U fight song: "Min-ne-so-ta hats off to thee, to thy colors true we shall ever be..."

I'm out of school on a Thursday, dunking in warm-ups like Dr. J in my Uncle Sam pants. On the bus, Mike played McFadden and Whitehead's "Ain't No Stopping Us Now" on his Sanyo box with the single honeycomb speaker. And we *are* unstoppable, scoring over and under and around North Branch's giant en route to a 54–41 cakewalk. Mike is interviewed postgame by Tom Ryther on channel 11. Back in our room at the Saint Paul Radisson, we wait through the weather to see our highlights on the ten o'clock news.

The next morning, the *Star and Trib* headline reads: KENNEDY'S RUSHIN PUTS RUSH ON FOE.

I don't know what that means, but it's a thrill to see my name in the Sports section. I can see Mom at home, scissoring the article out and pasting it into the maroon scrapbook. Dad will come home from 3M, sit in his Archie Bunker chair, snap open the paper, and stare through the hole where the piece used to be in sitcom-Dad exasperation.

The story begins: "Kennedy's 'forgotten man' introduced himself to the fans and North Branch Thursday.

"Steve Rushin, a 6-foot-4 senior forward, averaged around seven points and seven rebounds a game during the regular season. Yesterday he got 14 points and 12 rebounds to lead the Eagles past North Branch in the opening game of Class AA."

There follows a quote from me so anodyne ("The ball and the opportunities seemed to come to me today...") that it reads like a ransom note cut and pasted from all the clichés uttered by all the other athletes in the rest of the day's Sports section.

Outside our window at the Radisson, on top of the First National Bank building, is a red glowing number 1, fifty feet tall. We take it as a portent, our neon destiny. It doesn't occur to me that every other kid on the other three remaining teams—including our next opponent, unbeaten and top-ranked Minneapolis North—is looking at the same number 1 and feeling identically destined.

The Saint Paul Civic Center is another hallowed venue, site of the televised state high school hockey tournament, whose iconic see-through Plexiglas dasher boards make the rink resemble a Lucite lottery drum. This is where I saw my first concert—Earth, Wind & Fire in eighth grade. This is where I watched professional wrestling—Tom threw potatoes into the ring on a Friday night, then watched the taped broadcast on channel 9 after Mass on Sunday morning to see the potatoes rain onto the wrestlers. Before one of those matches, in the crowded ticket lobby, I watched a heavy man fall dead of a heart attack while the mass of spectators moved around him and into the arena to see the insuperable tag team of Jesse "The Body" Ventura and Adrian Adonis.

The high polish of the basketball court reflects the arena lights above. Three months from now, Bruce Springsteen will play in this building and pull a young woman in jeans and a white T-shirt out of the front row to dance with him onstage as director Brian De Palma films them for what will become the Boss's "Dancing in the Dark" video. We don't know that she's not a local girl from Fridley or South Saint Paul but an actress from Alabama named Courteney Cox. The thrill will be in seeing the Saint Paul Civic Center in heavy rotation on MTV, and in looking for Tom in the crowd shots. But the biggest thrill of all will be to say that Bruce, Mick, Keith, Dylan, and Prince played on that stage *and so did we.*

We're playing Minneapolis North on channel 11. *TV Week* says we're on opposite *Dallas, Webster, The Dukes of Hazzard,* and, on subscription cable, "**The Untamed** / Private eye tells a writer his romantic adventures. Kay Parker, Paul Thomas. 1978. Language, nudity, mature themes." I've stepped inside my TV.

Minneapolis North is in the "inner city," the setting of my favorite songs, and their black players are whom we imagine ourselves to be when we're listening to R&B on KBEM on our boom boxes. But we've been pretending long enough now to feel at ease against any opponent on any court—playground or civic center—and by the time I get a rebound and putback to give us a 40–37 lead, we're one quarter from playing White Bear Lake in the state championship game, if we can just hold it together for eight more minutes.

But North starts pressing, we turn the ball over for layups, struggle to get past half-court. In the ensuing avalanche, I'm reminded of casually opening a closet door and having all its contents fall on me. When my head finally emerges from the mountain of fallen boots and tennis racquets and suitcases, the last item in the closet—a bowling ball—falls off the shelf, causing birds to circle my noggin. We lose 59–52. The mimeographed box scores that circulate in the locker room after all our games—I like to press their purple ink to my face and drag in deeply the heady fumes—will show I had 10 points and 6 rebounds. I don't care. My teammates and I are in tears. I mimic the heroically vanquished Larry Bird, after losing to Magic Johnson in the 1979 NCAA championship game, and hang a towel over my head.

The consolation game the next night provides no consolation, beyond twenty-four more hours in the hotel and thirty-two more minutes of basketball against the hometown team, Saint Paul Central. It's almost a relief when we lose on a shot heaved from nearly half-court at the buzzer. As the horn sounds and the shot rips through the net, I retrieve the ball and spike it so hard into the court that it rebounds up toward the rafters.

I will never play another competitive basketball game, one with a scoreboard and a clock operator and referees in striped shirts and coaches and 13,997 spectators who hired babysitters and paid to get in and parked in a downtown parking garage. For ten years I've been handed a uniform and bought new shoes and molded a mouth guard marinated in boiling water, sucking the air out of the rubber to form-fit it to my teeth. Permission slips, participation fees, tryouts. Hockey sticks curved over the red coils of the stovetop. Like monks illuminating manuscripts, Mike and Ope and I illustrated our rubber basketballs with ballpoint ink. At the center of every one of these rituals was a contest of some kind—a game. And there would always be another game. Games were inexhaustible. We were too. But in this instant my athletic career is over.

As on a game show, it ends with a buzzer. Never again will I be part of a real team competing in a real league covered by real television channels and newspapers. That part of my life lasted three days. I've never been better at basketball and will never again play it competitively. I'm seventeen and a door has closed behind me with a thud and a click.

Emerging from the Civic Center locker room, hair wet from the shower, I'm greeted by Mom and Dad and Amy and John, but also by Jim, who had flown up for the weekend from Chicago. In years past, Jim would have consoled me with something like "Nice game—you want a medal or a chest to pin it on?" But tonight Jim greets me with a smile. He has seen something he admired, and these are the first words out of his mouth: "Nice spike."

We return to school as if it never happened. Orwell's Winston Smith makes his first diary entry on April 4, 1984. The Twins have lost their opener to the Tigers at the Metrodome, a predictable result, yet not one foretold by Orwell. I have an application in to work a concession stand at the Dome. I'm seventeen, and have to be nineteen to sell beer there, so Dad takes my birth certificate to Mickey Mining, makes a copy, whites out the last number in my birth year, rolls the Xerox into his secretary's glorious IBM Selectric II, changes 1966 to 1964, rips the paper out of the typewriter with a flourish, and—voilà—I am now nineteen, old enough to sell Grain Belt.

At least I'll have a job this summer. I'll have graduated by then. Sometimes I allow myself to think about the consolations of leaving home, though most of these balms are an end rather than a beginning—*not* mowing grass, *not* pulling weeds, *not* shucking corn, *not* working jobs that require smocks and visors for net wages FICA'd into fractions of an infinitesimal gross. And then I realize I will still be doing all of these things over the next four summers.

Hall & Oates have a new song called "Adult Education," and while I don't care for it, there's a line I can't get out of my head: "Believe it or not, there's life after high school."

I have preemptive homesickness, having not yet left home. I want to—in the words of John Cougar Mellencamp—hold on to sixteen as long as I can. Even though I'm already seventeen and am really holding on to age ten.

As one of my final acts in the school year, I finish Orwell's *1984*. On the penultimate page, before Winston Smith abandons his humanity and embraces Big Brother, he allows himself one last look back. "Uncalled, a memory floated into his mind." Winston is in his bedroom, "a boy of nine or ten, sitting on the floor, shaking a dice-box, and laughing excitedly."

He might as well be playing Strat-O-Matic.

6.

# One More Summer

We all look the same in our caps and gowns. But as members of the Class of '84 are called to the stage in alphabetical order, and I wait one more time for the *R*s—flanked by Rud and Rynchek in the countless roll calls of student life—I find myself at eye level with the shoes of those *A*s and *B*s and *C*s matriculating before me: the wafflestompers and Weejuns, the high heels and Hush Puppies, the high-tops and flip-flops. And I know who they all are, from the ankle down.

I'm on the floor at Met Center. Ordinarily, Willi Plett of the North Stars and Knuckles Nilan of the Canadiens would be exchanging haymakers on this very spot. Next week, Blue Öyster Cult will be playing "Don't Fear the Reaper" here, and the week after that, Rush will play "Subdivisions." I have grown up in a subdivision—South Brook—whose poet laureate is Geddy Lee and have absorbed half the Rush discography through open windows. "In the high school halls, in the shopping malls...In the basement bars, in the backs of cars."

It's strange to be in this arena without hockey or heavy metal playing. They have the same hair, the North Stars and rock stars. I should be up in the seats, selling popcorn. Instead, I'm on a folding chair, the ambient hum of "Pomp and Circumstance" playing. We're not yet through the *E*s. Hell, we're not yet through the Ericksons. "Jennifer Erickson...Lars Erickson...Margaret Erickson...Teresa Erickson..." I don't recognize my friends until they're on the stage, summoned there by formal, unfamiliar names. "Daniel Keane." *Hey, that's Gator.*

There's at least one student I don't recognize by name or face. He's known to me as Ferret and I've only seen him in costume, as the Kennedy Eagle mascot, flapping his wings at basketball and football games. Ferret smokes. Oly claims Ferret smokes *inside* the Eagle head, and that if I look closely, I might see smoke curling from the beak. In the last few months of school, with seniors walking across the street to Burger King at lunchtime and never returning to class, Ferret's been hosting a matinee poker game at his house. Even his dad, who sometimes participates in the games, calls him Ferret. But what his real name is, or what he looks like, or if he's already been summoned to the stage, I don't know. He's just an Eagle named Ferret.

They move their tassels from one side of the mortarboard to the other. Some collect their diplomas and shout that they're free. Individual families up in the hockey seats squeal when their common surname is called. Some of these kids are done with school, some are attending the U, others are off to Normandale Community College in Bloomington, what Jim and his buddies always called Harvard on the Hill. It's June 6, 1984, the fortieth anniversary of D-Day.

I collect my diploma. A gold plastic "84" is tied to my tassel. "Here we come," I tell Mom later, "storming the beaches of Normandale."

Forty percent of my classmates told the yearbook staff that they're going to a four-year college, eighteen percent to Normandale, eighteen percent to vocational schools, ten percent into the military, and the remaining fourteen percent are unsure what they're going to do with their lives but have all summer to think about it.

In the yearbook—*Prime Times*—staff members predict their future vocations and avocations. Almost every prediction is a (successful) effort to sneak a sex reference past the faculty advisor. One will have "a sex-change operation to experience the other side of whoopie." Another will become a madam on Hennepin Avenue (what passes for Minneapolis's red-light district). One will "give up a life as a flasher to write the *Penthouse* Forum column." One will become "a photog for *Swank*." And on and on it goes, for two pages: "Florida G-string critic," "stripogram agent known as the Molten Mountain of Human Desire," "porno film star," "transvestite maid at the Grab and Stab Family Inn."

A few make earnest attempts to forecast their future, ranging from "Gets Nobel Prize in medicine for curing AIDS" to "Marries Adam of the Ants and moves to Edina." The most poignant entry reads: "Marries a Jefferson graduate, settles down for a mediocre life in Richfield."

Mike's going to play basketball at a small college in Kansas City. On graduation night, in his basement, he and Ope and I watch the Celtics play the Lakers in Game 4 of the NBA Finals. The Lakers' Kurt Rambis, who wears a mustache and black-framed glasses, a cheap detective's disguise, is driving for a layup when McHale clotheslines him. The three of us surround the ancient TV, Richie the C, cheering McHale.

"Kick his ass, Kevin."

"Sit down, Rambis, you *Revenge of the Nerds*–looking motherfu—"

Dory has left the prison tray of snacks and drinks at the foot of the basement stairs and silently retreated to the safety of the kitchen.

We laugh when announcer Tommy Heinsohn, a former Celtic, says of McHale's violent act: "It's part of the game, ya know." We roar our approval when the Lakers' James Worthy misses a free throw and the Celtics' Cedric Maxwell makes a choking gesture at him. And we are high on life, cheese popcorn, and 7 Up when the Celtics beat the Lakers in overtime 129–125 behind Larry's 29 points. At the Castle, we try to eat one slider with vinyl for every one of Larry's 21 rebounds.

On Saturday, in the screened porch in our backyard at 2809 West 96th, I'm the guest of honor at my own graduation party. Mom and Dad give me presents: a soft-sided suitcase the color of a new penny and a ProKennex wood-graphite hybrid tennis racquet with an oversized head. Ope and I sometimes play tennis on park courts, cursing and racquet tossing like McEnroe and Connors. Tennis will ease me into a life of recreational competition. Mom and Dad play tennis. As for the luggage, it has an unmistakable message: *Get the hell out of here.*

Mom and Dad's friends file in and out of the screened porch, handing me cards with cash in them, congratulating me, urging me—now that I'm practically a grown-up—to call them by their first names.

"Hello, Mrs. Parker."

"Call me Rita."

But I don't call her Rita, and I can't, and I know (even now) that I never will, no matter how long we both shall live.

One Thursday night on *Magnum, P.I.,* the world-famous professional football champion "New Jersey Blazers" are training in Hawaii in July, as no team has ever done or ever will, but so what, because here's Dick Butkus as "Dumbo," an assistant coach in beltless Bike brand polyester coaches' shorts, Spot-Bilt coaches' shoes, striped tube socks pulled to the knees, and a whistle around his neck, like every coach I have ever had but will never have again.

I settle in on the maroon love seat. The orange afghan that Grandma Boyle knitted is folded on the ottoman, and all I know of these ancient Middle Eastern peoples—the Afghans and the Ottomans—is our home furnishings. I wonder if houses in Kabul and Istanbul have little accessories—throw rugs and armrest covers—called "South Brooks" or "Bloomingtons."

On *Magnum,* someone wants to murder the Blazers' philandering quarterback. Magnum and his helicopter-pilot pal T.C. investigate while Higgins holds down the fort at the Robin's Nest. It's all so comforting. Watching *Magnum* in our family room while the dishwasher gurgles in the kitchen is something I will miss in a matter of months.

After Magnum cracks the case, there's a short coda, just long enough to justify a final block of commercials on CBS. The quarterback knows his playing days and womanizing nights are near their end, and Magnum has wrapped up his own brief but happy return to football, and both men are content, having wanted only one thing at the twilight of their athletic careers: one last golden hour on a field of play.

The episode's title, displayed an hour earlier in big gold letters, now makes sense: "One More Summer."

That's what I have, One More Summer. One More Summer sharing a bedroom with Tom, who's home from Iowa State. We still fall asleep to *Katy Lied* on cassette, still sleep until midmorning, when Mom opens the door, complaining of the unspeakable smell. She dashes to the shades, pulls them open, and dashes back out the door, holding a handkerchief to her face as if fleeing a fire.

We both work nights. I sell pops and Dome Dogs out of a concession stand at the Metrodome when the Twins are in town, and Tom works the pass at T.G.I. Friday's on the Strip. In his spartan childhood in Fort Wayne, Indiana, Dad was pressed into a Dickensian world of child labor—toiling as a pin monkey in a bowling alley, stoking the hellfires of a Gary steel mill—and he thinks it did him a world of good. I'm told to get a second job, for when the Twins are on the road. It must be a short enough drive that Mom can drop me off. Which is how I answer a want ad in the *Star and Tribune* for a dishwasher position at Bennigan's on the Strip. When I submit my application and shake the manager's hand, he doesn't let go, and indeed tightens his grip, as if I'm pulling him back into a building from a window ledge. And perhaps I am. His only question after glancing at my application is "Can you start today?"

I show up at four in the afternoon in khakis and a white button-down, instead of more appropriate attire, like a scuba suit or a yellow rain slicker or nothing whatsoever, for unbeknownst to me I'm about to take a nine-hour shower.

The man I'm replacing has the mustache, girth, and shiny skin of a seal, saturated by "the Hobart," which is what Cody calls the dishwashing machine that stands before us belching steam. "It has the chemical conveyor," Cody says, slapping the Hobart, "the resin-rinse nozzle." Cody talks as if he's trying to sell me the Hobart. "The patented Opti-Rinse technology." He might as well be trying to put me behind the wheel of a Cutlass Supreme across the street, at Wally McCarthy's Lindahl Olds. Above me is a showerhead on a hose whose purpose is to power-rinse the dishes before they're fed to the Hobart. It reminds me of the microphones that drop from the rafters into the hands of a tuxedoed ring announcer before a heavyweight fight. "All of this," Cody says gravely, "is your responsibility."

Cody has been promoted to busboy but seems reluctant to leave the Hobart. I wonder if he's had intimate relations with that resin-rinse nozzle. After three minutes of feeding the Hobart filthy dishes and extracting clean ones, I'm soaking wet. My white shirt is translucent, adhered to my skin. I have the shriveled fingertips that were once the hallmark of a blissful afternoon in the Airport Beach pool.

"The nice thing," Cody says, "is you can get ahead of the dishes." He gives me a conspiratorial look, as if he and I are gaming the system. "Buy yourself some free time. If you wanna go out back and smoke a cig, you can go out back and smoke a cig. If you wanna take a nice twenty-minute dump, you can take a nice twenty-minute dump."

But you can't get ahead of the dishes, any more than you can get ahead of time itself. On a Friday night they keep coming, great piles of cheap crockery, arriving in busboy tubs on a conveyor belt, like crowded trains at rush hour. The plates and bowls and glasses themselves are still half full, covered in ranch dressing, cigarettes stubbed out on salad plates, fork tines plugged with chewed gum and chewed meat.

Each one of these unfinished plates and drained beer mugs is evidence of a grown-up Bloomington life on the other side of this wall. It's in the lipstick on a lowball glass, in the tongue-tied stem of a maraschino cherry, in the phone number on this paper napkin, scrawled with hope an hour ago, but consigned by its recipient—through me—to the Rubbermaid dustbin of history.

My first shift is four to midnight, and I never get a break. The twenty-minute dump is a pipe dream. I don't finish the dishes until after 1 a.m., when I stagger into Cody's Plymouth Volaré, for he has offered me a ride home. The June air is cool on my wet clothes. When we pull into South Brook, something about the subdivision looks familiar to Cody. But he can't quite put his shriveled fingertip on it. As we pass the little traffic island on Upton, which the ladies of South Brook plant with flowers every spring, a light bulb buzzes to life above Cody's head. "I passed out in that flower bed one night." It's nearly two in the morning. My next shift at Bennigan's starts at ten. The Hobart dominates my dreams.

Two hours into my Saturday shift, the manager tells me there's a "mouse" in the garage off the kitchen where the dumpsters are. Would I mind "taking care of it"? He hands me a push broom. I've seen enough Mafia movies to know that "taking care of" something means the opposite. I walk into the garage in the dark, wondering if I'm being hazed, if I'm on *Candid Camera,* if Allen Funt is going to pop out and interview me after a madcap mouse chase in the dark.

I stand in the garage for five full minutes doing nothing. And then I return to the manager and hand him the push broom and say, "I'm quitting." He doesn't betray the slightest surprise. This position has weekly, if not daily, vacancies. The two of us stand there in the kitchen for a moment, he with the broom, me looking hangdog, *American Gothic* in an imitation Irish pub.

"Can you finish the shift?" he finally says.

I do, and when Mom picks me up at four she says, "How was work?"

"Terrible."

"It will get better. When are you scheduled to work next?"

"I quit."

"You *what*?"

"They asked me to kill a *rat* with a dustpan and I—"

"You will have another job *next week.* You will *not* lie around the house all summer. Do you understand me?"

"Yes!"

We ride the rest of the way home in silence.

Working Twins games more squarely aligns with my career aspirations. During home stands, I don a polyester V-neck work shirt and brimmed hat, like the Twins themselves. Of course mine isn't a cap but a visor, and the "shirt" is a brown smock with a brown-and-orange plaid pattern across the chest and shoulders. If the Burger King were a real Scottish monarch, this would be his tartan.

From my concession stand, a small patch of right field is visible. Every once in a while, Tom Brunansky will run across it in pursuit of a fly ball. For three seconds at a time, a dozen times a night, I get to know the right fielders of the American League: Dwight Evans, Larry Parrish, Harold Baines, Saint Paul's own Dave Winfield, George Bell, and the exquisitely named Rusty Kuntz.

Across the polished concrete floor of the Metrodome concourse is a door that blends in with the wall. This is the entrance to the press box, and I spend most of every three-hour game wondering how I can bridge the endless forty feet from this workplace to that one.

For now I tong hot dogs from a Roller Grill into buns, roll the dogged buns into foil, stack the wrapped dogs like cordwood in a stainless-steel warming drawer, and sell them when the revolving doors to the Metrodome are unlocked. I pull beers, dispense pops, and pump molten nacho "cheez" with the viscosity of 40-weight motor oil into the little nacho-cheez hot tub in the corner of the tray. Every time I depress the cheez plunger, I imagine I'm buzzing in with an answer at the start of *Family Feud*. Dad and I still watch it after dinner at 6:30 and howl at the answers.

"Do you believe these bozos?" Dad says.

Richard Dawson: "During what month of pregnancy does a woman start to look pregnant?"

Bozo: "September."

Dawson: "Name an animal that has three letters in its name."

Bozo: "Frog."

With the exception of ABC's annual airing of *Brian's Song,* it's the only time I see Dad cry, nearly hyperventilating with laughter at *Family Feud.*

When the Twins are on the road, true to my word, I get another job, this one at "the Thumb," our local branch of the Tom Thumb chain of superette convenience stores, whose mascot is an elf. Not an elf like Ernie Keebler, of the Keebler Company, whose headquarters in a hollow tree was in Elmhurst, Illinois, when I was born there nearly eighteen years ago; nor is it Hermey, the misfit elf and aspiring dentist in *Rudolph the Red-Nosed Reindeer.* Rather, the elfin mascot of the Thumb is there to sell cartons of Salems, copies of *Penthouse,* and six-packs of three-two Pabst Blue Ribbon to Bloomington's thirsty, horny, Marlboro-jonesing citizenry.

I work from four to midnight scooping Polka Dot ice cream into cones for kids coming straight from baseball practice wearing the same uniforms of the Bloomington Athletic Association that I used to wear. I sell hot dogs from the little hot dog Ferris wheel on the checkout counter, as distinct from the Roller Grill at the Dome. I imagine a little hot dog amusement park, like Minnesota's own Valleyfair but devoted to rides exclusively for wieners: Roller Grill, Ferris wheel, log flume. So much of my work night is devoted to daydreaming.

Occasionally, friends come into the Thumb and stroll past the register with a wave. "Hey, man!" They leave the store with frozen pizza-shaped goiters or six-pack-sized tumors under their shirts. The next day, the manager will tell me, before leaving for the night, that the till was $14.32 short on my previous shift. I'll plead ignorance. And then I'll get busy "fronting" the milk: putting the soon-to-expire milk in the front of the dairy case. At home, I'll front my socks and underwear—moving the least recently worn to the front of the drawer—and fronting the plates and glasses in the cupboard whenever I unload the dishwasher.

In the back room at the Thumb is a pallet of shrink-wrapped nudie magazines that the manager shelves on his own. I'm never asked to front the *Playboys*. Two-Minute Tommy Kramer comes in on two separate nights, and the quarterback of the Minnesota Vikings takes three tins of Copenhagen from the rack on the counter and I ring him up, resisting the urge to tell him that he's Tommy Freaking Kramer. But he already knows, and he knows that I know, and for anyone who doesn't, he's wearing a polo shirt with the Vikings logo where the alligator ought to go.

Another night, a drunk puts nine separate items on the counter and when I ask "Would you like a bag?" he says, "No, I'll juggle them to my fucking car."

At times like this I fantasize about being Brad, working at All American Burger in *Fast Times at Ridgemont High,* when the middle-aged customer keeps demanding a refund because he wasn't "one hundred percent" satisfied with his breakfast. "Mister," Brad tells him, "if you don't shut up I'm gonna kick one hundred percent of your ass!"

I tell the drunk: "Then start juggling, because you're wasted and I'm calling the cops." He gathers his packet of bacon, his Winstons, his Slim Jim, his Mountain Dew, and sundry other ingestible vices and hauls ass for his car while I call the Bloomington PD to report a drunk driver. The phone number is taped to the counter just below the register. The Thumb doesn't have one of those giant rulers adhered to the doorframe to help me estimate the height of a departing armed robber, but I eye every customer who walks in for his larceny potential. I'm prepared to fork over the contents of the till and all the cigarette cartons he can carry.

If Mom's worried that her seventeen-year-old, posing as a nineteen-year-old, is closing a convenience store at midnight, she doesn't say anything, perhaps because I called her bluff and got the job within a week of my breakup with Bennigan's.

When I lock up the Thumb at midnight, and Tom gets off around the same time at T.G.I. Friday's, he picks me up, and we take a Tombstone from the Thumb's freezer case. At home, in the basement, we gorge ourselves on pizza, Mountain Dew, and rented videos. We only watch comedies: *Bananas, Sleeper, The King of Comedy, The In-Laws.* In the basement, punch-drunk with laughter at two o'clock in the morning, we wait for a *ding* to signal that our Steak-umm and Velveeta sandwiches have melted in the microwave. Like Pavlov's dog, we salivate at the sound of a bell. It's like old times, but not exactly. We laughed together as kids, but *at* each other, not *with* each other. We fought in this basement, with and without boxing gloves, and at some point—still in grade school—Tom rode away on his bike and I couldn't pedal fast enough to keep up. Somewhere down the block he achieved escape velocity from his little brother.

We were on muscle bikes at the time, Schwinn Sting-Ray knockoffs, designed to look like little motorcycles and make each of us in South Brook a tiny Evel Knievel. When he got to Iowa State, Tom suggested to Mom and Dad that he might buy a motorcycle to commute to class, and Mom replied, "If you do, we won't pay your college tuition." But Dad casually told Tom that evening, "If you *did* get a motorcycle, your mother would never know."

He bought a blue 1972 Suzuki Enduro 250, and on the first day of class he hit a car that had blown a stop sign. Tom was thrown over the car, sending him skidding on his pants across the pavement. The canvas uppers of his Top-Siders were torn from their soles, but Tom sustained only a broken pinkie toe. His white sweater was unmarked. "Obviously, I didn't make it to class," he told me. "But the next day I did. And the chick sitting next to me was the driver who caused the crash."

The motorcycle was totaled. He buried it in the grave he blasted for his fictional frat brother (and very nearly for himself), then got another, a '75 Honda 250, on which he jumped over the same grave, so strong was our childhood impulse to emulate Evel Knievel. On landing, Tom drove his front teeth through his lower lip.

His hospital visits tipped Mom and Dad off to his motorcycles, and I heard them talking in the kitchen about how one of their sons was a motorcycle daredevil and the other—me—wouldn't even get his driver's license. Daredevil and fraidy-cat, extrovert and introvert, party animal and wallflower. Tom and I have in common our nightly comedy video film fest. The next afternoon we'll quote whole monologues verbatim from *Sleeper:* "Do I believe in God? I'm what you would call a teleological existential atheist. I believe that there's an intelligence to the universe—with the exception of certain parts of New Jersey."

Peter Falk in *The In-Laws* lamenting the horrors he witnessed in an African village: "Tsetse flies...the size of eagles...carried their children off to almost certain death." At 3 a.m., it's the funniest thing either of us has ever heard. The names of these protagonists—Sheldon Kornpett in *The In-Laws,* Rupert Pupkin in *The King of Comedy,* Fielding Mellish in *Bananas*—will stay with us for the rest of our lives. We'll never again run from any trouble without suddenly zigzagging while shouting another Peter Falk line: "Serpentine, Shel, serpentine!"

I would never tell Tom, but I've come to cherish these nightly film fests, what I now think of—in homage to Bob Dylan, our fellow Minnesotan—as the Basement Tapes.

Back in mid-June, six days after graduation, Mike and I watched Game 7 of the NBA Finals on Richie the C in his basement. I had started to write stories about the games on my typewriter and save news clippings about them in a manila envelope. When the Celtics beat the Lakers in Boston Garden, where it was 91 degrees on the floor at game time, we celebrated so loudly that Dory checked on us in the basement, and we hugged her. She only shook her head, as baffled by our joy as by our anger when they lost.

Throughout the summer, we continue to play in Flip Saunders's backyard every weekend. Flip is half a foot shorter than I am but has longer arms. We see him shooting his cuffs on the sideline at Williams Arena as a Gophers assistant. Mike and I have been going to Gophers games for years, getting the pocket schedule at Coach Liquors—on the counter next to the Dum Dum suckers every kid gets for accompanying Dad on his Saturday morning mission to top off his supply of Hamm's Preferred Stock. Flip has enormous hands that easily palm basketballs and playing cards. He's a self-taught magician. *But his greatest sleight of hand is on the basketball court,* I think, watching him dribble while composing a feature story in my head, for I'm now writing stories about the games we play in the backyard or driveway or playground.

In the coming weeks, we gather enough players in Flip's backyard to contest fierce games of three-on-three. Tournament brackets are drawn up. Flip makes a trophy, wrapping a Cool Whip tub in aluminum foil so that it looks like the Stanley Cup. Flip tells me, as the resident word nerd, to come up with a name for the tournament. Madison Square Garden has the National Invitational Tournament. I decide this will be the Saunders Hoop Invitational Tournament. The acronym is written in Magic Marker on a piece of white hockey tape and adhered to the Cool Whip tub, and thus is born Bloomington's answer to the NIT: the SHIT.

Flip's friends have all played college basketball—one or two will play in the NBA—and while Mike and I are getting dunked on in Flip's backyard, we're equals in the bantering, to our blissful disbelief, getting away with saying things like "I'm gonna beat all a y'all motherfuckers in the SHIT."

Flip's life is a revelation to me, that you can still live like this—shooting hoops, cranking Rockwell on a boom box, making coins disappear with the tap of a wand—at the advanced age of twenty-eight.

The SHIT is contested on a perfect Saturday afternoon, June 23. It is a joy to have my shots blocked by men with thirty-two-inch vertical leaps and, when forced to sit out, to watch the baseball *Game of the Week* on NBC, Cardinals and Cubs from Wrigley Field. I've been to Wrigley on family trips to visit our old neighborhood in suburban Chicago, fallen in love with its ivy-covered brick walls, and even envied the cheapskates on the rooftops along Waveland and Sheffield looking onto the field for free: baseball's Peeping Toms. Above all, I love the inebriated fans inside the park—both the bleacher bums and announcer Harry Caray, now a regular in my house thanks to cable TV. John and I watch the Cubs religiously. We're captivated by the concept—games piped into our house like tap water, on WGN-TV. It doesn't matter that the Cubs are in third place in the National League East and trail the Cards 9–3 today.

The Cubs score 5 in the sixth, each run bringing more SHIT participants off the court to the TV in Flip's family room, until the court is empty and a semicircle of sweating basketball players stands around the set, watching Cubs second baseman Ryne Sandberg, his team down 9–8, face the Cardinals' fearsome reliever Bruce Sutter with the bases empty in the bottom of the ninth.

Sandberg swings. "Into left center and deep," screams Bob Costas. "This is a tie ballgame!" The ball is swallowed by the bleachers, a writhing mass of tube-topped women and shirtless men in nut-hugging jorts. It looks like the happiest place on earth. Flip, who played college basketball at the highest level, going 24–3 his senior year with the Gophers, appreciates the pressure Sandberg must feel with 38,079 watching him in Wrigley, and thousands more on the rooftops, and millions more around the nation gathered around their TVs.

It doesn't matter that the Cards go up 11–9 in the top of the tenth, or that Sandberg comes up again with two out and one on in the bottom of that inning, unlikely to vanquish Sutter (again), tie the game (again), and restore the joy to Wrigley (again). Costas is already reading the closing credits. "Coordinating producer of baseball, Harry Coyle," he says as Sutter delivers. "One-one pitch." Another gorgeous Sandberg swing. Costas: "Do you believe it?"

The shirtless rabble in the left-field bleachers is fighting for another Sandberg home-run ball. The drunks on the rooftops are slapping each other five. Sandberg is calmly shaking hands with the third-base coach on his way to the plate like he's just sold an order of ball bearings at a business meeting in Omaha. And the entire field of the first annual Saunders Hoop Invitational Tournament is rocking Flip's family room to its foundation. Ryne Sandberg is who we want to be—cool, clutch, handsome, nonchalant, circling the bases in the late-afternoon sun-and-shadow of Wrigley Field. "If I ever have a son," Flip says, "I'm naming him Ryne.

"Deb," he says to his wife. "We're naming our son Ryne. Ryno. Ryne Sandberg Saunders."

The Cubs win it 12–11 in the eleventh. I don't want to leave here, but I now also can't wait to get to Marquette, to Milwaukee, a ninety-minute drive from Wrigley Field, and become one with the bleacher bums in the bucket hats.

The courtside boom box is pumping "When Doves Cry." Prince's movie *Purple Rain,* filmed in and around Minneapolis, will premiere in Hollywood in a few weeks. Prince's success confirms my impression, formed in the previous decade by the Vikings and *The Mary Tyler Moore Show* and Cheerios and Lucky Charms and Tonka toys and a thousand other things that came from or were set in Minnesota, that I've grown up

in the center of the universe, however many galaxies remain
to be explored.

Even Dad knows Prince, and he's remained steadfastly immune
to the power of celebrity for his entire adult life. "Recording
artist?" he says, hearing Prince described as such. The *real*
recording artists, he'll tell you, are the men engineering and
selling Scotch brand recording tape to the coked-up candy-
asses constituting rock and roll's motley crew (including
Mötley Crüe).

Very few popular music lyrics have been caught in the lint
trap of his brain. The three lines he knows by heart are "On
the road again," "Hop on the bus, Gus," and the title phrase
from a Jerry Reed song: "When you're hot, you're hot, and
when you're not, you're not." Mom can actually identify and
listen to current soft-rock titans Christopher Cross and Dan
Fogelberg. And last year, when *The Thorn Birds* miniseries
unfolded on ABC over what seemed like 487 hours, Mom was
transfixed by Richard Chamberlain as the handsome Catholic
priest with impure thoughts for Rachel Ward—the same
impure thoughts for Rachel Ward that I've had since seeing
her in *Dead Men Don't Wear Plaid*.

Dad wouldn't know Rachel Ward from Monkey Wards,
as we call the Southtown outlet of Montgomery Ward. It's
maddening because he spends endless hours in New York and
L.A., in recording studios and television networks, in close
proximity to rock and TV and even movie stars whose faces
he doesn't recognize and whose achievements he doesn't
esteem. Every year, Dad attends a dinner in L.A. at which the
Academy of Motion Picture Arts and Sciences hands out its

Scientific and Technical Oscars. These are real Oscars given to illustrious nerds at a black-tie ceremony held five days before the televised Oscars for all the other categories. Dad rents a tux in L.A. and returns to Bloomington with infuriatingly vague descriptions of the movie stars he encountered during the previous week: "Some guy from *Star Wars*," he might say, or "the gal who was in that thing your mother and I saw last year" or "that guy from that airplane movie you and Tom liked."

"Leslie Nielsen? You met *Leslie Nielsen*?!"

"No, it was definitely a guy."

He's even worse with rock stars. When Dad walks into the family room to see a small man with a mustache and perm playing guitar on MTV, shirtless beneath a leather blazer, exposing a small woodland of chest hair, he squints and says, "Think I'll walk into Mickey Mining tomorrow dressed like *that* guy, see how that goes over."

"That's John Oates," I say, just to wind him up. "You don't know Hall & Oates?"

"I know 'Mairzy doats and dozy doats and liddle lamzy divey,'" Dad sings, and it's a perfect rejoinder, reciting a novelty song from 1943, the last time he was attuned to popular culture. Until now, that is, because now—suddenly, impossibly—Dad knows Prince.

Prince is everywhere, a constant presence on MTV alongside Diamond Dave, who traded in his marble bag for a school-bus driver's uniform in Van Halen's just-released "Hot for Teacher" video. Someone has worked out that the numbers on the chalkboard in the video—20, 9, 8, 19, 25, 12, 15, and 8—correspond to letters of the alphabet.

What they spell—TIHSYLOH—has to be read backward: HOLYSHIT.

To notice this, of course, you have to record the video, then play it back and pause it when the blackboard appears, but thousands of boys are doing that anyway, pausing the video as the bikinied teacher sashays across the classroom. Those boys have been enabled by blank Scotch brand videocassettes, and thanks to Dad we have an endless supply of them, stacked in the basement like gold bars at Fort Knox.

In his ongoing mission to bind the planet in magnetic tape, Dad makes one of his regular flights to Los Angeles. On returning, he casually mentions that Northwest Airlines had upgraded him to first class on the flight from MSP to LAX, and he was seated in row 2. The two seats in front of him—seats 1A and 1B—were empty. "The doors were about to close," Dad says, "when three people got on. Two of them were bodyguards, and the other one was your buddy."

"My buddy?"

"Prince."

The two bodyguards, Dad says, were enormous men in matching blue suits, "impeccably tailored," and leather dress shoes "polished to a high shine, without a millimeter of wear on the heels." Only Dad could see Prince and focus on shoeshines.

Prince, immaculate in a white jumpsuit, platform shoes, and the kind of mustache that would have Jim suggesting the cat lick it off, sat by the window in 1A. Dad sat in 2B, kitty-corner to greatness. One bodyguard sat next to Prince on the aisle in 1B, and the other took an aisle seat in the last row of first class. Prince didn't say a word until the flight attendant took drink orders, at which time he whispered into the body-guard's ear, and the bodyguard in turn stood and whispered in the flight attendant's ear.

"Funny thing is," Dad says, "you could hear Prince stage-whispering, *'Mineral water.'* And you could hear the body-guard stage-whisper to the stewardess, *'Mineral water.'* And then you could see the stewardess pour a mineral water and hand it to Prince."

I'm hanging on every word.

"Somewhere over the Rockies," Dad says, "Prince had to take a leak, and this elaborate protocol kicked in."

Bodyguard Two in the back row walked to the can and knocked on the door. Finding it unoccupied, he signaled to Bodyguard One in seat 1B, who blocked the aisle while Prince got up. Once they secured Prince in the toilet, Bodyguard One stood sentry with his arms folded and his back against the john, while Bodyguard Two took Bodyguard One's seat, presumably so no one could rifle through Prince's carry-on valise. Naturally, given the complications of undoing a jump-suit in an airplane bathroom, Prince took a while.

"When we landed at LAX," Dad says, "before the plane stopped taxiing, the process repeated itself." Bodyguard Two walked to the front of the cabin, Bodyguard One blocked the aisle to let Prince out, and the two behemoths made a Prince sandwich while deplaning. Dad was the next passenger off, directly behind them, and watched with an air of wonder as Prince and his bodyguards boarded a chauffeur-driven golf cart in the terminal and cleaved a path through the throng. If anyone was disinclined to notice this trio, a red light affixed to a pole on the back of the cart turned like a cop car's beacon, and the world's biggest rock star, wearing a jumpsuit and flanked by giants, made his way as conspicuously as possible through LAX at a stately rate of three miles per hour.

*Purple Rain* has its premiere at Mann's Chinese Theatre in Hollywood on July 27. MTV broadcasts the spectacle live to my basement. The red carpet is a *Who's Who* (and occasionally a *Who's He?*) of 1984 celebrity: there's Steven Spielberg, Paul Stanley from Kiss, Henry Thomas from *E.T.,* Donna Mills from *Knots Landing,* John Cougar Mellencamp, Morgan Fairchild of multiple *Love Boat*s, Lionel Richie, and Lindsey Buckingham from Fleetwood Mac. Little Richard tells the MTV veejay Mark Goodman that Prince is "the me" of 1984. Eddie Murphy is wearing a cheetah-print blazer, sleeves pushed up, collar popped, with no shirt underneath. Weird Al Yankovic, whose "Eat It" video is in heavy rotation on MTV, tells Goodman, "We all knew Prince was a great actor, but who knew he could sing?!"

Prince himself emerges from a purple stretch limousine, in a purple lamé coat, and ignores the waiting press. He hasn't given an interview in three and a half years. The kid from Bryant Junior High is the biggest star in Hollywood.

We see *Purple Rain* at Southdale. The audience cheers when First Avenue comes on the screen because we've all been there or driven past it and now by some strange magic it's on a movie screen. We try to identify any Kennedy girls in the concert scenes, filmed at First Avenue last summer. There's an explosion of laughter when Prince tells his costar, Apollonia Kotero, "You have to purify yourself in the waters of Lake Minnetonka." As Apollonia sheds her all-leather ensemble of boots, pants, gloves, and blouse, I can hear my own mom, from the shore, shouting that she should wait a half hour after eating before going into the water.

In its first week of release, *Purple Rain* replaces *Ghostbusters* as the most popular movie in America. This national recognition of Minnesota couldn't be more gratifying. If Ronald Reagan uses his next State of the Union address to extol the virtues of Jimmy's Lemon Tree restaurant or *National Geographic* devotes its August cover to Nine Mile Creek, I'll not be as taken aback as I am to hear Lake Minnetonka—a place only we know—immortalized by Prince, whom everybody in the world now knows.

Morris Day, Prince's *Purple Rain* costar and front man of the Time, is on *Letterman*. "It's interesting to me that Minneapolis is producing stars in rock and roll music, and now film stars, and actually that major movies are being made there," Dave says. "How does that *happen?*"

"It's a mystery to me," Morris says, to studio-audience laughter. It's a mystery to all of us. Dave is from Indianapolis, a place often confused with Minneapolis, and Prince's fashion sense, androgyny, and contradictory persona—reclusive but ubiquitous—clearly amuses Dave. "For those who haven't seen the movie," he begins a question to Morris, who interrupts: "Come on, everybody here has seen the movie."

"I haven't," Dave says, to applause. A few nights later, he introduces Apollonia as "the first guest we've ever had named Apollonia, and a former Ridgid Tool calendar girl." When he asks her what Prince is like, she says, "He's very good at basketball. I beat him once, though."

"Well," Dave says, smirking, "he must be very good. He must be a regular Bob Cousy if he's only lost once."

I love Dave's invocation of a Celtics legend, his skepticism over Prince's hooping skills, and his inability to take *Purple Rain* half as seriously as its stars do. Dave is utterly insincere, in open mockery of his guests, sending up the conventions of show business—"Please welcome the lovely and talented" so-and-so—while conferring an ironic grandeur on his recurring bits. I look forward to his readings of his "voluminous viewer mail." Or Stupid Pet Tricks: "This is just an exhibition, this is not a competition—please, no wagering."

What I love even more than Dave is New York itself. *Late Night* opens every show with a camera panning Manhattan in the wee small hours—traffic lights blinking, steam pouring from strange street orifices, yellow cabs, blue police cruisers, chalked pavement, signs for the Lincoln and Holland tunnels, a marquee on 42nd Street—BAD GIRLS at the Victory Theatre. Announcer Bill Wendell always opens with a joke about the city: "From New York, where *Minnesota Twins* is playing in Times Square..."

Dad has filled the bottom drawer of his filing cabinet in the basement with maps—places he's been and will return to—and I know from his map of Manhattan, which I've spread on the concrete floor and pored over like MacArthur with a map of the Philippines, that the camera is moving uptown in *Late Night*'s opening title sequence: from Times Square to Lincoln Center, then east to Radio City Music Hall. From there, the camera pans across 50th Street to 30 Rockefeller Center, and through a window into studio 6A, where Dave talks every night about New York's weirdos, comical cost of living, and general hostility. "I was at a restaurant last night," he says. "There was a ten-dollar service charge to get the Heimlich."

But I can tell he loves it—who wouldn't?—and that New

York is superior in some way to Los Angeles, the city that fascinated me in the 1970s, with its *CHiPs* and its *Brady Bunch* and its *Bad News Bears*. Dave gets to make fun of everything and everyone *for a living,* the way my brothers and I used to at the kitchen table. Jim has started tearing Mike Royko columns out of the *Chicago Tribune* and mailing them to me: a thousand words in April on how the columnist has wasted a significant portion of his life watching the Cubs—270 full days in all, by his calculation—and he's through with them forever: "Unless somebody can get me a couple for the home opener."

Dad brings home Jim Murray columns from the *Los Angeles Times.* Murray refers to San Diego as "San Di-don'tGo... America's retirement home." San Diego seems more exciting than South Brook, but I'm laughing anyway, because the whole point is to make fun of something.

To be a professional smart-ass doesn't seem achievable. But it's fun as an amateur pursuit. For years, in addition to the Twins and Celtics game stories I compose on my typewriter, I've written phony letters, news columns, and epic poems. I pull one out of an accordion file folder, about the doctor who jogs through South Brook in his shorts in the winter.

> *'Twas the week before Christmas,*
> *The temp minus thirty*
> *Not a creature was stirring*
> *Except for Doc Verbie*
> *To whom someone should make*
> *The following disclosure:*
> *While keeping in shape*
> *You'll die of exposure.*

At seventeen, I'm affecting the hard-earned world-weariness of the thirty-seven-year-old Letterman. Of course I don't show my stories or poems to anyone. I think of the line from "Nights in White Satin," a song that scared the striped pants off me when I was little: "Letters I've written, never meaning to send." That's what all my writing is.

In a week I'll leave South Brook with my copper soft-sided suitcase and set out for the bright lights of the big city. If Milwaukee is not quite Manhattan, it's 343 miles closer to it than Bloomington. Mom has taken me shopping for a bathrobe to wear in transit to and from the communal showers in my dorm, a hot pot for heating SpaghettiOs and Lipton Cup-a-Soup, and a portable black-and-white TV set, the size of my typewriter case, so that I can watch Dave on the desk in my dorm.

One late August morning I leave South Brook with my bathrobe, hot pot, and portable TV, looking like the movie poster for Steve Martin in *The Jerk*.

PART II

# I Have Only Come Here
# Seeking Knowledge

# 7

# The Beer That Made Milwaukee Famous

Milwaukee's low-slung skyline of smokestacks and church spires is broken only by the raised middle finger of the First Wisconsin bank building downtown, forty-two stories of flipped bird aimed at Chicago, whose suburbs send so many freshmen to Marquette. These FIBs, as they're called in Wisconsin, for Fucking Illinois Bastards, come from Arlington Heights, Downers Grove, and Hoffman Estates. "Hoffman's Mistake," Dad said every time we passed a sign for it in our wood-paneled Country Squire en route to Chicago or Cincinnati in the '70s.

Mom, Dad, and I now arrive in Milwaukee by Oldsmobile Cutlass Supreme, to a scratch-and-sniff city of odors: west of campus, the Miller brewery smells like hops. In Milwaukee, every morning is the morning after. I'm reminded of the wreckage left by Mom and Dad's dinner parties, how I'd rifle the living-room couch for change the next morning and sniff the tops of lipstick-smeared beer cans, inhaling the scent of stale beer and stubbed-out cigarette.

To the east of campus, the Ambrosia Chocolate Factory is a real-life Roald Dahl phantasmagoria, pumping out Wonka-like bars for the Charlie Buckets of Milwaukee and issuing a kind of visible aroma for the rest of us, like those vapor trails of pleasing smells—fresh-baked apple pie on a windowsill—that travel up the nostrils of hoboes in old Warner Bros. cartoons. The leather tanneries south of campus carry the scent of animal hides on the wind. They have us surrounded, these smells, reminding me of the three stages of life—candy, beer, and death. I'm now entering that middle stage: beer.

Many of Marquette's myriad bars are Irish pubs, neighborhood joints, places called O'Donoghue's, O'Paget's, Glocca Morra, Murphy's Law, Hegarty's, the Ardmore, the Gym, and—most belovedly—the Avalanche, home of the Naked Beer Slide. This last, I'm told, involves divesting oneself of one's clothing, lubricating the floor with pitchers of Red White & Blue, then Pete Rose–diving across its foamy surface—from the men's room to the jukebox—on an alcoholic Slip 'n Slide.

These buzzed high jinks ought to come naturally. I'm descended from a long line of happy inebriates. In stories overheard at Mom and Dad's cocktail parties, or told among Tom and Jim and their friends from college, or howled at over Hudepohls during family reunions in Cincinnati, the men—they're always men—are the heroes of drunken misadventures: fistfights in banquet-hall parking lots, downhill ski races in business suits at happy hour, shoeless walks from Wrigley Field after imbibing a vague but underreported quantity of alcoholic beverages—"a few beers," "a couple of pops," "a belt or two."

The drinkers in my family tree—the drinkers falling *out* of my family tree, onto other family members, at picnics—are always happy. Even their hangovers have a kind of magnificence when being recounted days after the day after. After hearing about some of my blood relations' apocalyptic hangovers, it made sense to me that ABC called its nuclear-holocaust movie *The Day After*. Drunkenness, at least in the retelling, is a kind of poetry. The adjectives alone are lyrical: "plowed," "blitzed," "blotto," "wasted," "hammered," "schnockered," "smashed," "shit-faced." I have never been any of these things. I still have never had a beer.

The drinking age in Minnesota is nineteen, but it has always been eighteen in Wisconsin, which is why high school friends make the sixty-five-mile round-trip to Hudson, across the border, to buy a six-pack of Leinie's and transport it back across state lines, like Burt Reynolds and Sally Field bootlegging four hundred cases of Coors from Texarkana to Atlanta in *Smokey and the Bandit*. Underage drinking is illegal, so I want no part of it.

On July 1, seven weeks before I left for college in Wisconsin, the state legislature raised the drinking age in the Dairy State to nineteen. To remain in accordance with the law, I have no intention of drinking until my sophomore year, at which time it will become compulsory if the stories Tom and Jim tell me are true.

Last year, a few months before he graduated, Jim hosted Mom and Dad at Providence College for Parents' Weekend, or what our Uncle Pat in Cincinnati insisted on calling "Family Weekend," to explain why he'd also flown in for the festivities. While attending a Friday night welcome dinner, a Saturday matinee hockey game, and a Saturday night postgame reception, Uncle Pat managed to befriend every one of Jim's teammates with his irrepressible bullshit. "Uncle Pat was being Uncle Pat," Jim said last Christmas, when he told me this story for the first time, ten months after it happened. "He wasn't exactly a wallflower, but he never got out of control, and by ten o'clock on Saturday night, when the last function had ended, he and Aunt Sandy and Mom and Dad went back to the Providence Marriott. They all had early flights out the next morning, so I'd arranged for my friend Father McPhail, the VP of student affairs, to say a private Mass for Pat, Sandy, Mom, and Dad early on Sunday morning."

"How did that go?" I asked.

"It was going fine," Jim said. "But just as the four of them are finishing their drinks at the Marriott bar and getting up to go to their rooms, a couple of guys from my team walk into the bar with their parents, see Pat, and say, 'Hey, we know where your nephew is right now. Wanna go meet him at this party?' It's eleven o'clock on Saturday night, there's a snowstorm starting outside, and of course—of *course*—Pat says yes."

"How old is Uncle Pat?" I asked.

"Forty-three," Jim said

"Go on," I told him.

"So it's late and the party is already kind of over by the time Pat gets to this off-campus house in Providence," Jim said. "We're all out of beer, but there are still enormous quantities of vodka on the kitchen counter. Pat opens one of the bottles and fills a sixteen-ounce plastic cup with straight vodka to the brim. No ice, no Coke. Straight, warm vodka. He proceeds to drink it like he's drinking beer. And then he casually pours himself another one."

Jim was telling this story like a fifteenth-century mariner returning from an unmapped world with tales of dragons and cannibals. In his four years at Providence, he had never seen drinking this prodigious, and he was a college hockey player.

"As Pat is drinking these cups of vodka, there's now a classic, full-blown nor'easter happening outside," Jim continued. "You wouldn't want to drive a block if you were sober, but as the party breaks up, somebody volunteers to drop Pat off at the Marriott. They somehow make it there. Pat gets out of the car, completely schnockered, and slips on the ice, badly twisting his ankle. He falls, and lands—I shit you not—in a shrub in front of the hotel."

Needless to say, Mom and Dad have never mentioned a word of this to Tom or me. We sat there listening to Jim in slack-jawed wonder.

"He lies there for a while," Jim said, "unable to get up. He told me later that two college kids eventually walked by, laughed at him, and said, 'Look at the drunk guy in the bush.' Pat yelled, 'Goddammit, I'm not a drunk guy. I sprained my ankle and fell into this bush.' So the kids went into the Marriott and got two bellmen, who came out and lifted Pat into a wheelchair and wheeled him up to his room. Which is how Aunt Sandy woke in the middle of the night to find two Marriott bellhops dumping her husband out of a wheelchair and into bed with his clothes on."

Uncle Pat is Mom's little brother. Where Mom is abstemious, Pat is Dionysian. The last thing Mom had said to Pat in the Marriott lobby on Saturday night was "Father McPhail is saying a special private Mass for us in the morning so don't do anything stupid tonight."

"So what happened in the morning?" I asked.

"Mom and Dad and Sandy got to my apartment early Sunday morning to head over to the little chapel on campus for Mass," Jim said, "and I can see immediately that Mom is *pissed*. But I had to pretend that I didn't know what was going on, that I hadn't seen Pat drinking full cups of straight vodka last night. I asked them where Pat was, and they said he wasn't feeling well, maybe he'd meet us at Mass. And I was thinking, *Meet us at Mass? There's a better chance he's dead than he'll meet us at Mass.*"

Needless to say, Pat didn't go to Mass, didn't make his flight, and was wheeled through the airport on Monday morning with ligament damage in his ankle, and I already know that "Family Weekend" of 1983 at Providence College will be spoken of with amazement for decades to come among Patrick James Boyle's nephews.

Alcohol is a Rubicon I'll have to cross. If I can swim that river of beer, swallowing most of its contents, girls will be waiting on the far shore, probably in bikinis, to believe the Bud Light commercials that air during every football game.

As if to acknowledge all of this, Marquette houses some of its freshmen in a cylindrical high-rise dorm that resembles a 16-ounce tall boy of Old Milwaukee. McCormick Hall was completed in 1967 in a style that could best be described as Beer Can Brutalism. Its architect was Joseph Schlitz, or possibly Frederick Pabst. The building is twelve stories tall, and my room is on the third floor, and because the students on the upper floors have discovered a glitch—hold down the LOBBY button and the elevator will take you directly to the lobby, an express train bypassing all other floors—I climb the stairs holding a milk crate filled with my every possession. A flexible desk lamp peers over the edge of the box like a pet goose.

The dining hall downstairs is catered by a food service called SAGA. Hans, my resident advisor, says, "SAGA stands for Soviets' Attempt to Gag America."

Just last week, Ronald Reagan announced during the sound check for his weekly radio address, "My fellow Americans, I'm pleased to tell you that today I've signed legislation that will outlaw Russia forever. We begin bombing in five minutes." This jocular threat of nuclear annihilation is hilarious and was the source of endless jokes in the past several days.

On the third floor, Hans and I pass what used to be a large lounge, now evidently a storage area for decrepit furniture. Each floor used to have two of these TV lounges, but now there is only empty cabinetry where the TVs used to be. We're told—can it possibly be true?—that students threw the TVs out the windows on the night, in 1977, when the Marquette Warriors beat North Carolina in the national basketball championship game in Atlanta. I try to imagine that joyous aftermath, the Zeniths—each one as heavy as a safe—falling from the windows, their seaweed-green screens shattering on the pavement below, all those MU freshmen defenestrating TVs like the rock stars of that era.

Just beyond the lounge and the express-train elevator is my

room, number 304, a tiny pie wedge of this circular building with just enough room for bunk beds, a mini fridge, a desk facing either wall, a window, and a wall-mounted, rotary-dial telephone the color of Silly Putty.

My roommate gets up from his desk chair and extends his right hand. "Zeke," he says. He's dipping Skoal.

Zeke is in ROTC and has preceded me by several weeks. The room is already festooned with U.S. Navy recruiting posters. The tiny fridge is already filled with cans of Old Style. In a city that smells like beer, we're living in a giant beer can, which is in turn filled with many smaller beer cans.

Zeke has already selected the bottom bunk. He's spitting tobacco juice into a plastic cup, which is resting on the radiator, heating it like soup. I know from the profile card Marquette mailed to Bloomington a month ago that Zeke, my randomly assigned roomie, is from Cincinnati, and we discuss Hudepohl beer, Skyline chili, Graeter's ice cream, the Big Red Machine, King Kwik convenience stores, and WLW radio for three full minutes, after which I'm relieved to meet Mom and Dad at the corner of 22nd and Wisconsin Avenue, in front of the M & I Bank, to open my first checking account.

I don't receive a free toaster or a handheld calculator, though I've been conditioned by newspaper ads and TV commercials to believe that such *Price Is Right* prizes come standard with the opening of any bank account. But I'm given something called a TYME card—which stands for "Take Your Money Everywhere"—and it allows me (get this!) to withdraw money from a machine just outside the bank, at any time of the day or night. I don't have to wait in line for a teller. The machine is an *automated teller*.

I've seen them on the news and in the newspapers: "Automated teller machines, for those still unaware, are the space-age machines near bank lobbies and shopping centers that permit customers to punch a keyboard to conduct their routine business, gaining access through plastic bank cards and personal identification numbers." Norwest Bank has thirty-five of them in the Twin Cities, and customers using "ATMs" nationwide use them to withdraw, on average, thirty-seven dollars. Ninety percent of transactions in the Twin Cities are withdrawals, because customers don't trust the banks to post cash deposits. "It is very difficult to encourage consumers to use that machine for anything more than getting cash," a Norwest manager told the *Star and Tribune* in March.

The card for the automated teller machine—the TYME machine—goes into my Velcro wallet alongside my Hennepin County library card, my phony YMCA membership card, and my brand-new Marquette University student ID card. This growing collection of cards is physical proof that I am developing my own identity, independent of my parents, even if my YMCA identity is technically somebody else's.

With less ceremony than the occasion warrants, a kind lady in a tweed business dress also presents me with a checkbook. The checks—they don't yet have my name on them—start sequentially at 0001. I read somewhere that a person's credit rating is commensurate with the numbers on his checks: the higher the better. So instantly I've gone from a nothing to a something. The next check Mom writes, if I have to guess, will have a number on it like 659327. She wields her checkbook like a gunslinger, drawing it from her purse, writing the check, memorializing the date and amount and check number in the check registry, then folding the check along the perforation and tearing it perfectly from the book with a flourish before handing it over to the clerk. All of this takes a second and a half. Mom cannot stress strongly enough the importance, in life, of balancing one's checkbook.

My checkbook, like hers, has a blue vinyl cover and non-scenic checks. While my eye gravitated to the checks enlivened by lighthouses and hot-air balloons, I understood instantly that scenic checks were not for the Rushins. I will never write "seventeen dollars and thirty-seven cents" across the Rocky Mountains at sunset, never sign my name on a dolphin breaching a cerulean sea. It just isn't who we are. We never bought the Crayola 64-pack with built-in crayon sharpener, we don't rest our bottoms on the pew when kneeling at Mass, and none of us will ever write a check with a dolphin on it. No male descendant of Don Rushin will ever wear a mustache or drive a pickup truck. Plenty of other people do all of these perfectly reasonable things, but not the Rushins. Mom and Dad have never stated any such precepts outright. But I understand them instinctively. I know them to be true.

At the same time, I'm already becoming my own person. Mom and Dad don't have TYME cards. Mom would no more use an automated teller than an automated doctor. She insists on walking into Community State Bank in Bloomington, is comforted by the pointy-ended ballpoint pens tethered to the teller counter by nine feet of beaded chain. In a pinch, she'll use the drive-through lane, depositing checks in a clear capsule that resembles our blender. The capsule rockets through a pneumatic tube to the teller, seated at a microphone behind eight inches of bulletproof glass, talking to Mom through a

Muscle cars replaced muscle bikes as our Sting-Ray afternoons yielded to nights in White Castle. (Car Culture / Getty Images)

At the dawn of the 1980s, one redhead and four shitheads gather in their South Brook driveway. Left to right: Tom, John, Jim, Amy, and the author, in khakis.

Stewardesses sun themselves beneath a jumbo jet at Airport Beach on the Strip, as Bloomington boys look on, filled with wonder and milkshakes.

John celebrates Christmas 1982 in front of the TV and its state-of-the-art VCR, whirring with Scotch brand videotape.

Santa delivers Amy an argyle sweater to go with her plaid skirt and monogrammed wardrobe straight from *The Official Preppy Handbook*.

I will spend many high school afternoons marooned on this maroon love seat, waiting—in khakis—for cable TV.

Leaning jauntily on a typewriter (just out of frame), I'm photographed by Mom for the dust jacket of a future book. Say *cheese,* indeed.

Eddie Money performs in a North Stars jersey at Met Center, where I vend popcorn at concerts and hockey games—two tickets to paradise in Bloomington, Minnesota. *(Jim Steinfeldt / Getty Images)*

The 1979 disco hit "Ain't No Stopping Us Now" is our basketball anthem, played on the JFK team bus en route to State.

In pants inspired by Uncle Sam, I attempt to dunk at the Saint Paul Civic Center, where Bruce Springsteen will soon pull Courteney Cox onstage for his "Dancing in the Dark" video.

The IBM Selectric II hums to life when I turn it on, and that turns *me* on. Twenty of them going off like guns in typing class makes writing an act of violence. *(Indianapolis Museum of Art at Newfields / Getty Images)*

On high school gradua-tion day, Dad gives me a Silver Handshake, partially absolving himself of finan-cial responsibility for me. The Golden Handshake is still four years away.

Jim receives a second, superfluous Golden Handshake after earning his MBA from Notre Dame.

As a Marquette freshman, in signature khakis, I fuel up on McDonald's before joining the tank-topped, tube-topped rabble in the Wrigley Field bleachers, September 1984.

Mom, in new white hair and new white coat, dreams of a new white kitchen in which every surface is spotless.

Flip Saunders shoots over Mike McCollow at the Saunders Hoop Invitational Tournament, aka the SHIT. *(Courtesy of Mike McCollow)*

Resplendent in jean shorts, the young baseball writer for *Sports Illustrated*—or is it *Jorts Illustrated*?—enjoys a spectator's view at an Angels game in Anaheim, 1992. *(V. J. Lovero / Getty Images)*

The author (left) with pen-pal-turned-colleague Alex Wolff at the 1994 Winter Olympics in Lillehammer, Norway.

The lion in winter: Dad, near the end of his Mickey Mining career, enjoys Milwaukee's most famous export on a December getaway in Palm Desert, California.

Beyond the great blinking neon harp of the Dublin House on West 79th Street in Manhattan, I meet my future wife. Daddy don't live in that New York City no more.

tinny speaker. When I was a little kid, this mysterious ritual of adulthood never failed to fascinate, a 1950s vision of the future that already had a retro, Jetsonian, "space-age" feel. I loved to watch her consign deposit slips to that tube, a message in a bottle, but more often I hated running errands with Mom. Now I already miss them.

Despite my fancy new TYME card, Mom suggests I use the checkbook whenever possible. Her check registry is filled with impeccable cursive. She can legibly squeeze anything—"Oxboro Dry Cleaners"—into those tiny rectangles in her beautiful Palmer Method script. Her non-scenic checks are light blue, so I order mine in the same light blue, the color of my oxford button-down shirts. I don't know it yet, but I will fill my check register with page after unbroken page of $7.04 withdrawals made out to Domino's Pizza.

But for now, Mom and Dad are preparing to leave me, armed against the world with my empty checkbook. It's getting late in the afternoon, and they have a long drive ahead of them. "Call us," Mom says.

"Every Sunday," I promise, though I wish I could call them five minutes from now, when they're westbound on I-94, just to hear their voices. I've seen ads in the paper for "cellular car phones" that allow drivers to make and receive calls on the "analog cellular telephone network," whose tentacles, apparently, have newly spread across the U.S. this year.

But I'll have to wait until Sunday evening, after dinner, because that's when Mom and Dad get their calls from Tom and Jim. Dad listens on the extension for three minutes and says, "I'll let you talk to your mother."

In the parking lot of the M & I Bank, Dad shakes my hand

and Mom hugs me, resisting the urge to wet, with her own saliva, a wadded Kleenex fished from her purse. Never again will she wipe a smudge of something off my face.

And then they're gone. I watch the Cutlass Supreme head west down Wisconsin Avenue, its turn signal blinking back a tear, before hanging a left toward I-94, the Minnesota license plate — 10,000 Lakes — disappearing from view.

I resist the urge to wave a hanky as if the car is a departing ocean liner, never to return. And in fact, back in McCormick Hall, I do have a hanky among my meager personal effects, a snot-rag that is another rite of passage into manhood. The biblical edict to put away childish things said nothing about replacing them with the personal effects of manhood, but here are some of them in room 304: cloth hanky, terry-cloth bathrobe, and a fridge filled with Old Style.

Back in our rooms, shorn of our parents, the freshmen of McCormick are summoned to the urban "lawn" outside the hall for a mandatory "mixer." The men and women and at least one seventeen-year-old boy are told to remove one shoe and place it on a pile. Then we're instructed to choose a shoe other than our own, find its rightful owner, and receive our own missing shoe in turn. I put my hand inside this Everest of Nikes, Top-Siders, and shower sandals and pull, like a rabbit from a hat, a single white Reebok Freestyle high-topped cheer shoe. As a taxonomist of footwear, I recognize this as a winning lottery ball. For a moment, I entertain the fantasy that a beautiful freshman cheerleader limping around in this shoe's mate will have also found mine and recognize (in my Converse high-top) a kindred Larry Bird fan.

And in fact, a beautiful girl does smile at me and say,

"I think you have my shoe." I blush, as if I've stolen it, or sniffed it or been caught in some other act of depravity, and—*without a word,* utterly contravening the entire point of the exercise—I bow my head and grimly return the Reebok. The girl pauses for a moment, as if to say something, for I am physically incapable of breaking the ice. It occurs to me, having recently read about the Soviets trying to free three thousand beluga whales trapped in the frozen Bering Sea, that what I need is a...Rushin icebreaker.

As I lose myself in this inane wordplay, a bearded dude with several inches of boxer shorts exposed above his sweatpants approaches, my missing right Converse in his meaty hand. I grimly accept it while the girl walks away, leaving me where I was five minutes ago: alone, risk averse, and fully shod. "Goody Two Shoes," as Adam Ant put it.

Back in my room, Zeke has his wool-socked feet propped up on the radiator, sending cartoon stink squiggles into the air, one more smell in this city's polyglot miasma. He never bothered to go out to the lawn for the shoe ceremony. I would have enjoyed seeing his own unspeakable Top-Sider returned to him in a zipped Mylar bag, pincered between salad tongs, held at arm's length by a man in a hazmat suit.

"Brewski?" he says, cracking a beer and handing it to me. I sit in my desk chair, three feet from Zeke's, and sip. It tastes of carbonation and refrigeration. Slightly metallic. A full swig makes my tongue go numb for a second, the way it did when I'd lick a 9-volt battery to see how much juice it had left. Tom and I used to take the Rayovac 9-volts from our basement smoke detector and use them in our handheld Mattel electronic football game. Now I'm sharing a room with this stranger instead of my brother. Tom would have asked—while handing me my first beer—if I wanted to drink it out of the can or would I prefer a baby bottle. But Zeke doesn't know this is my first beer, and I certainly don't let on, and anyway, we're both distracted by the middle-aged homeless alcoholic hanging out by the dumpster that our room overlooks.

Hans the RA informed us that this "bag man"—the masculine equivalent of New York's "bag lady" phenomenon I've seen on TV—is known to generations of McCormick residents as Richard the Bum. I admire the formality of it, like a European monarch—Ethelred the Unready or Sverker the Clubfoot. Richard the Bum is not a genial drunk like Otis on *The Andy Griffith Show* or the guys on *Cheers*. The drunks on TV—Foster Brooks on *The Tonight Show* and Dean Martin roasting celebrities—are happy-go-lucky men whose only side effect isn't liver disease but chronic hiccups.

Richard the Bum, on the other hand, is at this very moment shouting profanity at the upper floors of McCormick, whose open windows are coming alive with music and laughter and young people using their first night of semi-independence to deploy the word "party" as a verb.

Near as I can tell, Richard the Bum has been panhandling in the parking lot. Some students have rewarded his efforts by showering him with coins from open windows. Hans the RA—another title from the Western Civ text I've peeked at, like Charles the Bald or Richard the Lionhearted—said some past students heated coins in their hot pots before tossing them out their windows. I picture the penny-sized stigmata in the center of Richard's palms and think of Jesus.

"Whatsoever you do to the least of my brothers," we sang as nine-year-olds at Nativity of the Blessed Virgin Mary, "that you do unto me."

This isn't Bloomington. A few blocks down Wisconsin Avenue, just past campus, in downtown Milwaukee, the storefronts are full of mounted wigs. Mannequins wear double-breasted jackets and matching slacks in mustard or purple. A man in the market for a crimson fedora has more than one shop window to browse. But there are familiar sights and sounds too. Comforting ones. I hear a siren song down the hall: "Love, exciting and new..." A small crowd has gathered around a small TV to watch a rerun of the *The Love Boat*, and when I casually walk past, as if on my way to somewhere else, a drunk guy standing in the door sings, "Come aboard. We're expecting youuu."

They're playing a game called Chug Boat, which involves selecting a character on tonight's episode—Isaac, Julie, Captain Merrill Stubing—and drinking every time he or she appears onscreen. This particular episode guest stars Tony Dow (Wally Cleaver from *Leave It to Beaver*), Grant Goodeve (David Bradford from *Eight Is Enough*), and Claude Akins (Sheriff Elroy P. Lobo from *B.J. and the Bear* and *The Misadventures of Sheriff Lobo*). I attempt to point out these exciting cameos but am drowned out by freshmen chanting, "Chug! Chug! Chug!" Bidden to chug, I comply.

And the evening passes, McCormick thumping like a human heart, my fillings vibrating to "We're Not Gonna Take It" blasting from another floor, as my inaugural beer buzz deepens with every appearance on *The Love Boat* of Beaver Cleaver's older brother. The hours wear on and the music de-escalates, until the distant purr of "Drive" by the Cars gives way to silence.

On every floor of McCormick Hall, freshmen in brand-new bathrobes like mine are trudging down the hall in flip-flops, a toothbrush in one hand and a bar of soap in the other, on their way to or from the communal bathroom. This parade of the pajamaed brings an oddly comforting domesticity to the hallway on my first night away from home. From every room glows a desk lamp, or a goosenecked lamp clamped onto a bunk, or the graphic equalizer bars of a stereo turned low.

I resist the urge to remove my set of brand-new hankies from their box to have at the ready: one in case the tears come in the middle of the night and the other to cling to as a tiny security blanket. For the first time in my life I'm spending the night with strangers, entirely bereft of friends or family, a foot below the ceiling and two feet above my first-ever roommate unrelated by blood. How many more roomies await in my future I can only guess at. In this recumbent state, as the tiny room starts ever so slightly to spin, it occurs to me that I'm simultaneously two things for the first time in my life: drunk in a bunk. If only Dr. Seuss had written a bedtime story by that name, and Mom were here now to read it to me, for I'm already missing home.

I make friends named Mike, Mike, Steve, and Steve. These were, respectively, the first and thirteenth most popular baby boy names of 1966. To distinguish the two Mikes on our floor, they're renamed Hodes and Vill. The three Steves become Steve, Steph, and Stever, like the conjugation of some Old English verb (presumably meaning "to remain recumbent until the noon hour"). I'm Steph, and I cleave to the kids on my floor—from Milwaukee, Minnesota, and Chicago—who like sports. I am already contracting my horizons, narrowing my gaze.

On a gorgeous blue-skied day in early autumn, we drive to Wrigley Field to watch the Cubs play the Phillies. The home team has a 7-game lead on the Mets in the National League East. We walk up to the bleacher box office and ask for four seats and pay three bucks apiece for the tickets. There are 28,964 of us in the Friendly Confines, leaving 10,000 empty seats. We sit in left field and chant, "Right field sucks!" The right field bleacher bums chant in reply, "Left field sucks!" This goes on for many minutes until we finally agree to disagree. We are drinking beer at noon on Tuesday: tube-topped women, tube-socked men in jorts, pot smokers, eschewers of shirts, sunscreen agnostics, the whole shower-sandaled rabble of North Side truants and deadbeats and day drinkers, the unemployed and the unemployable.

Just last season, Cubs manager Lee Elia called those of us sitting out here "the fuckin' nickel-and-dime people who turn up. The motherfuckers don't even work. That's why they're out at the fuckin' game. They oughta go out and get a fuckin' job and find out what it's like to go out and earn a fuckin' living. Eighty-five percent of the fuckin' world is working. The other fifteen percent come out here—a fuckin' playground for the cocksuckers." It should perhaps go without saying that Lee Elia is no longer the manager of the Cubs, but still, we embrace his depiction and—looking around—struggle to refute its central points.

Midway through the game, Phillies left fielder Jeff Stone

loses a shoe while chasing down a drive to the gap. He simply runs right out of one half of his pair of spikes—the left one—and when the play is dead and he returns to retrieve it, a selfless shit-faced spectator seated near us removes his own left shoe and throws it toward Stone as a remedy. Quickly, the bleachers cough up another shoe, and then another, and within a minute, single shoes are raining down on the Wrigley sod, a hailstorm of unmatched sneakers, Sperrys, flip-flops, and wafflestompers. It's like the freshman mixer all over again, except that the groundskeepers picking up the footwear have no intention of returning anything to their rightful owners.

After the game—a 6–3 Cubs loss, Lee Smith giving up 4 runs in the ninth, blowing the save to cost Dennis Eckersley the win—a half-shod crowd of happy inebriates limps away from Wrigley. They board the elevated train at Addison, stand in line at McDonald's, and stumble into Murphy's Bleachers bar the way Mom often found me adrift in a daydream when I was supposed to be getting dressed: with one shoe off and one shoe on.

Nobody cares about the late defeat, or their unshod feet, or anything beyond the comfort of the crowd, our shared shoe joke, the brick-and-ivy of the ballpark, and this gorgeous blue-skied hookie-playing Tuesday, whose date—September 11—holds no significance whatsoever, except as a perfect day in a blessed season for an otherwise star-crossed franchise.

## 8.

# Home Again, Home Again, Jiggety Jog

College is intimidating—though truth be told, I have not been "made timid" by my first weeks here, as my dictionary suggests. Rather, I arrived timid and have simply remained so: afraid to walk into the basement of Johnston Hall, where the College of Journalism is housed, and ask an editor at the *Marquette Tribune* for an assignment, any assignment. My academic advisor is the sixty-seven-year-old former journalism dean and Irish Guy from Chicago on whose massive head breaks a surfable wave of white hair. Between the hair and the owlish black-framed glasses, he's a living cartoon, an Al Hirschfeld caricature, black ink on white paper. His voice is a deep rumble that rattles windowpanes while digressing far and wide from the matter at hand. He was the press secretary to President Lyndon Baines Johnson in 1964 and 1965, and LBJ once said of him: "That man George Reedy knows more about more things that I could care less about than anyone else I've ever known. You ask him what time it is and you'll get a history of clock-making." Reedy is, in short, my kind of guy.

He's the kind of guy who paid his way through the University of Chicago as a saxophone-playing circus clown, which somehow makes everything—from the Oval Office to the College of Journalism to journalism itself—seem marginally less august and intimidating. He tells me to march into the *Trib*'s offices and demand an assignment, and so I am assigned a six-paragraph story on intramural flag football—"Marquette's own version of Monday Night Football," as my lede puts it—and I have my first byline, my first clipping, which I mail to Mom and Dad. In the return address, I identify myself as Bud Ding Journalist.

This newfound courage does not extend to girls. One night the wall-mounted rotary-dial phone in my room at McCormick rings and I answer it and a female voice asks for me.

"Speaking," I say.

"My friend Mary Kate O'Herlihy is in Western Civ with you and was wondering if you'd want to meet at the library tomorrow night to study."

My armpits instantly inflame. "I have tickets to the Bucks game tomorrow night," I say, and when a long silence ensues, I fill it with this clincher: "It's the opening game and they're playing the Bulls." I feel like a secular priest, vowing fealty to basketball, and when I replace the phone receiver on its cradle I feel a simultaneous sense of relief and despondence.

I could be a real priest. Father John Patrick Donnelly, SJ, bestrides the thirty-two-foot stage of the Varsity Theatre like a colossus—perhaps the Colossus of Rhodes, which he can tell you all about as he declaims off-the-cuff to 1,075 freshmen while lecturing on Western civilization, in Western Civ, with an authority handed down from God. My friend Vill (one of the Mikes) and I develop a devastating impersonation of Father Donnelly's oratorical style—part John Houseman in *The Paper Chase,* part white-bearded God of the Old Testament—and especially his description of Christ's duality, "His two natures, *yuman* and *diviiine.*"

Walking into Western Civ, up the theater aisle to find a seat, a girl waves at me, pointing at the mortified girl sitting next to her while mouthing: *Mary Kate O'Herlihy.* My armpits reignite as I take a seat several rows behind them, and across the aisle, and crack open our textbook and feign absorption in an upside-down page about the Protestant Reformation.

Mom wouldn't mind if I became a real priest, a Jesuit priest, member of the Society of Jesus, and I like the name of the building where the Jesuits live at Marquette. Officially it's the Jesuit Residence Hall, but everyone calls it the Jes Res. And because my full name is Steven Joseph Rushin, I'd be S. J. Rushin, SJ.

I like the symmetry, the near palindrome, and wonder if this kind of wordplay is worth staking a vocation on: S. J. Rushin, SJ, c/o Jes Res.

On September 22, 1984, my floor mates present me with a 40-ounce screw-top bottle of Schaefer in a brown paper bag to mark my eighteenth birthday. Schaefer's most famous advertising slogan was "The one beer to have when you're having more than one," and I am evidently having more than nine. I'm carried out of McCormick on a litter and taken out to "the Bars," to O'D's, where a bored bouncer will inspect our fake IDs with a flashlight, gaze up at our faces, then back at the IDs, as if playing a Spot the Difference game in *Highlights* magazine. Even though I'm six foot five inches, with a permanent five-o'clock shadow, I sweat out the agonizing interval of those five seconds at the door, perhaps because my Iowa driver's license identifies me as a five-foot-ten-inch twenty-two-year-old from Council Bluffs, and surely the bouncer can see me mouthing my "birthday"—May 19, 1962—over and over as a mantra, just in case I'm asked.

At one time there were fifty-three "bars or grocery stores" on or adjacent to campus, according to a history of Marquette, and collectively they're a single destination: "the Bars."

"What are you doing tonight?"

"Probably hit the Bars."

The Bars are a low-rent version of the Strip. None of these places has a membership fee, as at Maximillian's "disco restaurant" on the Richfield side of the Strip. On the contrary, the Avalanche—almost entirely devoid of furniture—barely charges for its beers: Pabst Red White & Blues cost fifty cents.

There are no White Castles in the benighted state of Wisconsin. The nearest one is on Harlem Avenue in Chicago. But there are plenty of substitutes, joints that are, like their patrons, luridly lit. We go to Cousins to sword-swallow submarine sandwiches at midnight, or to Real Chili, a Marquette landmark since 1931 whose bumper sticker slogan ("Not just for breakfast anymore") concedes that the most robust patronage is in the wee small hours of the morning. The harsh lighting, the limited foodstuffs, the bouquet of odors—it's like eating inside a bachelor's fridge.

I've settled into the comforting routine of college life.

I make a collect call to Mom and Dad once a week on Sunday evenings, and Dad—perhaps because he's incurring the charges—hangs up the extension in the master bedroom after three minutes and returns to his Archie Bunker chair while Mom acts like the chair of a congressional committee who has five minutes to ask all of her questions: am I studying, am I eating, am I doing my laundry, and have I "met anyone," to which I reply that I'm meeting all kinds of interesting people.

For instance, Hodes (another Mike) and I met a gentleman on the Trailways bus. We were going to Chicago, where Jim would pick us up in the Loop and drive us to South Bend, Indiana, for the Notre Dame football game versus Air Force. The bus left Milwaukee at 6 a.m. and was nearly empty, so Hodes took one row of seats and I took another, and we both gazed out our respective windows, anticipating ninety minutes of sleep. But just before the bus pulled out of the station, a small, middle-aged man in a short-sleeved dress shirt boarded and—surveying the empty rows—chose the upholstered seat directly next to Hodes. Hodes made panicked eye contact with me, and I began to laugh, silently but soon uncontrollably. By the time the man next to Hodes pulled a clipboard from his backpack, and secured in its clamp a child's word-search magazine, and set about solving it with a pencil—circling diagonal "DOG" and horizontal "HEN" and upside-down "DUCK"—my shoulders were shaking.

The gentle shaking of my shoulders and the vibration of the road and the hypnotic hum of the Trailways engine soon dispatched me to dreamland, where I remained for many minutes, until I was awakened by a burst of profanity, a small scuffle, and the middle-aged man with the word-search magazine rubbing his biceps and running to the back of the bus.

Hodes had nodded off shortly after the trip commenced, he told me later, and slipped into a pleasing road coma somewhere in the lawless border region between Milwaukee and Chicago, a landscape relieved only by Mars Cheese Castle, a twenty-four-hour "adult bookstore" in Kenosha, and an official state tourism sign for the Bong Recreation Area, named after a World War II fighter pilot from the Dairy State called Richard Bong, but now a backdrop for young stoners having their pictures taken as tractor trailers roar past at seventy-five miles an hour. It was somewhere near Bong, as Hodes enjoyed a deep and dreamy REM sleep, that he felt someone—the guy in the seat next to him, it turned out, his word-search magazine still clamped in the clipboard—*caress his thigh.*

Which is why I was awakened by two outbursts: Hodes's short volley of profanity, followed by the word searcher's yelp of physical and emotional pain after Mike punched him in the biceps, dispatching the man to the back of the bus, where he nursed his wounded arm and pride. Neither Hodes nor I, it scarcely needs saying, ever went back to sleep. Instead I spent the rest of the ride—on a Trailways bus out of Milwaukee, with a simple-minded sex offender circling his CATs and BATs in the back seat—dwelling on one fact: nothing like this ever happened in South Brook.

But I also thought: *I can't wait to tell this story to my friends and my brothers.* It was why I wanted to be a writer, this need to bend and shape various experiences into a narrative balloon animal.

As his seat springs began to squeak, and he became

preoccupied with what I could only assume was the clipboard on his lap, Word Searcher (it slowly dawned) was doing something in the back seat that—in Bloomington at least—is always euphemized as an act of animal cruelty: choking the chicken, flogging the dolphin, spanking the monkey. Word Searcher ducked into the bus's only bathroom. And the Trailways sped on, whooshing under the Lake Forest Oasis, where on childhood trips to suburban Lisle, to visit old neighbors in the city of my birth, we'd stop at the HoJo's and Amoco station suspended above the tollway, press our noses to a window (smudged with the noseprints of a hundred other kids), and watch the traffic pass beneath us.

Now the HoJo's is a McDonald's and I am that traffic, never again to be that kid, innocence yielding to experience on an almost daily basis.

Another fall day, another bus. I'm returning home for the first time, for Thanksgiving, on a chartered coach full of other students from the Twin Cities, many of them surrounded by the spent shells of Miller Lite cans. By the time we stop at the Burger King on I-94 in Tomah, Wisconsin, and everyone stands in the aisle waiting for the doors to open, a dude at the back of the line vomits on the passenger in front of him, and the chain reaction is like a string of fireworks popping, so that by the time we arrive at a parking lot in Midway, the seething air brakes signaling our arrival, I disembark smelling of barf and Burger King, but also with a powerful gratitude. Mom is picking me up here, and pulling into our driveway I'll have to fight the urge to kiss the tarmac, like the pope does on airport runways, so happy will I be to get home.

But where *is* Mom? I scan the crowd of waiting parents and don't see her.

"Steve!" It's her voice issuing from a different head.

She gives me a kiss, walks me to the car, drives through Minneapolis while giving me a happy interrogation, but I don't hear any of it. Who is this woman? We pull into our garage, where Dad said after every car trip of my childhood, just before turning off the ignition, "Home again, home again, jiggety jog." I walk into the house as if for the first time, suddenly in love with the full-size fridge and its copious contents, Dad's briefcase (in its familiar spot under the yellow telephone that is tethered to the wall mount by fifty feet of coiled cord), and every familiar dish, cup, and cupboard, down to the floral pattern of the shelf paper. Everything in this kitchen is cozily familiar, with one significant exception.

"Do you notice anything different about me?" Mom says.

I nod in reply.

"What?" she says.

I can barely say it: "Your hair."

"What *about* my hair?" She's laughing at my deep discomfort. She seems to find it fascinating.

"It's white."

"Were you going to say anything?" Mom wonders. "I picked you up an hour ago. You didn't mention it."

After a long interval of silence, I manage to say, "Why did you dye your hair white?"

She laughs, cocks her head slightly, looks me in the eye, gives me another kiss on the cheek, and says, "I *stopped* dyeing it. On September 27. My fiftieth birthday."

Three months ago, and for all my life before that, Mom's

hair was as black as a Kingsford charcoal briquette. Now it's the opposite, as white as the guy's on the Quaker Oats box, as white as her own fur coat, which matches the hair exactly. If this kitchen ever gets the white cabinets and countertops Mom wants, she will look—while standing in this very spot—like a benevolent version of the White Witch in the permanent winter of Narnia.

It has never occurred to me until this afternoon that while I am growing older so are Mom and Dad.

Our kitchen is full of things I never knew I loved and didn't know I'd missed. The kitchen table, for starters. For three months now I haven't sat down to eat, taking all my meals while lying in a bunk bed, walking down Wells Street, or standing at the counter in Amigo's, ingesting nachos out of a Styrofoam clam box.

Iceberg lettuce, kept crisp in a seafoam-green Tupperware lettuce keeper, is the first vegetable I've eaten in three months that wasn't on a pizza. I've come to think of vegetables as toppings or—in the case of carrots—an onion-dip delivery system. I gaze into our glorious, harvest-gold Frigidaire, feeling like a Soviet defector walking into Red Owl for the first time, marveling at the cold cuts, cheeses, nectarines, the roast wrapped in its fishnet swimsuit.

But I also see my family on these shelves and in these crisper drawers. There's the grapefruit Mom will cut in half in the morning and eat for breakfast with a golf ball of cottage cheese, and the Grey Poupon Dad prefers to the French's yellow mustard the rest of us like, and the packaged Jell-O puddings Mom has apparently purchased for Amy and John after caving in to their supermarket demands. Jim, Tom, and

I always ate her homemade pudding with the trampoline of rubber skin on top, but Mom is fifty now, and white-haired, her defenses worn smooth like the paint on the banister.

"Would you mind closing the fridge," Mom says, "or are you tanning yourself by the light bulb?"

I've probably stood here for a solid minute, staring into the fridge as if it were a crystal ball. And it is, in reverse. Gazing into it, I can see the past. A can of frozen orange juice from concentrate is thawing on the top shelf. It's about the only thing I know how to make—squeezing it out of the cardboard tube in a single citrus defecation, filling the empty can with water, then pouring it into the Tupperware juice dispenser and mashing up that semi-frozen bullet of concentrated citrus with a wooden spoon, stirring it, eating the occasional undiluted bit of frozen flotsam, a speedball of vitamin C. I know, even as I'm doing it, that I'll never buy juice from concentrate as an adult, not when they sell it ready-made in cartons from Tropicana. These are the little inconsequential decisions I've already made about how I'll live my grown-up life, my infinitesimal rebellions.

Two nights before Thanksgiving, I attend a Kennedy basketball game in khakis, maroon argyle sweater, button-down oxford, and belted raincoat, even though it isn't raining and no rain is in the forecast. Collar turned up against the cold, I see myself reflected in the glass entrance doors as a double for Sam Spade, Humphrey Bogart's hard-boiled detective. Alas, Oly's greeting in the gym—"Help take a bite outta crime!"—lets me know the private eye I really resemble is McGruff the Crime Dog, the Ad Council's cartoon canine who urges children, in public-service announcements, to narc on any suspicious characters in their neighborhood.

Still, as my penny loafers scuff against the highly polished hardwood in the JFK gym, I look back on that golden time now long vanished when—five long months ago—I was young and carefree, with no need of a belted raincoat.

As the current crop of Eagles runs our still-familiar offense—one of them is wearing my number 32, which I half imagined had been hoisted to the rafters by now—I remove a cotton handkerchief from my raincoat pocket (one of the twin tokens of my newfound sophistication) and ostentatiously blow my nose.

The next night, the eve of Thanksgiving, is the busiest bar night of the year, according to a story I read in the paper. Oly and Roy are leaving O'Gara's in Saint Paul when they see a guy in short sleeves standing outside, having a smoke. "You should put a coat on," Roy says to him, and a moment later—halfway to their car, while walking through an alley—he and Oly are jumped by five guys, including the Short-Sleeved Smoker. In the cartoon melee that ensues—a rolling ball of fists and feet and ampersands of profanity—Oly's glasses are broken and his face is bloodied. He doesn't want to meet Mike and Ope and me at Whitey's because he doesn't want to stand in line bleeding and battered in broken glasses.

"Are you kidding?" I tell Mike when he relays the news. "Oly would be, like, one of eight guys in line who look like that."

Indeed, in the Castle, nothing has changed. At a table near the counter, an old man festooned with sailor's tattoos is wearing a fancy admiral's hat from another country's navy, or possibly from a military surplus store on Neptune, or more likely from Ragstock on Penn Avenue.

At another table, another party of one wears a professional bowler's brace on his arm, or perhaps—on closer inspection—it's a falconer's arm protector. He has come from either Lyn-Del Lanes next door or the bar at Fong's across the street, or he is patiently awaiting the return of his peregrine. It's possible that all three of these circumstances are true, for White Castle is in that category of places—bus stations, DMV lines, ER waiting rooms—where an admiral and a falconer don't turn a single head. I want to pair them up for dinner, or possibly cast them in a televised cop drama, but instead I order a sack of ten sliders with vinyl, a box of nails, and a fifty-five-gallon drum of Coke and take a table by the window with Mike and Ope, as we've done so many times before, except now we're living in the Future we used to talk about as a concept, as a mythological location.

Like the kid gazing down at the traffic on the Illinois toll road from his perch at the window in the Lake Forest Oasis—then finding himself in that traffic, on a Trailways bus to somewhere else, as another kid gazes down on him—I have been fast-forwarded, to borrow a phrase from Dad's magnetic-tape empire. I'm suddenly on my way somewhere, or so it seems, in my belted raincoat.

Even now, the only occupations I can conceive of ever holding down are the ones depicted in Richard Scarry's *What Do People Do All Day?,* whose vaguely Bavarian municipality called Busytown has a detective (the private eye wears a deerstalker and holds a magnifying glass), a shoemaker (the cobbler hammers away at boot heels inside his shoe-shaped shop), a barber (a white-coated pig sits beneath his candy-striped pole), an automobile dealer (the car salesman is literally collaring a passerby and pulling him into the show-room), and an eye doctor (an anthropomorphic owl, fitting another owl for glasses).

Above all, Busytown champions the arts, and writing in particular, for in its quaint downtown are a newsstand offering several daily papers, the office of *The News* (whose editor is in the window, puffing away on a cigar), and—next door to ABC Book Publishers—the Remarkable Book Shop, whose proprietress, "E. Kramer," stands in the doorway, showing off a book to a passing child, who stares at its pages in rapt fascination. A newspaper reporter runs through the streets with a notebook in one hand, his fedora in mid-flight from his head, while a poet—quill at the ready—stares out the window of an artist's garret. There are two other garrets atop the same building: in one, a painter in a beret sits at his easel; in the other, bent over a typewriter, a smiling raccoon composes his masterpiece. He is, according to the caption, "a story writer." In Richard Scarry's illustrations, in that book buried somewhere in Amy's bedroom now—all of us long since having outgrown it—the banker and the mayor and the janitor and the story writer are all of equal prestige and importance and, as far as I know, earn equal pay. Mike wants to be a basketball coach, whistle around his neck. Ope wants to be an accountant, poring over a ledger, presumably in a green eyeshade. And I want to be a writer, flailing away at an olive-green Selectric.

We eat our sliders, Mike and Ope and I and the admiral and the falconer and some high school kids talking too loudly.

The steamed bun has fused with the burger, creating a gummy stratum where they meet. God, it's good. In its own way, this is Thanksgiving dinner, an act of gratitude, surrounded by loved ones and a few crazy uncles, some of whom will be passing out shortly after their meal.

Or during their meal, as it happens, when the admiral rests his cheek on the cool surface of the stainless-steel table and succumbs to the loudmouth teens, the onions sizzling on their stainless-steel grill, the grill itself irrigated with water from a squeeze bottle, the ice dispenser paying out like a slot machine over at the pop machine, and the kids peeling out of the parking lot in their muscle cars—a symphony of sounds that feels like home, the full White Castle lullaby.

Thanksgiving dinner is the opposite of last night's repast at White Castle. For starters, we eat in the formal "dining room," something we'll also do on Christmas and not again until the following Thanksgiving. If it's odd that 200 square feet of our 2,800-square-foot house is reserved exclusively for two meals a year, nobody says so. This is part of what makes Thanksgiving dinner special, along with the various table leaves, the white tablecloth ironed for the occasion, the heirloom china that emerges once a year from its hiding place, like that Pennsylvania groundhog on the *Today* show.

Part of the annual rite is sitting in the dining room, this otherwise forbidden space, staring at ourselves in the mirrored wall opposite the table. I'm drinking white wine in front of Mom and Dad. I've only ever sipped wine in Mass, but that's the blood of Christ, which is why the priests would often glug down the remainders from the various chalices.

My graduating to wine at Thanksgiving is a milestone, same as when I matriculated six or seven years ago from the Kids' Table at various large get-togethers.

There is another matriculation the day after Thanksgiving. Among all the other graduations of recent years—bicyclist to motorist, high school to college, teetotaler to inebriate—this is perhaps the greatest: I'm allowed to eat in the family room in front of the TV while watching football, as Dad has done for years.

This is a ritual he usually reserved for Saturday afternoons, a plate on his lap—turkey, swiss, iceberg lettuce, and deli mustard on rye, garnished with Old Dutch potato chips—and a glass of ice water on the end table. Only now I'm invited to enjoy my sandwich in this sanctum sanctorum—this football salon of the front room—with Dad. Like him, I set down my drinking glass gently on a coaster. Since childhood, Mom's admonition—"That will leave a permanent ring"—has left a permanent ringing in my ears whenever I have a beverage in hand.

Dad has allowed me into his exclusive fraternity of arm-chair eaters. And it is a fraternity. Mom doesn't do it. Amy doesn't do it. I doubt they have ever wanted to. But sitting on the maroon love seat, eating a bologna sandwich while Boston College and Miami are locked in mortal combat on CBS, is everything I imagined it to be: decadent, manly, and fun. I settle in with my sandwich in front of the hundred-pound Zenith, as solid and permanent as Dad himself.

The football is almost an afterthought to the sandwich, but the game is compelling. Boston College's quarterback, five-foot-nine Doug Flutie, is an unsinkable runt in a mesh half shirt that exposes his midriff, one of those great journalism words that always makes me wonder if there is an upper or lower riff as well.

The game is in Miami and everything looks sun-kissed. This is one of the great vicarious joys of watching football on TV in Minnesota with winter approaching. The field is bright green, reflecting the blinding South Florida sunlight I recognize from our visits to Grandma Boyle's condo in Hollywood, north of Miami. We were there last over the Christmas holiday in 1980, a few weeks after John Lennon was shot, when Tom and I—then fifteen and fourteen—sat inside the fifteenth-floor apartment doodling mustaches and missing teeth onto magazine covers while cranking up Grandma's AM/FM clock radio, which played Lennon's new songs, "Watching the Wheels" and "Woman," seemingly on a loop, until Mom came up from the pool and ordered us outside, into that punishing Florida sun, but not before she expressed her grave disappointment at our vandalism of Grandma's copies of *Redbook* and *Reader's Digest*.

BC and Miami are scoring at will. The twelfth-ranked Hurricanes are defending champions, but the Eagles are the number ten team in the nation. Still, Miami is at home, with a six-foot-five All-American quarterback, Bernie Kosar. In September, he was on the cover of *Sports Illustrated*'s college football preview issue, and for good reason: Kosar has thrown for a ridiculous 447 yards in this game, giving the Canes a 45–41 lead as Boston College gets the ball back at their own 20 yard line with twenty-eight seconds remaining.

Dad is not literally on the edge of his seat. He is deeply ensconced in his Archie Bunker chair, probing his incisors with a toothpick. But he has issued enough involuntary hoots and whoops to acknowledge that this game has been worthy of his respect. Dad played college football at Purdue before transferring to play at Tennessee and looks down on many of today's players on television as "pansies," "hot dogs," and "candy-asses," but he has made no such assertions today.

After three quick passes, Flutie has moved BC out to their own 48 yard line. But there are only six seconds left, time for one last desperate fling. He has already thrown forty-five times, for 420 yards, and is further encumbered by his ridiculously large shoulder pads, which make him appear nearly as wide as he is tall. On CBS, Brent Musburger and Ara Parseghian go silent for a moment. I sit forward on the love seat. Dad stills his toothpick. The ball is snapped.

"Flutie flushed!" says Musburger as this tiny dynamo flees the pocket, races back to his own 37 yard line, and heaves a ball—like some sacrifice to the gods—into the sky, where a thirty-mile-an-hour wind offers one more redundant obstacle. "Throws it down!" cries Musburger. It will be several minutes before he utters another sentence that isn't punctuated by an exclamation mark. It appears that every player on both teams besides number 22 for the Eagles—Flutie—is racing to the end zone. As the ball comes down, nearly all of them fall like bowling pins.

*"CAUGHT BY BOSTON COLLEGE!"* screams Musburger. *"I DON'T BELIEVE IT! IT'S A TOUCHDOWN! THE EAGLES WIN IT!"*

We're only rooting for Boston College because it's a Catholic school, and yet the family room is now a storm of iceberg lettuce, Old Dutch potato chips, and sandwich crumbs raining down on the raked carpet, Dad and I both having leapt out of our seats with our lunches on our laps.

A writhing pile of football players in Miami is transmitting unfettered joy to Bloomington via the CBS television network, thanks to Doug Flutie and his receiver, Gerard Phelan. "Phelan is at the bottom of that pile!" Brent is shouting. "Here comes the Boston College team!" They are pouring onto the field from the bench, a flash flood of humanity.

In the next day's *Boston Globe,* in a column I won't see for several days, after returning to Marquette, to which some New England student has returned from his own Thanksgiving break, bearing his hometown paper, sports columnist Leigh Montville recorded the dialogue of two Boston College offensive linemen. One, Mark MacDonald, said in the postgame locker room: "That wasn't Gerard Phelan who caught that ball. God caught that ball." As a Catholic boy at a Catholic university, I eat this up with a spoon. But it's the next line that gives me goose bumps. "No," big Jim Ostrowski said softly. "God threw it."

The following Wednesday, when *Sports Illustrated* is published, I will do what I do every Wednesday at school (and every Thursday in Bloomington, for the magazine arrives there a day later): I'll go to the mailbox to see whom the magazine's editors honored with the cover. THE MAGIC FLUTIE reads the headline, over a picture of the dynamo heaving the ball heavenward. "Boston College's Sensational Doug Flutie Stuns Miami."

On another Friday after Thanksgiving, a few years from now, I'll be sitting inside, watching football with my brothers, when we'll hear tires squealing outside the window, and look out to see a late-model sedan receding down West 96th Street and six rolls of toilet paper hanging from the birch tree in the front yard. They're strangely beautiful, the two-ply tendrils dripping like Spanish moss, turning our house into a small New Orleans of Quilted Northern bathroom tissue, to judge by the plastic wrapper these dipshits have allowed to escape the car window. Tom picks up the bag and crumples it in his fist. He squints into the distance like a TV detective. Tom has TP'd more than a few houses in his time and recognizes this as an amateur job. Who buys quilted two-ply to TP a house? Tom also knows what the rest of us don't: they'll be back. In the same way that arsonists often return to a smoldering ash heap, these perpetrators will make another pass in their mom's or dad's car to properly admire their handiwork. "And when they do," Tom says, parting a curtain of toilet paper on his way back into the garage, "we'll be waiting."

It takes five minutes to circumnavigate South Brook by car, during which time Jim, Tom, John, and I wait in silence in the dark garage. We hear it before we see it—the sweet song of a Buick Skylark growing louder, until it heaves into view on West 96th. As it crosses over Washburn Avenue and passes Mr. Cole's house next door, we make our move: the Boys run into the street. We form a human barricade. The stunned driver slows the Skylark. She's a girl, as are her three passengers, presumably the same girls who call at 3 a.m. and ask, "Is Johnny there?" Or are they? We have no real way of knowing, for the car slowly swerves around us, horn sounding. If it's possible to read a horn's honk, this one—to my ear—is more terrified than taunting. Our hands slap the hood as the Skylark slaloms past, and the car disappears at speed around the bend, where 96th turns into Xerxes.

Retreating to the backyard, feeling semi-defeated, Tom brandishes something long and thin and metallic. It glints in the late-afternoon sunlight.

"I snapped off their antenna," he says, and we all take a turn holding it, swinging it about like a swashbuckler's sword, happy to have a trophy.

In three months away from home, by far the longest absence of my life, I've missed my siblings, a notion that had never really occurred to me, but I take comfort in the fact that being one of the Boys, as Mom has always called us, is like being a member of the Mafia. It's a lifetime commitment, an irrevocable status, and it's—perhaps more important—a kind of muscle memory. The way we are and have always been around each other, since childhood, will reflexively kick in whenever we're together, time and distance immaterial.

What I'll remember most about *this* Thanksgiving, though, isn't the Doug Flutie play, or the BC–Miami game itself, but the shared experience of sitting with Dad in front of the tube, admiring these athletes in silence, eating our sandwiches. From now on, the day after Thanksgiving will be special to me, long after retailers have turned it into a door-busting start to the Christmas shopping season.

Before a bus returns me to Marquette, I make one last batch of "nachos," of the sort Tom and I used to eat by the pound in our summertime, middle-of-the-night movie marathons in the basement. These nachos are home on a plate—an edible Bloomington, a microwaveable Minnesota, that begins with a blanket of Kraft singles or thinly sliced Velveeta pulled over a pile of tortilla chips like a sheet over a corpse. The chips are always Tostitos, introduced to a grateful America in 1980 with a TV commercial featuring a "restaurant owner" named "Fernando Escandon" saying, "My favorite Mexican snack doesn't come from Mexico." Tostitos (in Traditional Flavor and Nacho Cheese) come from someplace more authentic: Frito-Lay.

I nuke the pile of Tostitos and Velveeta in the microwave until the cheese forms a thin fluorescent yellow membrane, like skin blistered by the sun. Then I spoon on Chi-Chi's brand salsa—for it was Chi-Chi's that brought Mexican food to the 494 Strip before spreading its refried gospel to dozens of other cities around the country.

Chi-Chi's is the love child of the Strip's two greatest ghosts: flight attendants and footballers. It was opened in 1975 by a Minnesotan named Marno McDermott and his business partner, former Green Bay Packers wide receiver Max McGee, who is best known for picking up an American Airlines stewardess in Los Angeles and partying all night on the eve of the first Super Bowl. The oldest player on either team, McGee wasn't expecting to play that Sunday but was promptly summoned into the game with a crippling hangover. The Packers beat the Chiefs, McGee was the game's star, and with the relative riches he accrued—and in the spirit of the times—he opened a restaurant on the Strip called the Left Guard. *Time* magazine called the Left Guard "the nation's ultimate singles bar." The nation's ultimate singles bar! *In the 1970s!* And it was ours! Ours, even if my friends and I, at seven years old, could neither comprehend nor take advantage of it.

As the popular culture changed around the Left Guard, McGee and McDermott converted it into a wicker-and-fern disco called Maximillian's. "It's a place where a girl can get picked up respectably," an employee told the *Tribune*. "She knows [he's] not going to be a low roller."

Tommy Kramer—himself no low roller, springing for three tins of Copenhagen at a time at Tom Thumb—used to hang out at Maximillian's, which charged an annual membership fee of $100, ensuring that only millionaires (or anyone with a hundred bucks) could apply. I'm sure some of the parents in South Brook went there to do the Hustle, in shirts unbuttoned to their navels, but Don and Jane Rushin were not among them, though they *have* brought us to Chi-Chi's, a favorite of Mom's when she has lunch with other moms. Nine years after the original Chi-Chi's opened on the north side of the Strip in 1975, there are now seventy-four of them across North America. Wouldn't it be wonderful if Minnesota's own Marno McDermott brought Mexican food *to* Mexico *from* Minnesota?

Chi-Chi's (named for the founder's wife, Chi Chi McDermott) has its salsa on grocery shelves, the only salsa I'll spoon on my nachos, and now McDermott is the CEO of an upscale hamburger restaurant on the Strip called Fuddruckers, kitty-corner to Mother Tucker's, a pair of joints evidently christened in the hope that our parents will accidentally utter a four-syllable swear word.

Even so, there is a sense—now that I'm eighteen—that I've missed the Strip of my parents' heyday. Perhaps my affinity for soul and R&B and disco is what has me pining to go to '70s-vintage Ichabod's South, colossus of the Strip, with its thirty-thousand-dollar sound system and stainless-steel dance floor, or Eddie Webster's, with its sunken dance floor and house band—Five Easy Pieces—and all the glorious hotel bars that lead to and from Minneapolis–Saint Paul International Airport like a string of runway lights: the Exchange at the Marriott, the Captain's Table at the Ramada Inn, the Pow Wow Lounge at the Thunderbird Motel, the Grand Portage Saloon at the Registry Hotel, the Lounge at the Rodeway Inn, Mr. C's at the Radisson, or Le Bar at L'Hotel Sofitel, where Billy Martin punched out a marshmallow salesman, costing him—Billy, not the marshmallow salesman—his job as the manager of the New York Yankees.

If my friends and I have been deprived of Daddy's—another '70s Strip fixture, with its singing waitstaff and crab-legs specialty—well, so has my own daddy, who married Mom when they were both twenty-two, at which time the newlyweds were stationed in Fort Sill, Oklahoma, "courtesy of Uncle Sam's Army." The notion that I could be married or in the army (or both) four years from now is ludicrous. Even after I've returned to Marquette, I find myself blinking back the punishing light of the Castle. There, off-Strip—Off-Off-Strip, to use the Broadway analogy—is our slightly less glamorous version of Henrici's or the Decathlon Club or the Arthurian-themed, lavishly turreted Camelot, another faux castle in Bloomington. But that faux castle is not *our* faux castle. At White Castle, at what Dad sometimes calls Le Chateau Blanc, there are no high rollers picking up women, respectably or otherwise. In fact, I've never seen a woman getting picked up at the Castle, unless—as occasionally happens—she was being picked up off the floor by a put-upon worker in a paper hat, trying to mop the tiles around her. But for now it's a kind of heaven.

## 9.

# Spending Warm Summer Days Indoors

Twenty of us sit side by side in four neat rows at olive-green IBM Selectrics whose collective racket sounds like a thousand sets of novelty wind-up teeth chattering across a factory floor. Bashing out our timed deadline exercises in a News Writing class in Johnston Hall, we're disproving the notion that five hundred monkeys bent over five hundred typewriters will eventually compose the collected works of Shakespeare.

And we *are* monkeys, college freshmen not fully evolved. When we return from our three-week Christmas break, one of my friends named Steve—Stever, as he's known—opens his dorm-room door and is confronted with a profound stink. Tugging his T-shirt over his nose and mouth, Steve makes a brief investigation of the tiny room but turns up no rotting eggs, no lunch meat that has fallen onto the radiator. Feeling ridiculous but wanting to be thorough, he disassembles the handset of the room's wall-mounted rotary-dial telephone. Unscrewing the ear- and mouthpieces, he makes a grisly discovery.

Someone has concealed within both of them a dollop of shit. Steve suspects it was more than one person—two people with whom he had fought outside a bar. As he puts it to me an hour later, still incandescent with indignation but summoning all the dignity the phrase will allow: "They *shat* in my *phone*."

I've grown up with three brothers whose atrocities are always imaginative. Tom is a Marquis de Sade of scatological torments. He once invited me to sniff an empty aspirin bottle into which, unbeknownst to me, he had quite recently farted. Something about the tiny plastic receptacle, and the bed of cotton at the bottom, acted as the ideal vessel for his scheme. When I took a deep draw, the smell nearly rendered me unconscious—and was so strong it could have also revived me if indeed I *had* passed out. It was both knockout punch and smelling salts.

McCormick Hall is a tower full of Toms. Every floor has at least one visionary joker, a Walt Disney of depravity. My next-door neighbor is a quiet six-foot-six Milwaukeean with a cheerful disposition and a striking poster above his desk of a beautiful woman in a peach toga and pearls, with her name—Whitney Houston—across the top. In the evenings, B.Q.—as everyone knows him—enjoys decanting a six-pack of beer into a pitcher liberated from O'Paget's and using it as his personal mug. He sits on his desk chair with the door open. Like a prison toilet, it's the only place to sit that isn't the bed.

But here is B.Q.'s brilliance, the divine spark that reminds me of Tom. Whenever a floor mate's parents arrive for a visit—or parents of a prospective student tour the dorm—B.Q. is tipped off to their presence by one of his informants. And because the floor is circular—since the building is a cylinder—those parents usually make a full circumnavigation of the floor while looking for their son's room. As a result, B.Q. has just enough time to divest himself of his clothes, sit at his desk with his legs casually crossed, and give a jaunty wave while quaffing 60 ounces of beer from a pitcher at eleven o'clock on a Tuesday morning.

In this atmosphere of anti-domesticity, the mere presence on our floor of any mom puts all of us but B.Q. on our best behavior. I want these visiting moms to tuck me into my upper bunk or hand me a bologna sandwich. My diet is abysmal. At least three times a week I order two chimichangas from Amigo's across the street and ask for extra sour cream and salsa. I dip the chimi into the little plastic receptacles on every bite. One night, ravenous, I return from Amigo's in a downpour and the bottom of the paper takeout sack—already translucent with grease—falls open. My two chimichangas drop into a puddle in the McCormick parking lot. I look at them for a moment with regret, this tortilla flotilla, and make a decision: with both hands, I reach into the murky depths of the puddle and pull out both chimichangas. I am tempted to hold them up to the sky in triumph. They feel good in my hands, like an Olympic sprinter's baton. Back in my room, I put the chimies on the radiator. When they have dried, I eat them.

In fact, every menial task is a minefield. Clean clothes, I've discovered, require a descent into the coin-operated under-world of the dormitory laundry room, or the neighborhood Laundromat, both places teeming with other people's under-wear, the cotton-candy remnants of the lint traps, sheets of Bounce fabric softener stirring on the floor like autumn leaves whenever the door opens, bringing in new strangers with their bras and bedsheets and pajamas on full display. If there is value in the proscription against airing one's dirty laundry in public, none of us can afford to care.

Someone else's wet clothes have evidently been abandoned in a washing machine whose cycle has long since ended, and I'm left to bundle their twisted jeans and pink pillowcases in my arms and solemnly place them on a plastic folding table. (The table itself folds but is also used for folding clothes. Imagine a coffee table that also makes coffee.) I'm careful not to touch the sodden panties or to gaze directly at the off-white bra while silently praying that their owner doesn't walk in just as I'm transferring her frilly unmentionables across the black-and-white-tiled floor. And then I sit and watch my own underthings do somersaults in the foam-lashed porthole of an industrial Maytag.

I write Mom a letter to tell her what I can't in our Sunday night telephone conversations: that I now appreciate how difficult it is to do on my own all the things she has previously done for me. Even this requires me to buy envelopes and find the post office and procure a single twenty-cent stamp. The stamp they sell me was just issued. It bears the likeness of the great Roberto Clemente in a white Pittsburgh Pirates cap. How can the United States Postal Service depict one of the most famous players in the history of the game wearing a *white* cap when he and his teammates famously wore black or mustard caps? I want to write the Postmaster General and express my outrage, but then I remember who the stamp is for: Mom. I address the envelope to "Jane Rushin, 2809 West 96th Street, Bloomington, Minn. 55431."

In the upper left corner of the envelope, I write "The Zoo, 1530 W. Wisconsin Ave., Milwaukee, Wis. 53233." Then I take one last look at Clemente in his white hat and—turning the stamp over with a sigh—I lick it and stick it and send it on its 343-mile journey. Mom will be reading my letter in two or three days.

Among the visions I have of the distant future, fed by TV and newspapers and popular music, are those thin TVs that hang like paintings in the living room carrying as many as fifty channels into my den. On one of the cassettes Tom and I listen to on the boom box between our beds during summer and holiday breaks, Donald Fagen, late of Steely Dan, sings of a streamlined world of spandex jackets, ninety minutes from New York to Paris, undersea by rail. That song, "I.G.Y.," is about a kid in 1957 thinking about the impossibly distant world of 1976. Here I am, in 1984, contemplating a similar far-off Valhalla, as described in the *Minneapolis Star and Tribune,* which claims that someday—when I'm thirty-five, maybe, and on the brink of decrepitude—I won't be licking stamps and mailing letters. In fact, the paper tells me, that day has already arrived for some.

"Today," this story claims, "information that might otherwise require costly long-distance calls or delays for postal delivery can be exchanged across town or around the world virtually in an instant via 'electronic mail'—a computer-to-computer communications system regarded as the most revolutionary since the telegraph and telephone replaced horseback couriers more than a century ago."

"Electronic" mail. "Cellular" telephones. "Cable" TV. All

these magical modifiers. Surely flying cars cannot be far off. They certainly can't arrive fast enough for my liking. In March, four months after taking a Trailways to South Bend, I go there again. It snowed the previous night, the "lake-effect snow" in which cold air sucks up the warm water from Lake Michigan and drops it heavy and wet on Milwaukee. This is heart-attack snow for middle-aged shovelers. It leaves an icy coat on Interstate 94. My friend Vill is driving us to Notre Dame to watch the Irish host Marquette in basketball. Ten minutes south of downtown, we hit a patch of ice on I-94. As the Chrysler LeBaron starts to spin at sixty-five miles an hour, the revolving landscape seems to slow down, as if passing by on a merry-go-round.

While I remain stationary in the shotgun seat, the world leisurely turns around me. Or so it feels. The other cars, the highway signs, the churches and houses fringing the freeway, all go by slowly, a lazy Susan landscape, while I wonder if this is how it all ends—on Saturday morning, March 2, 1985, with the radio playing "I Want to Know What Love Is" by Foreigner.

When the spinning stops, the LeBaron is facing the oncoming freeway traffic. After a short moment of bewilderment, Vill harnesses years of watching *The Rockford Files* and executes a perfect Rockford Turn, reversing at speed, jamming on the brakes, throwing the car into drive, and continuing southbound on I-94. No words pass between us, and we drive to South Bend without further incident, as if nothing happened, as if that perfect J shape of burnt rubber was left by somebody else.

But our morning spinout confirms what I—and I can only

assume Vill—have suspected all along. That we are immortal. Indestructible. Eighteen.

The downside of this immunity to Death: we'll have to earn a living forever. And so, on our safe return to Milwaukee from South Bend, I write an account of the Irish victory over the Warriors. The game story is for my eyes only. I will never show it to anyone. I can't wait to get home for the summer, when school breaks, and return to Flip Saunders's backyard, and write more game stories about our three-on-three contests that I won't show to anyone. Is it possible to make a living this way, writing stories for myself that pile up in one Mead folder after another in the back of my closet, like the crated Ark of the Covenant warehoused among a million other identical crates at the end of *Raiders of the Lost Ark,* never again to see sunlight?

God, I hope so, because that's my plan.

In my weekly Sunday evening call home from the prison phone in my dorm room, before he hands the receiver to Mom, Dad tells me, "That was a nice letter you wrote to your mother. I can tell you've really matured." I'm wearing a bathrobe at 8 p.m., eating nachos from a paper sack, and watching *Knight Rider,* a show about a sentient, self-aware 1982 Pontiac Firebird that talks back to its driver.

"Thanks," I say, as my fellow freshmen do lap after lap around our circular hallway on wheeled office chairs in an impromptu Indianapolis 500. "I guess I *am* growing up."

Summer arrives faster than I expected. Within days of my returning to Bloomington, a letter arrives from the dean of the

College of Journalism, which Mom puts into my Tupperware memory box, a see-through sarcophagus memorializing all of my worldly achievements: Kool & the Gang ticket stub, state tournament basketball programs, letter-jacket letter—they lie in repose like Vladimir Lenin in his bulletproof tomb in Moscow, transparent testament to past glory.

"Dear Steven," wrote the dean, whose first paragraph is the only bit that isn't part of a form letter. "Congratulations on a successful freshman year at Marquette! I note especially your 'A' in J004 and encourage you to continue strong in writing."

The letter goes back into its envelope, and the envelope goes into my aforementioned Tupperware box, and the Tupperware box goes into the upstairs hall closet, with its bifolding doors that open to reveal the laundry hamper into which I frequently urinated during my sleepwalking rounds in junior high and high school. To the right of the hamper, just below my memory box, is Mom's sewing kit, with its fake-wicker exterior.

Every so often I open it up to inhale its mystical aroma, gaze into its fathomless depths. The sewing kit is Mom's memory box. It is tiered like a tackle box, displaying the various implements—scissors of various sizes, needles of differing circumferences, a solid bulb on which she darns socks, a measuring tape for reasons I can't discern, safety pins and thimbles and buttons of every description, and (at the center of it all) sufficient thread of every color to sew a Technicolor dreamcoat.

My memory box has my name in Mom's handwriting, block letters in permanent Magic Marker. There are four other boxes surrounding mine, for Mom is dutifully embalming each of our childhoods, preserving them in amber, socking away the very knickknacks that she ordinarily disdains as clutter.

Her favorite rhetorical question—"Can I pitch that?"—has always served as a death sentence for whatever object (stuffed animal, stray Shrinky Dink, ancient copy of *Sports Illustrated*) is in her crosshairs. Somehow this is the same mom who has saved every progress report, every newspaper clipping that mentioned any of us, every matchbook cover—CAMELOT: ADVENTURE IN DINING—that once cluttered one of our dressers as a reminder of that time we celebrated a special occasion at a fancy restaurant. She hasn't just socked away *my* birthday cards and graduation tassels and unsewn sleeve patches from long-forgotten tournaments (Tartan Basketball Classic 1981). She's done it for Jim and Tom and Amy and John as well. There's a box for every one of us. This closet is a Smithsonian Museum of the Rushin Children, their towering achievements preserved in airtight Tupperware for maximum freshness, to be snacked on whenever Mom gets hungry.

In June we contest the second annual SHIT in Flip's backyard, with the boom box blasting Whitney Houston, whom I'd never heard of when I first saw her on the poster above B.Q.'s desk. Now she's world famous. The boom box is the size of a Samsonite suitcase. The speakers pulsate like a cartoon thumb struck with a hammer. The wheels of the cassette tape turn slowly, inexorably. They are the wheels of a motorcycle, transporting me somewhere else: someplace grown-up, urban, racially diverse, and linguistically rich.

The *slap, slap* of high-end high-tops on the concrete court, the insults and warnings, the imprecations to "get that weak shit outta here," and—new to me—the elaborate slanders against one another's mothers. A player who pump-fakes three times—ball in both hands, elbows spread wide, pump-faking against a defender who isn't biting—is said to be "jacking off an elephant." Nobody does it again.

There's a real live NBA player here. Jim Petersen of Saint Louis Park and the University of Minnesota has just completed his rookie season with the Rockets. In Houston, he plays with Hakeem "The Dream" Olajuwon and Ralph Sampson. In Bloomington, he plays with Steve Rushin and Mike Mc-Collow and Keith Opatz. The resulting cognitive dissonance makes the SHIT slightly hallucinogenic. Arriving by Schwinn ten-speed at Flip's backyard court, "you're traveling through another dimension," as Rod Serling says. "A dimension not only of sight and sound but of mind."

In this dream state, Flip says his friend and former Gophers teammate Kevin McHale might come play in the SHIT, even though McHale and the Celtics have just played the Lakers in the NBA Finals. McHale doesn't show, but Flip's optimism, his can-do enthusiasm for basketball, and this backyard three-on-three tournament make me believe that an NBA all-star at any moment might walk through that sliding door from the kitchen and into the Saunderses' backyard, where McHale will clothesline me just like he clotheslined Kurt Rambis in last year's finals. And it would be a thrill, a privilege.

While the three-on-three games are going on, and the boom box throbs, and the traffic thrums past, I look up from the court to see a member of the Minnesota Golden Gophers basketball team staring pensively into the distance while sitting on the peaked roof of Flip's house. He is evidently upset, perhaps about the result of his three-on-three game, or possibly over a call (or non-call) in these self-policed games. "No blood, no foul" is the law here, though the truth is everyone acts unfazed even when their own blood is shed. *Especially* when their own blood is shed.

I don't know how the Gopher got on the roof, except to say that he—like almost all the players here—is of a higher physical order, capable of feats I can't fathom. He might have just leapt onto the roof, *Six Million Dollar Man* style, or vaulted up there off the picnic table. Whatever the case, he is unambiguously on the roof, brooding. Halfhearted efforts are made to coax him down. But they are for naught. The Gopher remains up there, marooned on a suburban roof like a Frisbee, as the sun sets on West 98½ Street, and I ride my ten-speed home, to the comforting drudgery of ordinary life.

Every Thursday I go to the mailbox in a fever of anticipation to retrieve my copy of *Sports Illustrated*. I have a fixed idea of who should be on that week's cover, and the instant I drag my copy into the sunlight of South Brook I know if I was right. But this Thursday is the Fourth of July. There is no mail. So I wait an eighth day, plus an extra minute—until the mail truck is two doors down, so I don't look like one of those elderly residents whose entire day is arranged around the arrival of the mail. (There's a kid on Xerxes who every day watches his live-in grandfather shuffle to the curb for the mail, then races out to snatch it from the box just before Grandpa can get to it.)

The cover of *SI* on this Friday is Dodgers left-hander

Fernando Valenzuela next to the headline MAKING HIS WAY IN THE U.S.A. The magazine is fat with advertisements, some of them rigid cardboard and scented with cologne. Three subscription cards fall out on my way from the mailbox to the front door. Leafing through this high-gloss leviathan, while walking barefoot up the scalding driveway, my eyes fall on page 62, on a story titled "The Only Game in Town." "On one spirited weekend each summer," reads the subhead, "tiny Lowell, Mich., turns into Mackerville, its streets, sidewalks, and front lawns given over to a three-on-three basketball bacchanal." I can scarcely believe it. *Sports Illustrated* has devoted eight pages to a makeshift, semi-ironic, quasi-suburban three-on-three basketball tournament in a Midwestern town and it reads like literature, thanks to the deft touch of its author, Alexander Wolff, whose name I recognize as the co-author of *The In-Your-Face Basketball Book,* which I ordered through B. Dalton Bookseller at Southdale in eighth grade and read almost in its entirety as Mom drove me home.

Upstairs, on the Brother typewriter in my bedroom, beneath Jim's handwritten copy of the Gettysburg Address, I compose a letter to the editor of *Sports Illustrated.* "Sir," it begins, in the style of all letters published in the magazine. "Lowell, Michigan, may have the Gus Macker, but Bloomington, Minnesota, has a better three-on-three basketball extravaganza: the Saunders Hoop Invitational Tournament, whose acronym is no reflection on the caliber of play..." It is a single paragraph, because letters published in the magazine are seldom longer than that, and I want to see this letter published in *SI,* see my name and town italicized at the end: *Steve Rushin, Bloomington, Minn.*

The Brother is forever warm this summer. It gives my desk the factory hum of enterprise. The Twins are hosting baseball's all-star game next week, and while I don't have a ticket, I do visit the Dome the day before, when it's open to the public for the official all-star workout. Though I have been in the Metrodome a hundred times, I'm now here to sketch its portrait, noting the quilted pattern of its Teflon roof, the white panels pushing through the grid like marshmallows through a tennis racket. The place is devoid of charm and atmosphere—if not for the organ music, it would be a sensory deprivation chamber—and I can't help but note the people here for the free workout will not likely be here tomorrow night for the game itself, when the stands and luxury boxes will be filled with (writes the righteous journalism student in his reporter's notebook) "fat businessmen" and "civic fat cats." I don't know why I think of white-collar workers as overweight. I'm not sure I know the difference between "corporate" and "corpulent."

The only thing I know is these imagined obese executives will be at the all-star game tomorrow night in place of me—a self-described "loyal box-score reader"—who will be forced to watch it at home, with "the armchair-and-six-pack crowd" (as I type in my eight-page single-spaced dispatch from in front of the basement TV, which I deliver in the historical past tense, writing for posterity):

I got my consolation, though. The game was a terrible bore, a lifeless 6–1 National League victory, complete with zero home runs, no American League extra base hits, and LaMarr Hoyt as the game's MVP.

Actually, my true consolation came the day before the all-star game, at the all-star workout, when members of both teams took batting practice at the Dome. A home-run hitting contest was held, and all the while that group known as The Media hounded anyone on the field wearing polyester double-knits (many of whom weren't ballplayers in uniform but members of The Media themselves).

That day I sat in the front row behind the National League's dugout, offering me a good view of Eddie Murray's high liner off the suspended speaker in right field, 175 feet off the ground and 350 feet out. I saw Ryne Sandberg send one over the wall in center, only to have a local high school kid who was fielding for the workout haul back a home run.

I also got to see Joe Garagiola and Vin Scully, Brent Musburger and a score of local writers whom I recognized. I was on a cloud. I pictured myself on the field, as did everyone else at the workout. But not only did I picture myself taking a Dwight Gooden fastball to the corner for a triple, I also saw myself with a luggage tag hanging from my belt and a notebook in my hand, following the neglected all-star batboys in search of a story.

But how, exactly, will that happen? How will I move from a seat in front of my television to a place in the dugout, clubhouse, and press box, that "luggage tag" of a press credential dangling from my belt loop? Where is the wardrobe door leading to *this* Narnia? My plan, such as it is, involves magical thinking. The key, I've decided—for reasons I cannot articulate even to myself—is to get my letter published in *Sports Illustrated.*

And so every Thursday I stand at the curb—the mailbox door still hanging open like a dog's tongue—and I flip to the back page, to the letters page, called 19th Hole, to see if the editor has chosen my letter. I don't know if the letters-to-the-editor editor—identified on the page as "Gay Flood"—is a man or a woman. I only know that he or she hasn't published my letter.

Every seven days, centuries go by. Entire geological ages transpire from Thursday to Thursday. How I wish I had access to "electronic mail," a phenomenon that now appears to be no different from four-course meals in pill form or flying cars. And so I wait another seven days for the next issue of *SI,* turning first to the back page, the letters page, reading the magazine from back to front like a Japanese comic book. My letter is never there. It is now dawning on me that it won't be published. The letters here refer to stories published weeks after the story on the Macker. The magazine has moved on. There is no magic wardrobe through which I can enter the world of *Sports Illustrated,* or New York City, or journalism in general. "You like to read, you like to write," Mom tells me, looking out for my best interests. "You might consider becoming a lawyer."

There's breaking news on the evening of Friday, August 2. Shortly after dinner—a reheated repast I eat alone at the kitchen table, having returned late from the New Orleans Court apartment complex, whose enormous grounds I am perpetually mowing this summer—the networks gravely report that Delta flight 191 from Fort Lauderdale has crash-landed in heavy rain and burst into flames on approach to Dallas/Fort Worth Airport. The pictures are horrific. Scores are dead. Some passengers, miraculously, are said to have survived.

It is thirty minutes after I get home and eat, then, that Mom absentmindedly mentions there's a letter for me on her desk in the kitchen. My name and address have been typed by a manual typewriter on the front of the envelope. There is no return address, but the postmark reads JUL 30 '85 NEW YORK, N.Y. I turn it over, and there's a return address on the back flap.

**Sports Illustrated**
Time & Life Building
New York, NY 10020

Typed above the *Sports Illustrated* letterhead is the name of my correspondent and what appears to be his office number in the Time & Life Building, kitty-corner to 30 Rock, where David Letterman broadcasts his show: A. Wolff 1931.

With trembling hands, I open the letter carefully, using a butter knife because a surgeon's scalpel isn't readily available. The stationery is creamy, on a stock of paper with which I am not familiar. At the top of the sheet is the same *Sports Illustrated* logo as on the envelope, just above the magazine's phone number, which doesn't appear to have changed in the previous quarter century. It is 212 JU 6-1212. I recognize these ancient telephone exchanges from bits of pop-culture flotsam. There's an old song called "PEnnsylvania 6-5000." The Ricardos' phone number on *I Love Lucy* reruns is MUrray Hill 5-9975. I've seen a novel at Penn Lake Library called *BUtterfield 8*. With this missive from JUdson 6-1212, I've taken one step into my television set, into a black-and-white '40s movie or a Signet Classic paperback.

I open the letter itself.

*Dear Steve:*

*The* SI *Letters Dept. recently forwarded to me your kind and informative letter responding to our story on Mackerville. My co-author, Chuck Wielgus, of* The In-Your-Face Basketball Book, *will likely call you soon to find out more about S.H.I.T., to help us research our sequel,* The Back-In-Your-Face Basketball Book.

*Thanks again for writing. Any help you could provide Chuck and me in our research would be greatly appreciated.*

*Sincerely,*
*Alex Wolff*
*Staff Writer*

I turn the envelope upside down and shake it, and a business card falls out. The card has raised letters, as if my goose bumps are contagious and have transferred to this inanimate object.

The business card has that Rockefeller Center address and a home phone number scrawled across the back in blue ink.

(Like the office number, it has that magical 212 area code.) On the front, next to Wolff's name, is the title "staff writer." How do you get to be that?

I put the business card on my desk. It looks like something that would arrive on a silver tray, proffered by a white-gloved butler, an engraved invitation to something in another, higher world. New York. Rockefeller Center. Time & Life Building. *Sports Illustrated.*

The card and letter sit on my desk for two weeks. I look at them every day, occasionally taking them to the couch downstairs, lying down and looking up at the letter as if into a lover's eyes. Soon I receive another missive, this one from Chuck Wielgus, "co-author" with "Alex" of *The In-Your-Face Basketball Book.* Could I send Chuck thumbnail sketches of the best pickup basketball hot spots in the Twin Cities—playgrounds, backyards, YMCAs—for possible inclusion in the book's forthcoming sequel? My electric typewriter hums. When I send "Chuck" several paragraphs on each playground—he has asked only for a few lines—he inquires, by mail, if I'd be willing to write similar sketches for other municipalities. By the end of the summer, I'm phoning parks-and-rec departments throughout Minnesota, Wisconsin, Iowa, Nebraska, and the Dakotas, asking whoever answers the phone to tell me where the good people of Bismarck or Yankton or Dubuque hone their spin moves and tomahawk dunks.

And then one day before returning to school I can't find the letter from Alex. I have misplaced it, as I misplace everything else in my life. Or perhaps Mom pitched it. Either way, I've lost this artifact—this Golden Ticket—and with it, Alexander Wolff's phone number and address, and any evidence that my correspondence with him was anything more than a fever dream. My pen pal is now Chuck, his co-author, who is himself a parks-and-rec director—in South Carolina—and not a staff writer for *Sports Illustrated.*

At the end of August, as she has done for the previous fourteen years, Mom buys me back-to-school clothes. The ritual hasn't varied in a decade. I try them on in my bedroom, I confirm they fit in the bathroom mirror, then I fish the scissors out of Mom's sewing kit to cut all the tags off.

Returning the scissors to the kit, I see it through the clear Tupperware of my memory box: the envelope from *Sports Illustrated* and, inside it, the letter and business card from Alex, tucked away by Mom for safekeeping. She'll never mention law school again.

## 10.

# Money for Nothing

Every morning at eight the next-door neighbors in my high-rise dorm crank "Money for Nothing," whose introductory guitar riff I come to think of as the theme song that runs over the opening credits of the sitcom that is my daily life. Over and over, background vocalist Sting sings a haunting refrain of "Money for nothin'" and "Chicks for free" before delivering the decade's most diabolical earwig: "I want my, I want my, I want my MTV." By embedding MTV's jingle within their song, Dire Straits has ensured endless rotation on MTV itself, which now has twenty-six million subscribers, all of us in the words of the Associated Press "peach-fuzzy viewers, notorious for their bite-size attention spans."

I've been hearing this since I was little. "Studies have shown that many children have short attention spans and suffer fidgets as the result of watching TV with its constant interruptions," the *Detroit Free Press* reported when I was eight. "Teachers fight the battle constantly. On *Sesame Street,* much of the show's educational material is done in a TV commercial style: short spurts to fit a child's short attention span." Of course, it's possible that children have always had short attention spans and adults have always lamented that fact and television provided a convenient scapegoat. This much is certain: when the video for "Addicted to Love" airs on MTV, as it seems to have done every hour on the half hour for weeks, I am powerless to look away for the full glorious duration of its three minutes and fifty-two seconds. Five sullen models identically done up in black dresses, bloodred lipstick, and slicked-back hair pretend to play instruments while towering over Robert Palmer, unintentionally dressed as a high-end waiter in black slacks, white shirt, and black tie. The whole tableau is enchanting. Even late at night, with the TV on mute, the syncopated gyrations of the pantomime musician-models render sound unnecessary. The song plays in my head. Likewise, when the song comes on the radio, the models are conjured from thin air. If any of this is wrong, I don't want to be right.

"Money for Nothing" is off Dire Straits' *Brothers in Arms* album. I know my neighbors are playing a vinyl LP because there's a brief interval of popping and hissing after "Money for Nothing" ends and before "Walk of Life" begins. This is the first album in chart history to sell more copies on compact disc than on long-playing record, and the first to sell a million CDs. The format is two years old and an unstoppable force. Digital has arrived, impatiently tapping its watch, waiting to usher analog off the stage.

CDs haven't replaced tapes and records. The downtown Milwaukee record store Radio Doctors looks and smells as if it's been here forever. And it has. The place opened as a radio repair shop in 1931 and still restores old Philcos and Zeniths to life. But most of its 22,000 square feet is devoted to a musical Tower of Babel, where pop, rock, funk, punk, comedy, country, classical, and jazz albums all call at once from their alphabetized bins. Bach and Bachman-Turner Overdrive, Coltrane and Cocteau Twins, Gerry and the Pacemakers and Echo and the Bunnymen—they're all here, as are their fans: hippies and yuppies in Frye boots and business suits, smelling of professorial tweed and undergraduate weed. Radio Doctors will always be here, in the aptly named Century Building, a shop both ancient and eternal. Here I discover the Smiths, whose songs about "spending warm summer days indoors writing frightening verse" somehow resonate.

Today, I buy a double album—Canadian classical pianist Glenn Gould playing Bach's *Goldberg Variations*—because I heard a professor extol it in passing. Gould will be shelved between the Gap Band and Grandmaster Flash in my alphabetized record collection.

A few blocks away is Renaissance Books, another Milwaukee institution that I'm certain will outlive me. Its five stories seem to totter precariously, like a pile of books. Inside, I have to wade through volumes stacked higgledy-piggledy to explore its heaving floors and buckling shelves. I feel like an EMT entering a hoarder's apartment in search of a body to carry out. The cracked spines and yellow pages and overpowering smell of age—old books, old customers—give the store the appearance of a skid-row hotel for the elderly. Indeed, the sign that hangs perpendicular to the front of the building, unmissable by any foot or automotive traffic passing by, are five enormous letters hung vertically:

**B**

**O**

**O**

**K**

**S**

Every time I pass by—or rather, every time I see it, finding it impossible to pass by—I read those five bloodred letters as:

**H**

**O**

**T**

**E**

**L**

Indeed, I buy a used paperback there called *The Hotel New Hampshire* because Professor Bovée praised it in a journalism class, and thus John Irving joins Julius Erving in the pantheon on my bookshelves. I make no critical distinction between Irving's *The World According to Garp* and the Erving-inspired *Dr. J: The Story of Julius Erving,* a 1975 Scholastic paperback by sportswriter Joe Gergen, except to say that I enjoyed them both equally, in different ways.

Much as moisture has found its way through the cracked grout in my shower at Tower (as my new dorm is called), so the occasional literary novel and classical or jazz or "college radio" recording has penetrated my collections, with a stealthy influence that I don't detect until it has become too late and pervasive.

If I'm to believe the news, I won't be buying records much longer. The news stories I read all the time now insist "it's only a matter of a few years" before digital kills analog, as video killed the radio star. I have faith, however, that my generation will continue to make mix tapes, if only to keep Dad, who is now fifty-one, employed for another dozen years, before he and Mom can retire to a condo on the Gulf Coast of Florida, following the migratory pattern of Minnesota snowbirds.

But it's difficult to believe this imagined future, these speculative news stories that come churning off the wire in the bowels of Johnston Hall, providing possible filler for the *Marquette Tribune*. "Many government agencies have not begun to deal with the prospect of worldwide weather changes resulting from the greenhouse effect, the name scientists have given to a global warming trend they say is occurring because of pollutants in the atmosphere." These stories read like *1984* and sound like "1999."

"Scientists," the story says, "warn of unprecedented catastrophes."

Sophomore year proves from the start to be every bit as sophomoric as freshman year. I'm in another high-rise dorm called M. Carpenter Tower, but this time on the sixteenth floor. The exterior rooms look onto Wisconsin Avenue, the city's main drag, and a few of my dorm mates are fond of dropping water balloons out the windows and onto the bus stop below, exploding at the feet of innocent Milwaukeeans, waiting freshly dressed-and-pressed for a city bus to take them to work.

I don't feel good about these "stunts," as Dad would call them if he knew about them, and he doesn't. Watching from a safe remove, I laugh along with everyone else, but maybe the guilt this time is less a fear of getting in trouble than a desire to do right, to grow up.

There are weekdays when I'll go sit in the century-old Church of the Gesù on campus—a dead ringer for Chartres Cathedral—and wallow in the near silence. The hum of traffic on Wisconsin Avenue reminds me of similar sounds from South Brook: the oscillating fan in my bedroom there; the churning and thrumming of the washer and dryer in the laundry room; the purr of the engine as Dad's car pulls into the garage and idles for a split second, signaling that dinner is imminent; the gurgle of the dishwasher after dinner, when Mom and Dad have their evening coffee. The muffled traffic on Wisconsin Avenue heard from a pew in Gesù is a reminder of home and hominess. I'm a sophomore in college and still a little homesick. Is it possible this feeling will never leave me, even when 2809 West 96th Street belongs to someone else and there is no longer a home for which to be sick?

There is comfort in the ritual of attending Mass, even if the ritual is rather different in Milwaukee—homeless men snoozing in the back—than in Bloomington (where the snoozing men have homes). Here, for instance, there is a Hangover Mass on Sunday evenings, attended almost exclusively by cotton-mouthed congregants lip-syncing through the hymnal. We place our faces in our palms to still our throbbing temples—but it looks like an act of piety. We are praying, yes, but mostly that the priest doesn't pass by with his brass censer, swinging a burning perfume in our direction.

At Notre Dame, there's a Sunday night Hangover Mass as well, and Jim is a regular attendee. My biggest brother is no longer collecting celebrity signatures on American Express receipts in the accounting office of the Sheraton O'Hare. He's a Notre Dame graduate student in pursuit of his MBA, which was the best method he could think of to become eligible for season tickets to the Fighting Irish football games. The happy result of all this is that Jim is home for a few days over Christmas break, when Mom requires all of us in college—Tom, Jim, and I—to register with an agency that will find us temporary jobs over the holidays. It happens every Christmas: I return home to register with this local authority, as if I'm a convicted sex offender or a parolee checking in with his PO.

The temp jobs are almost always ridiculous. At an auto-parts warehouse, we have to conduct the year-end inventory, pulling boxes off shelves and counting the number of spark plugs inside, then dutifully recording the number on a form that has six carbon copies. One of our fellow temps wears a Walkman with Iron Maiden spilling out the headphones. At least two temps climb to the third level of shelving, ostensibly to inventory the fan belts up there, and lie down among the boxes to take a nap. Tom and I stage what the papers call a "work slowdown," counting as sluggishly as possible, not out of any ideological labor protest but because we're apathetic. Lethargy is our school-break default setting. But Jim—Jim is doing his job and all of ours, happily counting box after box of wiper blades and gas caps and ignition coils and about a million other auto parts. How many? Only Jim can say for sure, because he's done a painstaking count of this entire warehouse—happily, enthusiastically, whistling while he works.

Each job is more tedious than the last. Our piecemeal assignments are given to us by a woman named Sally Ann. She is disembodied, faceless, a voice on the telephone like Charlie from *Charlie's Angels*. One morning she dispatches Tom, Jim, and me to the world headquarters of the Softsoap manufacturer in Chaska. Minnetonka Corporation is the maker of liquid hand soap flatulently dispensed from a pump at your kitchen sink or bathroom vanity. Our job is to look at hundreds of empty plastic bottles not yet filled with liquefied hand soap and note the number embossed on the bottom of each. Whenever we see a number 6, presumably defective, we are to cull that bottle from the herd. We do this for eight hours, with thirty minutes off for lunch, throwing the 6s into a separate bin. By the second hour, Tom and I are dispatching the 6s into their bin by means of hook shot, turnaround jumper, or tomahawk dunk. By the third hour, we are attempting to block each other's shots, vigorously defending drives to the basket, fouling the shooter when necessary. Talk about money for nothing.

"Thank you, everybody," the supervisor tells us when we've assembled in front of him at the end of the day. "Excellent work. We'll see you all here tomorrow morning."

He points at Tom and me. "Except you two. We won't need you back."

We find this hilarious. We'll just tell Mom what the guy told us—we won't be needed the next day. At some point in the past two years Tom and I have gone from combatants to coconspirators. But our transformation is nothing compared to Jim's. He finds joy in manual labor. Who is this guy? As a teenager hospitalized with two black eyes and a broken nose suffered in a hockey game—though his face resembled a Halloween mask and he couldn't see his interlocutor—he could still find the energy to say: "What are *you* lookin' at?"

This same guy now ingratiates himself with warehouse managers and happily performs the most menial tasks on offer. He has channeled his hockey-playing intensity into work. Here's a man, nearly twenty-five years old, on his way to an advanced degree, examining Softsoap bottles with the care and evident fascination of a jeweler gazing through his loupe at the Hope Diamond. Tom and I have the very same epiphany at the very same time: that Jim is becoming Dad, embracing work, recognizing the imperative of making money, and choosing to be happy in the necessary—in the salutary—pursuit of it.

I'm not there yet. One evening Sally Ann sends me on a solo mission to a suburban printing plant not far from the Softsoap site in Chaska. This is always the best part of temp work: getting the call. In that moment, Sally Ann is M, and I am James Bond being dispatched to an exotic location for an invigorating misadventure. And then I turn up at an industrial park an hour before midnight to spend the night shift in a windowless warehouse made of corrugated metal and lit like the White Castle parking lot, so that my coworkers have the skin tone and ocular health of the living-dead extras in the "Thriller" video.

My job is to stack pads of generic green restaurant checks and place them into boxes for shipping. These are the kind of pads on which a gum-snapping waitress (I think of Flo on

*Alice*) jots down your order before tearing it off and leaving it on the table as your bill. The stacked pads will only fit in the shipping boxes if their edges all align perfectly, and the quickest way to do this is to place the pads on a vibrating metal platform that shakes them into neat columns. After an hour of working the vibrating table, I've gone numb from the elbows down. Which is a blessing—in this condition, I don't feel the fresh paper cuts that score my fingers and palms. By 3 a.m., I find myself wondering if any of my coworkers has ever thumped his Johnson onto this vibrating plate just to feel *something*. By 5 a.m., I'm half contemplating it myself. Sometime after 7 a.m., when I've arrived home, long after Dad has gone to work but before anyone else has risen, I stick a Post-it note next to the wall-mounted phone in the kitchen. The Post-it note is another miraculous product from the 3M Company. Dad brings them home in bulk from the company store. On it, I write a poem I composed in my head while driving home:

*Sally Ann will ring this phone.*
*"Will Steve work?" she'll ask ya.*
*Tell Sally Ann to go to hell.*
*Or better yet, to Chaska.*

When I come down to breakfast at two in the afternoon, the note is still by the phone. Mom has left it there. If she didn't find it funny, it would be gone. But it isn't. Quite why this makes me so happy I cannot say, but making Mom laugh is still my primary aim in writing. Which is a challenge when the class assignment subject is a public-records search or a state congressional race or the theft of a bicycle. The best part of watching *The Carol Burnett Show* on Saturday nights as a kid was when Tim Conway made the other actors—usually Harvey Korman, sometimes Carol herself—"break." This was Hollywood shorthand for breaking character, but it appeared to me that they were literally breaking: their faces fissured with stifled laughter, tears appeared at the corners of their eyes, and their shoulders shook, as if some great rupture were taking place. That's what happens when I make Mom laugh at the dinner table. The impending rupture often involves her bladder, and she races to the bathroom five feet from her chair. In journalism classes I'm told to serve the reader, remember who my audience is. But there is only ever one reader, and really only one goal in writing for her. Breaking Mom.

In that golden hour of late afternoon, having just risen from bed, supine and concave on the maroon love seat as if lying in a wheelbarrow, I open the paper and turn first to the comics. It's a ritual as familiar as Mass but performed with greater religious zeal. It's also more comforting: even more than the soap operas that so many of my dorm mates at Marquette find absorbing—killing their afternoons with *Days* and *All My Kids*—the comics are unchanging and timeless. When exactly is *Blondie* set? Blondie herself wears a formal dress and a string of pearls to the movies, while Dagwood goes in a suit and bow tie. The boys in *Beetle Bailey* take leave in the big city, as if they're Gene Kelly and Frank Sinatra in *Anchors Aweigh* in 1945. (I saw it on *Mel's Matinee Movie* on a school sick day in the '70s, thermometer plugged into me like a Thanksgiving turkey.) There has happily been no character development in the comics in the fifteen years I've been reading them. Every husband and wife bicker: Hägar the Horrible and his wife, Helga; Andy Capp and his missus; and the passive-aggressive spouses in *The Lockhorns,* who remind me of Stanley and Helen Roper on *Three's Company,* or Archie and Edith on *All in the Family,* or Ralph and Alice on *The Honeymooners* reruns that have aired every weeknight for years on local TV. Even the comedians on *The Tonight Show*—Rodney Dangerfield, Henny Youngman, and Johnny himself—treat marriage as a combat sport.

Mom and Dad aren't like that at all, which may be why my favorite comics are about big families in chaotic houses. *The Family Circus* is about Bil and Thelma and their four kids, Billy, Dolly, Jeffy, and P.J. Their family isn't as big as our own, and is far better behaved, but they have the advantage of never aging, remaining forever nuclear, under one roof; the babies are forever babies, the teens perpetual teens. This has an appeal to me. The best comic strip of all, better even than the brilliant *The Far Side,* is *Calvin and Hobbes,* about an ageless boy and his faithful stuffed tiger, alive only to him.

On New Year's Day of 1986, Calvin approaches his dad, reading a book in an armchair like my own dad's, next to a lamp exactly like ours, and asks, "Dad, how come you live in this house with Mom instead of in an apartment with several scantily clad female roommates?" After Dad stares for a panel into the middle distance, Calvin has his TV privileges revoked. This is what it was like in our house, for the better part of a dozen years, which may be why I'm so happy at home, all seven of us under one roof: because these moments are finite, numbered, limited to Christmas breaks and summer vacations and Thanksgivings. And even during these brief homecomings, much of my time is taken up not reading the comics or watching movies in the basement but with temporary jobs of unbelievable, unrelievable boredom, each one a cautionary tale that betokens a potential future of daily despair, of existential ennui. I don't want any of these temp jobs to become my permanent job. I'm actively opposed to becoming a yuppie or a corporate fat cat, whatever my khakis and docksiders and kelly-green Izod cardigan might say to the contrary. I will live a modest life rich in fulfillment but bereft of luxuries, in the manner of Jesus, or James and Florida Evans on *Good Times*. I have no real interest in making money, and when I say so, Dad replies, "But you might someday. When you have a family to support."

A family to support. As with my long-ago dreams of flying to the moon, this distant land—A Family of My Own—is at once unreachable and unavoidable. Marriage seems inevitable and impossible. Even my literary hero, the divorced sportswriter Oscar Madison on *The Odd Couple,* had to get married before he became single, free to roam—in his Mets cap and sweatshirt, sandwich in hand—through his eight-room apartment in Manhattan. Which isn't to suggest that those dreams of flying to the moon have been entirely extinguished.

Shortly after returning from Christmas break in January, getting out of bed with just enough time to make it to Johnston Hall for my eleven o'clock class if I make brazen use of the elevator override button—evidently a universal feature in Marquette dormitories—I try to turn off the muted TV. But I can't immediately find the remote and see on the screen that the space shuttle is about to launch from Cape Canaveral. The sky is cerulean. A radio voice says, "T minus fifteen seconds." I was not quite three when my family moved from Lisle, Illinois, to Bloomington, stopping overnight in Wisconsin Dells, Wisconsin, where my parents tucked me and Tom and Jim into bed at the Shady Lawn Motel and watched the Apollo 11 moon landing. I was six when the men of Apollo 17 landed on the moon in the final Apollo mission. There followed a succession of astronautical bath toys and at least one Apollo rocket ship model that was broken when used as a pointy-ended billy club on my brothers. Childhood vacation tours of the Kennedy Space Center in Cape Canaveral, and of NASA headquarters when Uncle Pat and Aunt Sandy lived in Houston, and of the Smithsonian National Air and Space Museum when I was thirteen, remain vivid in my imagination. One of my unspoken dreams is to somehow slip the surly bonds of earth without slipping the cozy bonds of Bloomington.

I sit on the edge of the bottom bunk and watch. I am powerless to do otherwise. "We have main engine start," says a disembodied voice, though in my head that voice is attached to a man in a short-sleeved white dress shirt and skinny tie from the 1960s and the kind of glasses that Malcolm X wore. "Four, three, two, one, and liftoff. Liftoff!" The crowd is applauding. It's not a moon shot, but the goose bumps appear nonetheless. "The twenty-fifth space shuttle mission has cleared the tower." The great phallus climbs on a column of fire.

I stand to leave. The audio transmission is a beautiful mission-control mumbo jumbo about "engines throttling down" and the *Challenger* drifting "downrange," all said in that comforting Chuck Yeager Southern drawl first celebrated by Tom Wolfe in *The Right Stuff,* another book recommended by a journalism professor. That drawl has been adopted by every airline pilot in the U.S., if not the world. In that voice, danger is rendered routine, the heroic made mundane. "We apologize for the bumps," the Yeager-inspired pilot says as your 727 is tempest tossed. "Uh, we'll try to find us some smooth air so you won't spill your drinks. Flight attendants, please be seated..."

Textbooks in hand, I stand beside the bed for another beat, soaking it in. The shuttle is racing away from me now and so apparently is CNN, preparing to cut away from this enchanting tableau, their man on the scene—VOICE OF TOM MINTIER CNN CORRESPONDENT reads the chroma-key—wrapping things up neatly. "So the twenty-fifth space shuttle mission is now on the way," he says, pausing as another explosion—a booster, perhaps?—causes the white column in the rocket's wake to split into two. There is momentary confusion. "It looks like a couple of solid rocket boosters blew away from the side of the shuttle in an explosion," says the announcer, whose incomprehension slowly yields to disbelief. The smoky contrail is still rising upward like a wraith with two arms. "Flight controllers looking very carefully at the situation," says a tinny monotone. "Obviously a major malfunction."

I stand for thirty minutes, then sit back down on the bed. Every channel shows the same scene: the clear blue sky, the billowing white clouds, the anonymous death from above. I watch it again and again, this explosion that will have its echo on another bright Tuesday morning, fifteen years from now.

# 11

# Another One Rides the Bus

There are happier signs that point to a future that may be utopian rather than dystopian, more George Jetson than George Orwell. It's evident in a late-night commercial. "First came the pocket watch," goes the voice-over. "Then the pocket radio. Then, even, a pocket camera! But who would have thought of a pocket TV? Casio, of course!" Barely larger than a deck of cards, this TV runs on two AA batteries—included!—"sending a clear black-and-white picture from a name we know and trust." I have no intention of sending a check or money order for just $99.95 plus $5.00 postage and handling to a PO box in West Caldwell, New Jersey, but am fascinated to consider the result if I did: a television in my pocket. To get many of the channels I now watch, I'd have to be tethered to a prodigious length of coaxial cable. But with enough pockets, conceivably, I could walk around with a TV, a camera, a digital clock, and a Walkman—every one of them smaller than a house brick—at my immediate disposal.

But the *real* electronic marvel that holds me in its spell these days is the Canon Typestar, a sleek black half digital, half analog minotaur. It has a computer keyboard whose every key is responsive to the slightest touch, so that I don't have to strike them as if I'm Schroeder playing Beethoven on a baby grand. Above the top row of keys is an electronic "screen," four inches wide and two inches tall: every sentence I type passes through that window, never displaying more than two words at a time, each letter of every word composed of a series of dots, like the letters on the state-of-the-art electronic scoreboards at major-league stadiums. If I write "The quick brown fox jumped over the lazy dogs," I can review that sentence as it passes by, in two-word pairs, as if the sentence is boarding Noah's Ark: "The quick" gives way to "brown fox" gives way to "jumped over" and so forth, until I've forgotten what the start of the sentence was. But that hardly matters, for I can now edit on the screen before striking the carriage return and seeing those words transfer onto paper. The Typestar—its name evokes the retro-futuristic Telstar satellite of the early 1960s—still requires a sheet of paper scrolled onto a platen, as on Mom's manual Royal or my own electric Brother at home.

But I use it every day. My journalism teachers have made it clear that we can write about anything, find glory in the mundane, God in the everyday, literature wherever we happen to be. When I'm late for my journalism classes, I use the elevator override button in Tower, holding the L down as I bypass each floor on my descent from sixteen. The shouted obscenities and idle threats that issue as the elevator car passes each unrequited group on the other side of the unyielding doors gives me an idea.

For the first time in my life, I'm riding an elevator every day. One night I sit in my room in Tower and write an essay about the etiquette of elevator riding—avoiding eye contact, pressing buttons that have already been pressed, the suppression of flatulence, the repeated jabbing of the CALL button in the vain hope that the elevator will arrive sooner. I rip the thermal paper out of the Typestar, tri-fold it, stick it in an envelope, and mail it to 435 North Michigan Avenue, Chicago, Ill., 60611.

This missive to the *Chicago Tribune* is the second letter I've ever submitted to a publication, after the letter to *Sports Illustrated* about the SHIT. Beyond those, the only unsolicited essays I've ever mailed to anyone were thank-you notes, which Mom required us to write within forty-eight hours of Christmas. The unspoken obligation to fill out the entire blank space of the card—expressing my undying gratitude for that Billy Squier tape or the empty Rubik's Cube box—was my first exercise in creative writing. It was the literary equivalent of inventing sins to confess to Father Gilbert at reconciliation so that we had something to talk about in the confessional.

I buy the *Chicago Tribune* out of the coin-operated newspaper rack on Wisconsin Avenue every day. In Chicago, I've walked past the paper's neo-Gothic headquarters on Michigan Avenue, gazed up at its thirty-four stories—never has the word "stories" seemed more appropriate—and looked for Chicago psychologist Bob Hartley, who first appears to us, in belted trench coat, near here in the opening credits of *The Bob Newhart Show*. After Cubs games, I have gone underground, across the street from Tribune Tower, to the subterranean Billy Goat Tavern, haunt of Mike Royko and inspiration for John Belushi and Dan Aykroyd's "Cheeseburger, cheeseburger, cheeseburger" sketch on *Saturday Night Live*. I've walked along the Chicago River, past the squat box of the *Sun-Times* building and the majestic Marina City, twin towers, each one sixty-two stories, each story shaped like a sixteen-petaled flower whose architect—near as I can tell—was George Jetson. I imagine myself walking from work at the *Trib* or *Sun-Times,* in a trench coat like Bob Newhart's, to my condo in Marina City.

The centerpiece of this so-called Magnificent Mile is the turreted white Water Tower, fabled as the only building standing after the Great Chicago Fire of 1871, though I'm more interested in it as the alleged inspiration for the White Castle hamburger chain.

The *Tribune* costs a quarter in Chicago but thirty-five cents in Milwaukee. Every day I put my quarter and dime into the same metal box and pull out the paper with its U.S. flag on a blue masthead and fold it neatly and carry it in my armpit to class. On Saturdays, I put my coins in and pull out the paper and absentmindedly leaf through it in my room, which is where—on February 22, three and a half weeks after the *Challenger* explosion—I turn to the editorial page and see, beneath an editorial on loans to farmers, the title "Regimenting the Ups and Downs." The following thirteen paragraphs were written by me, in this very room, on my Canon Typestar, and now they're on newsstands on Michigan Avenue, being flung from Schwinns into box hedges in Bolingbrook, discarded on L trains, and carried onto airplanes. At the bottom of the story, my name in italics: *Steve Rushin,* leaning to the right, as if in forward motion.

Saturday is the least-read paper of the week and there is no Royko column and some of my immortal prose has been edited with less precision than I might have liked, but it hardly matters. I return to the coin-operated *Tribune* box. The box snaps shut with an echoing bang after you remove a newspaper. I put another thirty-five cents into the coin slot and this time remove five papers. The box snaps shut. It's a spring-loaded steel trap, this newspaper box, capable of snapping your arm off, or at least holding you fast, powerless to escape its clutches.

I'm fairly certain it has caught me.

The end of sophomore year rings the curtain down on two years that a biographer might call—were I a famous painter—my Bunk Bed Period. Never again will I climb a ladder to go to bed, or watch the bedsprings groan above me, for the only civilian adults I can think of who sleep in bunk beds—bunked hammocks, to be fair—are Gilligan and the Skipper. I am moving to an ungoverned combat zone called Off Campus, with two roommates, to an apartment where I'll have my own bed and bedroom. And thus begins a new era of my life: the Apartment Epoch.

Hodes and I and our mutual friend Todd furnish our third-floor walk-up at Canterbury Court with castoffs from our parents' houses. We put a TV cart in the corner, where the four divots in the carpet indicate the previous tenants' TV was. The avocado carpet, installed in a previous decade—*which* decade is unclear—tells us where the furniture fits. The four legs of the couch go here, the circular base of the floor lamp goes there. It's like an Arthur Murray dance chart, but instead of your foot you put your futon here.

Hodes secures for us a stereo and turntable housed in a walnut console the size and weight and finish of an upright piano. It's burnished to a sheen with lemon-scented Pledge.

Carrying it up to the third floor, I felt like Hercules. There are floral-print armchairs and a U-shaped rug that fits around the base of the toilet and a fuzzy blue cap for the lid—things I wouldn't know how to buy, refugees from various homes, a diaspora of misfit appliances and silverware and other aspirational kitchen implements: spatulas and wooden spoons and ladles, when all we'll ever need is a bottle opener and a couple of cereal spoons.

And still the kitchen sink is piled with dishes, a permanent art installation that sits for a month. The sink is "stainless steel," a phrase we've taken as a challenge while successfully staining it with petrified Ragú.

Inventors seem to have misplaced their priorities. The oven, never used, is self-cleaning. The shower and toilet, in constant use, are not.

Soon after we move into Canterbury Court I'm carrying a brown paper sack containing a six-pack of Miller Lite and a feed bag of Lay's Sour Cream & Onion potato chips across a vacant lot to our apartment building when three young men approach, presumably to ask me the time, and when I consult my watch to tell them it is 10 p.m., the oldest (or at least the largest) of the three says, "How much money you got?"

They've seen too many movies and TV shows. I have too. We're all improvising a stickup. They've arranged themselves in classic gangster-movie pose: the leader flanked by his two lieutenants, who stand a deferential step behind him. Together they form a greater-than sign pointing at me, which is appropriate. Three is greater than one.

"I just spent my money on groceries," I say.

"All of it?"

"Everything."

Unsatisfied with this answer, they flex their jaw muscles and rotate their heads by way of stretching their necks. The truth is, if they were to remove my wallet from the back pocket of my khakis and un-Velcro it they would find two dollars, which would yield each of them—I'm doing the math in my head—sixty-six cents. Giving them sixty-six cents apiece would almost certainly be worse than nothing at all.

"You're welcome to the groceries," I say, and then have a momentary panic that one of them is underage, and should the police happen upon this exchange, I'll be the one committing a crime by providing beer to a minor.

The boss peers into the brown bag, examines its contents, then looks back at me, assessing my veracity. His two stooges—I've come to think of them as Sour Cream and Onion—take all their cues from him.

"Come on," says the boss. "He ain't got shit."

Sour Cream looks disappointed. Onion still wants the chips. Me, I'm not sure what just happened. In the six years between 1985 and 1991, five students will be murdered or perish in fires in what the *New York Times* calls "the declining neighborhood that surrounds the campus here." I wasn't even mugged. These guys live here; I'm an interloper. Milwaukee is on its way to shattering its record for most murders in a year—set five years ago—and this neighborhood is among its least salubrious, though it hints at a glorious past.

A block and a half from Canterbury Court is Mashuda Hall, a Marquette dorm that was, in a previous lifetime, the downtown Milwaukee Holiday Inn. The Beatles stayed here in 1964, in the Governor's Suite on the seventh floor. I walk past it every day, secretly wishing I was housed there, wondering if the building is still redolent of tiny hand soaps and industrial towel detergent and plush carpet dampened by air-conditioning. But there is no sign of what it once was—literally no green-and-yellow sign, blinking outside, that made pulling up to a Holiday Inn in Arlington or Anaheim or Kissimmee (or Bloomington) such a thrill that I longed to live in one. This Holiday Inn has gone. I try but cannot conjure its ghosts—happy families disgorged from station wagons, John Lennon stepping from a limousine.

There are two oases on this western fringe of campus. The Glocca Mora will instill in me a lifelong love of dive Irish bars, and the Marquette rec center is a hotbed of pickup action. Pickup basketball, that is, though I'm sure others are picking up women there as well. My buddies signed me up for coed intramural basketball, but the only thing I can bring myself to say to my female teammates is "Switch!" or "Watch the screen!" or "Roll to the basket!" "Shyness can stop you from doing all the things in life you'd like to," I heard Morrissey sing on WMUR, the student radio station, narrowcasting to a three-block radius around campus.

Otherwise my neighborhood is a half century past its prime. Down the street is a nineteen-table poolroom called Romine's High Pockets. Around the corner is the ScrubaDub car wash.

Across from it is the Ambassador Hotel, a run-down relic from an art-deco heyday. A block from that is the Eagles Club, a 25,000-square-foot ballroom and boxing arena opened in 1926. It now stands as a Mediterranean revival reminder of the college culture that I'm not attuned to, for here play college radio acts like Siouxsie and the Banshees and the Replacements (from Minneapolis) and even—unbelievably—Limited Warranty, opening now for Eddie Money.

Limited Warranty are five guys from Bloomington who won Ed McMahon's *Star Search* talent show and got signed to Atlantic Records. Not since Kent Hrbek of Kennedy High School became the Twins' first baseman in 1981 has a Bloomingtonian been so exalted. They have big teased-up Flock of Seagulls hair and wear blazers with pushed-up sleeves over T-shirts. Teenage girls in Bloomington can still look them up in the phone book and call them even though they're opening for Eddie Money, whose "Two Tickets to Paradise" and "Baby Hold On" and this year's "Take Me Home Tonight" you can hear on the radio. The lesson is, you can come from my hometown and make it in the arts, at least the arts that were most esteemed in Bloomington in my childhood there: sports and rock and roll.

Dreaming of artistic glory, I schlep forty minutes by city bus to the Northridge shopping mall in Milwaukee to watch an old man do trick shots on a pool table in front of Sears for the momentary diversion of a couple hundred people walking from Foot Locker to Frederick's of Hollywood. A few more gaze down to pass the time while ascending the escalator, and a handful of others have brought books or magazines to be signed by the man who was the world champion of pocket billiards fifteen times between 1941 and 1957. I alone have brought a reporter's notebook and two pens, scribbling Willie Mosconi's every utterance for posterity.

This is Everymall, with a Spencer Gifts and a Cineplex showing *Lethal Weapon, Platoon,* and *Crocodile Dundee.* As a child, I saw Mosconi shoot pool in a tuxedo against Minnesota Fats on ABC's *Wide World of Sports,* and like anybody I have ever seen on TV, he retains both a gravitas and a kind of unreality, such is the power of the medium. I'm here to "profile" him for my Magazine Writing class. In my notebook is a list of questions. Only after I arrive and see this resplendent white-haired seventy-four-year-old pool shark—who appears with a statuesque blonde on his arm in George Thorogood's "Bad to the Bone" video, which still appears occasionally on MTV—does it hit me: I can't approach this man and introduce myself and ask him invasive personal questions.

As with girls, or North Stars fans who wanted popcorn vended to them at their seats, I decide to stand there in silence and hope that *he* will approach *me.*

That doesn't happen, of course, but I write down everything Mosconi says to the audience—"Nothin' to this game"—and eavesdrop in the autograph line, and on the bus back to campus I write in my notebook: "The old man with the custom cue knocks the balls off the table as if he were a schoolboy with a slingshot and the stripes and solids were so many crows perched on a telephone wire." It becomes the first sentence of the story that I compose on my Typestar and turn in to Professor Arnold, who has come to embody the career in journalism I've decided I want.

226 • NIGHTS IN WHITE CASTLE

He wears aviator glasses, a wardrobe of shirts and ties evidently acquired on the newsroom set of *All the President's Men,* and speaks in a pebble-dashed baritone that suggests a lifetime of coffee consumed from Styrofoam cups. If journalism issued its own currency, his would be the face on the one-dollar bill. Under the byline "James Arnold," he writes film criticism for Catholic publications, often defending movies like *Klute,* or the comedies of Woody Allen, against charges of immorality and licentiousness. As such, he has published a book called *"Seen Any Good Dirty Movies Lately?" A Christian Critic Looks at Contemporary Films.* He makes kind comments in red ink about various phrases in my Mosconi story and scribbles on the cover: "Don't let it go to waste." One day he announces in class that David Halberstam, the great author and Pulitzer Prize–winning war correspondent for the *New York Times,* used to get so nervous before calling an army general or other high-ranking mucky-muck in Vietnam that he'd have to pour himself a stiff drink before dialing the phone. I have no idea if this is true, but the mere possibility that a successful writer shares my phobia takes residence in my brain, throws open the shuttered windows in a dark room, and lets the air and sunlight inside.

At the same time, I've sent a copy of my Mosconi story to Alex Wolff. *The Back-In-Your-Face Guide to Pickup Basketball* has been published, with my name in the acknowledgments. Alex passes my piece along to one of his editors at *Sports Illustrated* named Bob Brown, who writes me a letter—on that creamy stationery, with the magical letterhead—thanking me for my submission, regretting that the magazine is unable to use it, and suggesting one idea that might improve my piece on Willie Mosconi: "Interview Willie Mosconi."

So I walk to the Milwaukee Public Library downtown, to their vast collection of U.S. phone books, select the Philadelphia White Pages, riffle to the *M*s and find, to my surprise, a listing for Mosconi in Haddon Heights, New Jersey. I write down the number, take it back to the bedroom in my apartment, sit on the edge of the bed, shotgun a Miller Lite in the absence of whatever a Vietnam correspondent would drink to steel his nerves, and then dial ten of the eleven numbers necessary to reach Mosconi before hanging up. I sit for five full minutes on the edge of my bed, then dial all eleven numbers. After half a ring, a gruff voice answers.

"Hello?"

"Hello, is Willie Mosconi there, please?"

"Who wants to know?"

I stammer through my rehearsed introduction, that I'm Steve Rushin from [cough] Marquette University trying to write a story for [cough] *Sports Illustrated,* somehow hoping he doesn't notice those eight qualifying words between coughs and only hears "Steve Rushin...from *Sports Illustrated.*"

He says, "Whaddya want?"

"When did you first learn to play—"

"I learned to play pool in dancing school," he says. "Summer of 1919." His uncle had a dance academy in South Philadelphia where Willie's cousins Charlie and Louie practiced when they weren't performing with the Ziegfeld Follies. "My uncle had a pool table in the corner of the studio," Mosconi tells me. "You know how kids are. I said, 'I can do that.' First I just picked up the balls and threw them around, but by the end of the summer I was running the whole table."

Unbidden, he recalls poking potatoes across the kitchen floor with a broomstick, his own father's five-table poolroom in Philly, how six-year-old Willie started performing for his cousins' show-business friends at the Friars Club in New York, about his barnstorming years, about the time in the '40s when he found himself at the Strand Theatre near Times Square waiting to begin an 8 p.m. straight-pool match with thirteen-time world champion Ralph Greenleaf. "I had tickets to *Abie's Irish Rose* that night, with an 8:30 curtain time. Greenleaf broke the balls, then I got up and ran off 125 points and did ten trick shots in seventeen minutes." He was in his seat browsing the *Playbill* when the curtain rose on *Rose.*

He tells me about Paul Newman, whom he worked with on *The Hustler* in 1961, and the film's costar, Jackie Gleason, who could shoot a little pool: "He was all right. I mean, he beat all those suckers at Toots Shor's." He talks about Minnesota Fats, his rival on those televised matches on *Wide World of Sports* that I watched on Saturday afternoons in Bloomington when Dad tired of whatever college football blowouts were on the other channels. We always rooted for Fats because he was from Minnesota, except that Mosconi tells me he wasn't. "He was Rudolf Wanderone," from New York City, and Willie did not enjoy his company in those televised exhibitions. "But my wife loved them," he says. "She got all the money."

By the time I hang up, my neck cramping from squeezing the handset between my ear and shoulder, every question on my handwritten list remains unasked, yet somehow answered.

All I had to do was get him started, like a pull-string doll, then listen to him talk for an hour.

I take Mosconi's voice, the stories of his childhood, the scene of him sitting in his theater seat on Broadway when the curtain rose on *Abie's Irish Rose,* and sprinkle them throughout the piece I've already written for class. They're yeast. They make the story rise. I write it up and seal it in an envelope addressed to Bob Brown c/o *Sports Illustrated.* Then I drop it into a mailbox on Wisconsin Avenue, a message in a bottle, tossed into a great big sea.

# 12

# We'll Give You the World

Suddenly, improbably, I'm going to New York for the first time, over spring break, to visit Jim, who has an apartment for six weeks in Stuyvesant Town, on the Lower East Side of Manhattan, paid for by the Metropolitan Life Insurance Company, which is training him for a job in Southern California. This means flying by myself for the first time, and taking my first taxi, and converting almost all of my money into American Express traveler's checks, per Dad's manifold instructions, which he delivers in the grave tone of a father giving his son the sex talk, not that he ever has, to our mutual relief.

"When you get to LaGuardia," he says, "go straight to the cab stand. Don't listen to anybody at Baggage Claim who offers you a ride. *Do you understand?*"

"Yes, Dad, for God's sake..."

"Then tell the cabdriver to take Crescent to the Fifty-Ninth Street Bridge. Got that?"

"For the tenth time, yes."

"If he tells you the Triborough is faster," Dad says, "tell him you don't care. Tell him Crescent to the Fifty-Ninth Street Bridge."

"*Okay!*"

"It's cheaper."

"So you said!"

I have forty bucks in cash, a hundred dollars in American Express traveler's checks, and Dad's folding map of the five boroughs, on which he has circled in ballpoint pen the intersection of 52nd Street and First Avenue, location of his favorite restaurant, Billy's, which has served beef and creamed spinach to New Yorkers since 1870, and pork chops to traveling magnetic-tape salesmen since 1970.

"Get the pork chops," Dad insists. "Best pork chops in New York." This is a man who has found the best pork chop in Jerusalem, a man who once said, "You can't undercook a pork chop" (you can), a man for whom the pork chop is the highest human art form: above music and literature and everything but the Cadillac Seville. As he describes the porcine succulence of Billy's on First Avenue, that checkered-tablecloth temple of grilled meats, I realize that this *is* the sex talk he never gave me. Except that it's not about the birds and the bees or the flowers and the trees. It's about a good pork chop and airplane etiquette (never recline) and dry cleaning (hangers not boxes) and how to calculate a 15 percent tip and how to buy Broadway theater tickets (at a 50 percent discount, from the TKTS booth in Times Square) and how to thwart pickpockets (wallet in front pocket) and how to hail a cab (in the street, downstream from the competition, waving madly like you're sending the *Lusitania* out of port).

Armed with this knowledge, I approach LaGuardia on March 5, 1987, sharking in over Shea Stadium, home of the defending world champion New York Mets. I have seen and heard these planes on TV, buzzing Shea and U.S. Open tennis matches, and now I am on one, already contributing to the noise of the city, already annoying someone down there, even before Northwest Orient Airlines delivers me to the terminal.

Following the crowd to Baggage Claim and Ground Transportation, I descend the escalator to a baying crowd of dour men whisper-shouting, "Need a ride?" A gaunt bearded man who smells of pine-tree air freshener seizes my softsided suitcase by the handle, perp-walks me past the long taxi line, and throws my luggage into the trunk of his 1974 Monte Carlo. He sees me into the fetid back seat and drives away. Only when we're in motion and he asks "Where to?" can I conclude with any confidence that I've not been abducted.

"Fourteenth Street and First Avenue," I say. "Take Crescent to the Fifty-Ninth Street Bridge."

"Triborough much faster," he says.

"Fine," I say.

Through Queens, thinking, *This is the home of Archie Bunker,* 704 Hauser Street in Astoria. My fingers are crossed that we'll pass through Brooklyn and see the sign—WELCOME TO BROOKLYN 4TH LARGEST CITY IN AMERICA—that welcomed back Kotter in *Welcome Back, Kotter*. My knowledge of New York City geography comes almost entirely from TV, from the reruns that still air in Minnesota of *Car 54, Where Are You?,* whose theme song I have in my head right now: "There's a holdup in the Bronx, Brooklyn's broken out in fights, there's a traffic jam in Harlem that's backed up to Jackson Heights..." Those after-school reruns were twinned with repeats of *The Patty Duke Show,* in whose theme "Patty's only seen the sights a girl can see from Brooklyn Heights..."

And then it appears through the window of the Monte Carlo, the *Honeymooners* skyline of Manhattan.

Climbing onto the Triborough, the theme to *Taxi* plays in my head, though the span in those credits was the 59th Street Bridge and I'm not technically in a taxi but an un-licensed, uninsured, and mostly unupholstered sedan driven by a man whose camel-colored Members Only jacket makes me wonder: *Who was* denied *membership?*

The Monte Carlo alights in Manhattan. Southbound on the FDR. On the East Side, site of George Jefferson's "dee-luxe apartment in the sky-y-y." Past the 59th Street Bridge, and I'm singing Simon & Garfunkel: "Hello, lamppost, whatcha knowin'..." The traffic is mad. At regular intervals, the driver blows his horn into the void, as if testing it. The radio ratchets up the tension, pounding out a frenzied nightmare soundtrack beneath the Voice of God, who gravely intones, "1010 WINS. You give us twenty-two minutes, we'll give you the world." There follows a litany of news stories involving rescued babies, arrested bankers, violent lovers, and a hard-luck man who tore up his winning lottery ticket. The traffic report makes liberal use of the words "standstill," "backup," and "bottleneck" at places that seem to be encrypted, a secret code to the city's drivers: Throgs Neck, Tappan Zee, BQE, GWB, LIE.

The Monte Carlo lurches to a stop on First Avenue, across from a vast complex of brown buildings. "Stuy Town," says the driver.

"What do I owe you?"

Dad insisted a cab ride via Crescent should cost no more than twenty bucks.

"Thirty," says Members Only.

"Does that include tip?" I ask.

He looks at me in the rearview mirror. I can only see his eyes. It's like he's looking at me through the food slot in the solid door of a solitary confinement cell, but the brows have gone up in the middle, like a parting drawbridge, an expression I take to mean: *Is this kid shitting me?*

"A tip would be nice," he replies.

"Do you take American Express traveler's checks?" I ask. Dad has assured me that they're better than cash, accepted everywhere, a kind of universal currency, the Esperanto of legal tender.

"I take cash," he says.

We're idling in front of a joint called Pete's-a-Place. I admire the cheap wordplay and pull two twenty-dollar bills out of my Velcro wallet.

He claims not to have change. I think he's inviting me to jump out of the Monte Carlo and jauntily say, "Keep it!" But any customer capable of such largesse would not be riding in this man's Monte Carlo, and he knows it. So he abandons the idling car and runs in to Pete's-a-Place to break my twenty. He emerges with a ten, two fives, and a half-eaten slice on a paper plate. I give him thirty-five bucks and he pops the trunk, releasing my suitcase and me into the wild.

\*     \*     \*

For three days I walk, until my feet are tender and my bladder is cast-iron. I walk from 14th and First to 50th and Sixth. On one corner is 30 Rockefeller Center, the GE Building, where I might see Letterman lean out a window with his bullhorn to mock Bryant Gumbel. On the opposite corner is Radio City: the Pretenders are there on the 31st, according to the marquee, but I'm only thinking of Steely Dan, "stompin' on the avenue by Radio City, baby." On the corner opposite that is the Time & Life Building, whose address—1271 Avenue of the Americas—I've committed to memory. I stand below this forty-eight-story temple to magazine journalism, fabled home of *Time* and *Life,* but not the home of Time Life Books, whose twelve-volume history of *The Old West* freaked me out in junior high whenever its epic two-minute infomercial aired. In volume one of *The Old West,* called *The Great Chiefs,* "you'll look into the eyes of Sitting Bull, the man who destroyed Custer," promised the ominous narrator, as the camera zoomed in on the chilling eyes of the Lakota chief. Eight weeks later, the lucky reader would receive *"The Settlers,* battling savage elements and bloodthirsty war parties" and—as the illustrations implied—tales of the Donner Party. Coming, as it did, as a jarring intrusion in the middle of *The Benny Hill Show, The Old West* promised to send me to bed dreaming of cannibalism and frostbite.

But that's not all, as they say in this kind of commercial. "They're all here," the narrator said with a leer, listing every hero and scoundrel of the American frontier—"in big handsome books with the look and feel of hand-tooled saddle leather." How I longed for those handsome volumes, suitable for reading or throwing over the back of an Appaloosa. "You'll meet the gunfighters," went the line we all quoted in school the next day, "men like John Wesley Hardin, so mean he once shot a man just for snorin'."

Above all, of course, the Time & Life Building looming above me now is home to *Sports Illustrated.* Unlike the rest of Manhattan, the pavement I stand on is done in alternating waves of gray and white terrazzo. The tiles mimic—or so I've read—the sidewalks at Copacabana Beach in Rio de Janeiro, a nod to our location on Avenue of the Americas. But I'm not looking down at the tiles, I'm looking up, to the eighteenth floor, familiar from my correspondence with Alexander Wolff and Bob Brown, in whose office up there—my eyes follow the vertical limestone facade until I've counted eighteen floors—my unsolicited manuscript sits under what I can only imagine is a Kilimanjaro of similar submissions. Even from down here, I can practically see it—or at least see the folly of having sent it. The vanity, the hubris—the *chutzpah,* to use a word that sounds like New York. In my apartment lobby in Milwaukee, I checked the mailbox every day to see if Mr. Brown had replied to my revised Willie Mosconi story. I see now, standing in a sea of people in Rockefeller Center, beneath this monument to magazines and midcentury modernism, that *Sports Illustrated* is doing just fine without me.

Jim's alma mater, Providence College, is playing in the Big East basketball tournament at Madison Square Garden, and I'm meeting him there. "MSG" is "the world's most famous arena," even more famous than the Met Center in Bloomington, for this is not just the home of the New York

Knicks and Rangers but also of singular spectacles like the Ali–Frazier Fight of the Century, the Concert for Bangladesh with Bob Dylan and half the Beatles, and Led Zeppelin's concert film *The Song Remains the Same*. Watching college basketball there, I can't help but see a silk-scarved Mick Jagger chicken-walking across a stage circa 1972. But mainly what I see are the courtside tables known as Press Row, preserve of New York sportswriters real and fictional, Red Smith to Oscar Madison. Madison Square Garden is a dump, but up here beneath the rafters in the notorious Blue Seats—so called for their upholstery but also the beer-fueled profanity of their drunken occupants—that is part of the charm.

In New York, dumps are temples. Anger is joy. Graffiti is art. The city's peculiar aroma—bagged garbage and straphanger BO—is a breath of fresh air. New York City will have 2,016 murders this year—nearly six a day, every day, without a holiday. Times Square marquees advertise NYMPHOID DREAMS and EROTIC LUST and PORNO HOOKERS. Volcanic steam issues from every manhole cover: the city is literally seething.

But walk a little farther up Broadway, to the Upper West Side, and kids sit on *Sesame Street* stoops. A few blocks east is Central Park, where Oscar and Felix do a little dance in the opening credits of *The Odd Couple*. New York is at once foreign and familiar, both Oz and Kansas.

In three days, I develop a routine. I never eat at Billy's, taking all my meals instead at a pizza place, including—but not limited to—Pete's-a-Place. There are so many joints to choose from—Ray's, Famous Ray's, Original Ray's, Original Famous Ray's, and Famous Original Ray's—an array of Ray's, none of them affiliated, in whose sweltering premises

I always get two plain slices before stopping at Smiler's Deli for two Coors Lights. Two slices, two Silver Bullets. I take them back to Stuy Town, as I've learned to call it, fall onto the sleeper sofa, and dine in front of the TV, with its own buffet of cable channels, one hundred offerings under glass, like the sneeze-guarded trays in the countless Korean delis I've passed.

Lights out, recumbent in my fold-out bed, still buzzing from the day, the sirens, horns, car alarms, and sighing steam brakes of the sanitation trucks rendering sleep unlikely, I flip through the muted channels, pausing at channel 35, which is airing an otherwise conventional talk show in which the host and guests are all naked. This is public-access television in New York. None of the participants is attractive, fit, young, or sane. The harsh lighting throws into sharp relief the guests' appendectomy scars and exit wounds. There is nothing remotely titillating about the program, though lying here in the dark I do idly hope that the sofa on set has been Scotchgarded with patented technology from 3M to safeguard against stains.

Every commercial on channel 35 is for an escort service, each catering to a specific clientele, including one whose telephone number is 555-PEEE. "The extra *E*," purrs the voice-over, "is for extra pee."

In the next show, an enraged man flips off the camera while excoriating everyone and everything—the phone company, his dry cleaner, the weather—that failed him this week. He's identified as the editor of *Screw* magazine, which I take to be a trade publication for handymen, available at the checkout counter at Hardware Hank, until he begins reviewing X-rated movies in straight-faced homage to Siskel and Ebert.

A woman in a crocheted bikini interviews strippers and adult-film stars, all of whom are also clothed. Each show on channel 35 is somehow less interesting than the last. There are commercials for phone-sex hotlines that are like listening to golf on the radio. And more commercials featuring the kind of nudity you avoid in a locker room.

Bathed in the blue light of the Sony Trinitron, the Lower East Side thrumming outside my window, I recall my unsuccessful efforts to find a split second of nudity when cable came to my basement in Bloomington. There, it was scrambled. Here, I long for a scrambler. I feel like a farmer who prayed for rain in a drought only to see his crops washed away by a monsoon.

A curious phrase keeps presenting itself in the summer of '87, my last in Bloomington before I graduate next spring and enter what Mom and Dad and even my friends have started to call "the real world," as if everything up to and including now has been a fantasy. *The real world?* It seems to me that the foregoing twenty years have passed in a very real environment of pressures and responsibilities: lawns that needed mowing, corn that required shucking, math tests that wouldn't take themselves. "Is this the real life?" I hear Freddie Mercury asking. "Is this just fantasy?"

What horrors could real life hold if the fantasy requires second graders to unburden themselves of sins in a confessional, and to sing "We Go Together" from *Grease* while jazz-handing onstage with their seventh-grade classmates, each of us wearing matching gingham shirts? "The real world" does not intimidate me when I've already been exposed—in eighth grade!—to three words more mortifying than any others: mandatory square dancing.

No, I've experienced the real life and would now like to try the opposite. I have a fantasy about getting paid to watch games, and write about them. Failing that, I'll work in "the real world." Doing what, I haven't a clue.

Tom has graduated from Iowa State and moved to Chicago, into an apartment within walking distance to (and stumbling distance from) Wrigley Field, where the Cubs still play eighty-one day games that somehow don't conflict with his new job at Metropolitan Life.

All my friends are now twenty-one. We can go wherever we want—to O'Gara's in Saint Paul or the Green Mill in Minneapolis or the Sports Page in Bloomington, though all those joints we used to pass on the Strip in Dr. McCollow's powder-blue Bonneville look, like the Bonneville itself, of another time. We still go to White Castle at one o'clock in the morning, but the talk there is less of infinite possibilities than of specific job prospects, the narrowing field of choices. We've reached that fork in Milton Bradley's Game of Life when you're required to choose a path that will lead inexorably to Millionaire Acres or the Poor Farm, one or the other, life as a zero-sum game.

On our last night together at the Castle in August, there is no sense of occasion, no acknowledgment that this may be the last time we ever gather here, that some of us may never live in Minnesota again, that our bodies might not always desire, much less be capable of digesting, a dozen sliders and a couple gobblers with glue at an hour when most grown-ups are in REM sleep.

Mike is telling the table about how we met, when I joined his kindergarten class at Nativity of the Blessed Virgin Mary, halfway through the school year, having been promoted out of Saint Stephen's Nursery School because *Sesame Street* had already taught me how to read and spell.

"We faced each other in the finals of the spelling bee," Mike says.

"Who has a spelling bee in kindergarten?" says Gator. He has returned to the Castle from his years in exile, Barney the rent-a-cop having either forgiven or forgotten the time Gator ripped a table from its moorings here.

"I was always a good speller," I say. "In third grade, I'd listen to the Lincoln cheerleaders say, 'R-O-W-D-I-E, *that's* the way you spell "rowdie"! Rowdie! Let's get rowdie!' and I'd tell my mom, 'That's *not* the way you spell "rowdy." It's R-O-W-D-Y.'"

"Well, if you're going to have a kindergarten spelling bee, at least give the kids a word like 'dog' or 'cow' or 'hen,'" Mike says to me. "That's what you got: some bullshit word like 'cat.'"

I've heard this story fifteen times but enjoy its annual embroidery, like an afghan that your grandma keeps adding to, always available for warmth and security.

"Meanwhile," Mike says, "I get 'picnic.' *Picnic*. I spelled it P-I-K-N-I-K. Because I passed Pik-Quik every day in the car. I didn't know grown-ups misspelled things on purpose."

"We used to buy Pixy Stix at Pik-Quik," I say. "How did we ever learn to spell?"

"Pixy Stix were kindergarten cocaine."

"We used to chop the grape powder into lines with a baseball card and snort them off our nap mats..."

And so it goes, long into the night, the banter moving on to other subjects, though I'm still thinking about kindergarten, how we were five years old then, with sixteen years of school ahead of us, and all but one of those is over, and now what? No matter how many times I press the SEEK button in Mom's Honda Accord on the drive home, all the radio ever seems to land on is the number one song in America. "I Still Haven't Found What I'm Looking For."

Before I return to Milwaukee for senior year, Mom takes a valedictory picture of me in my bedroom. Posters of Dr. J, Joe Morgan, Alan Page, and Fran Tarkenton that once adorned its walls are still evident in the orphaned pieces of Scotch tape that reveal themselves when the sun hits them just right. Wanton use of Scotch tape, a product of the 3M Company, has always been encouraged in our house.

On my dresser, introduced by Mom in my absence, are three potted plants, the first shots fired in a guerilla campaign to seize my room and slowly convert it to a "guest bedroom." My friends have experienced this same phenomenon, arriving home from school to find a carpeted cat tower in the corner, or a sewing machine squatting on what was once their home-work desk.

Of course this will always be *my* room. It's a child's great-est possession, his own room, and even though I shared this one, and it didn't have a lock, and Mom could (and did) ran-sack its contents on a daily basis, turning it over like a DEA agent, it was still *my* room, for if I told Amy or John or even Jim, "Get out of my room," they were required by unwritten fiat to comply. Likewise, whenever Mom or Dad yelled, "Go to your room!," enshrined in that command was an explicit acknowledgment that it was mine, these fifteen square feet of cobalt carpeting, these four walls covered in Benjamin Moore Blue Bonnet.

Jim, Tom, Amy, John, and I have spent most of our lives defending a small swatch of territory against each other's incursions, fighting over every inch of car seat or couch or church pew. As we scrambled to claim the best seat at a restaurant's cobbled-together table for seven, Mom and Dad became Churchill and Roosevelt at Yalta, assigning each of us our own chair at Mr. Steak. Our territorial natures manifest themselves in fantasies of owning real estate: building snow forts, buying hotels on Boardwalk and Park Place, gazing at the Pacific from the balcony of Barbie's Malibu Dream House.

But the only place I could ever truly call my own was this room, or at least this half of this room that I shared with Tom, with the Maginot Line running between our beds, bisecting the nightstand we shared, cutting the Kleenex box and bedside lamp in half. This is where, at different ages, I couldn't sleep the night before Christmas and couldn't wake up the morning after New Year's Eve. This is where my *Pigs in Space* poster on one wall and Tom's Farrah Fawcett poster on another engaged in a years-long staring contest. This is where I've spent the vast majority of my nights and a good number of my days. But I'll never again spend more than a week here, and when I do, I'll be something closer to a hotel guest than what I am now: a sultan supine on his daybed.

So the picture Mom takes of me is black-and-white, giving the occasion its proper weight of history. Seated at my desk, books arrayed on the shelf behind me, a framed *Sports Illustrated* cover of Larry Bird screaming back at the camera, I look back grimly at Mom, the way authors do on the dust jackets behind me. I'm wearing a pale yellow oxford-cloth shirt with broad vertical stripes. My right elbow, just out of frame, rests jauntily on my typewriter, as if I'm a middle-aged journalist who lives in Connecticut and uses "summer" as a verb and wears a V-neck sweater tied around his neck like a cape.

"Smile," Mom says, and eventually I comply.

"The author," she says, snapping the shutter, and I think if I ever write a book I'll dedicate it to her, the author of the author.

# 13.

# Golden Handshake

Six weeks after my senior year starts, a miracle draws me home, back to the bedroom that is no longer quite mine, my baseball cards in the closet now getting crowded by tablecloths and photo albums and other oddments.

The miracle is this: the Minnesota Twins, who have been bad for as long as I can remember—and who weren't even very good this season, getting outscored by their opponents 806–786 while winning only 29 of their 81 games on the road—have somehow been incapable of losing at the Metrodome, their fever blister of a football stadium, where just a few summers ago I sold Dome Dogs to the handful of paying customers who passed through the stadium's revolving doors.

In winning 56 of 81 at home, the Twins have won the American League West and will face the Tigers in the AL playoffs. What's more, Mike has somehow secured tickets for Games 1 and 2, and he and Ope and I sit in the bleachers and wave our Homer Hankies—white snot-rags emblazoned with a red baseball distributed for free by the *Star Tribune,* which has shed its conjunction. In the Metrodome, 55,000 people are waving hankies, and the national television audience doesn't quite know what to make of it all. It seems perfectly natural to me. Am I the only one who got a set of handkerchiefs as a rite of passage before going off to college?

When the Twins beat the Tigers in Game 5 of that series, having won both games at the Metrodome and two out of three in Detroit, they are suddenly—impossibly—in the World Series. The *St. Paul Pioneer Press* publishes a special insert, a Fall Classic preview, and the cover illustrates the Twins' fearsome home-field advantage. It's a full-page crowd shot of fans in the left-field bleachers at the Metrodome waving their Homer Hankies. And there, in the center of that mob, waving our hankies like three damsels in distress, are Mike, Ope, and me.

I'm back at school by the time that edition of the *Pioneer Press* is published, so Mom mails a copy to Milwaukee. Did she remove five papers from a spring-loaded street-corner box, the way I did with the *Chicago Tribune*? Will she someday buy five copies and give them to her bridge-club friends if I ever have a story published in the *Star Trib* or the *Pioneer Press*? Or am I duty bound to "buy five copies for my mother," as Dr. Hook will do if he ever appears on the cover of *Rolling Stone*?

This is the 84th World Series and the second in Minnesota. The first one, in 1965, was played in Bloomington four years before the Rushins arrived there from Chicago. The Twins beat the Dodgers' Hall of Fame pitchers Don Drysdale and

Sandy Koufax, the Lennon and McCartney of '60s baseball glamour, in Games 1 and 2 at Metropolitan Stadium. The NBC television network carried Bloomington to every hamlet in America. Seven weeks earlier, the Beatles, featuring the Drysdale and Koufax of rock and roll, played a thirty-five-minute concert on the very same field at the Met, using the Twins clubhouse as their dressing room and escaping in a dry-cleaning truck for downtown Minneapolis, where their rooms at the Leamington Hotel were raided, police looking in vain for underage girls.

Bloomington and its immediate environs were, well and truly, the epicenter of the world.

For Minnesota, then, hosting the World Series is not just a novelty but a return to its natural place of pop-culture supremacy. I'm stuck in Milwaukee, taking exams, and have to watch Games 1 and 2 on CBS, like thirty-five million other Americans. Under a Teflon sky, the Twins win 10–1 on October 17 and 8–4 on October 18 before traveling to Saint Louis with a 2-game lead on the off day. That evening, I turn on the network news to make sure that the Twins are the nation's top story. I don't know why it's so important to me that the rest of America pay tribute to my hometown. I only know that it is.

Tom Brokaw looks gravely into the camera. "A shattering six and a half hours on Wall Street," he begins. "The Dow off more than five hundred points. Paper losses more than five hundred *billion* dollars." I don't know what that means, or why news anchors speak in these sentence fragments, shorn of subjects, but five hundred billion sounds like a lot of money. Regardless of what Prince and Orwell and *The Day After* have taught me, the world may not end with a thermonuclear bang or the whimper of Winston Smith, a boot stamping on his human face forever. Perhaps it ends as a boxing match does, with a closing bell.

It's hard to say how frightened I should be, because the *NBC Nightly News* theme music is clearly designed, even on the sunniest of news days, to put the viewer on edge. I've taken to watching the *NBC Nightly News,* as Dad does, on the assumption that it's a gateway drug leading to the harder stuff of adulthood, like carrying a key wallet or owning a shoeshine kit.

"October 19, 1987," Brokaw continues, every syllable landing like a tombstone. "Wall Street's *Black Monday.*"

There follows footage of ulcerated men frantically waving papers on a crowded trading floor. When NBC finally gets around to showing Twins fans waving Homer Hankies, I think of them as a happy analog to those waving Wall Street traders, Gallant to their Goofus, the comedy and tragedy masks of Black Monday. One is the real world, I suppose, and one is not. But I know which one worries me more.

Black Monday is followed by the more serious debacles of Black Tuesday, Wednesday, and Thursday, as the Twins—true to form—lose all three games in Saint Louis, meaning Minnesota has to win Game 6 at the Metrodome on this Saturday night to force a Game 7. As I watch from my seat on the coffee table, a foot in front of the TV—Mom promised this proximity to the tube would leave me blind—I'm tempted to remove my thick glasses and theatrically clean them with a Homer Hankie. My brain can't yet process what my eyes have just seen.

In the bottom of the sixth inning of Game 6 of the World Series, Twins first baseman Kent Hrbek of Bloomington comes to the plate with the bases loaded and a 1-run lead. In the Metrodome, the crowd is standing. In Milwaukee, so am I. My brother claims that in high school—when Jim pitched for Lincoln and Hrbek played for Kennedy—he "owned" the six-foot-four left-handed behemoth, a fact that Jim's high school teammates have confirmed to me. Mercifully, Cardinals reliever Ken Dayley has no such mastery over Hrbek. Hrbie hits Dayley's first pitch to deepest center field and over the 408-foot marking for a grand slam. As Hrbek airplanes around the bases with his arms and fists thrust out to either side, it appears he might actually lift off, along with the roof of the Metrodome, for the crowd is making a noise commensurate with a 747 taking flight. I can almost see the roar lifting the roof, like a waiter removing the silver lid off a room-service plate.

The announcers go silent as Hrbek runs the bases. He rehearsed this a hundred times growing up. "I wish I could have run around the bases twice," he'll say in the next day's *New York Times,* which I'll buy for posterity. "I can't tell you how big a thrill it is with your family and friends in the stands."

And that's just it. Everyone here knows him and vice versa. In his yard a couple of miles from mine, Hrbek dreamed of doing this very thing. And now he has done it, and the Twins will play Game 7 of the World Series tomorrow night in a place where they are incapable of losing.

Hrbek has found a way to turn his backyard fantasy world into the real world. The same places where he dreamed, I did too: in the Met Stadium bleachers, on the Little League fields and in the municipal pool at Valley View Park, on the oiled lanes at Airport Bowl and in a window booth at White Castle, where anybody can drive by and see you on display, your grown-up self hatching in an incubator of dreams.

At 4:30 a.m. on Sunday, October 25, Hrbek receives a phone call from a buddy who says, "The ducks are flying." Hrbek goes duck hunting on the morning of Game 7, because he's from Bloomington, and this is what every Bloomington boy but me would do if his buddy called to say the ducks are flying.

Alexander Wolff of *Sports Illustrated*—I'm now invited to call him "Alex"—is in Milwaukee to write a story about the Bucks. When his work is done, he swings by my apartment to watch the end of Game 7. We are among the fifty-one million Americans who witness the Minnesota Twins win their first world championship, something the Vikings and North Stars have never done. I've now had goose bumps for seven straight days, like a happy version of the mumps, and Alex offers to drive me to the Lanche so that I might celebrate with my fellow Minnesotans.

On the short drive, Alex encourages me to apply for a job as a fact-checker at *SI*. The magazine can keep my résumé on file and if there's an opening someday and my clips are good enough, who knows? The fact that he is delivering me to an establishment that offers Red White & Blues nearly free of charge as a beverage but also as a lubricant for naked beer slides does not seem to disqualify me from consideration for working at the magazine.

The bloodred sign—AVALANCHE LIQUOR BAR—buzzes as Alex drops me at the curb and recedes down Wells Street, en route to his hotel, the Hyatt Regency, with its revolving rooftop restaurant, twenty stories above Milwaukee, affording a panoramic view of every steeple and smokestack in the quad-county area. Though I've never set foot in one, the very concept of a revolving rooftop restaurant has always dazzled me. These, surely, are our greatest temples of gastronomy and elegance. Polaris, as the Hyatt's restaurant is called, makes a full rotation every seventy minutes, so that every cosmopolitan diner ingesting duck à l'orange and Dom Pérignon is also on a very slow carnival ride. Not since third grade, when I scarfed cotton candy on the Tilt-A-Whirl at the Nativity school carnival—called Frontier Days—have I so desperately wanted to eat and spin at the same time. At thirty, Alex lives a life of almost unimaginable sophistication, chatting with NBA players before driving a Chevy Caprice to a revolving rooftop restaurant, a typical day in the life of a nationally known sportswriter.

I wrote about the basketball games in Flip Saunders's backyard and Alex wrote me back and now here I am, waving goodbye to a staff writer for *Sports Illustrated,* whose cover next week—headlined CHAMPS!—will feature a hog pile of Minnesota Twins, among them Kent Hrbek, who has given me the dangerous notion that maybe you can dream up a life in a Bloomington backyard and somehow have it come true.

In my meager portfolio is one masterwork of creative writing: the first draft of my résumé. Its style borrows heavily from the *NBC Nightly News,* rat-a-tat sentence fragments shorn of subjects that paint me as a Churchillian man of action. I want to run off a couple hundred copies at Kinko's, on the kind of paper ordinarily reserved for royal weddings, choosing a font

whose name I can only guess at: Baloney Bold, perhaps, or
Pig Lipstick.

Tom Thumb Convenience Store
Summer 1984
Fronted dairy case, tonged frankfurters and
shelved adult magazines for elf-themed purveyor
of cigarettes and sundries.

Bennigan's
June 17-18, 1984
Operated Hobart machine with patented Opti-
Rinse technology for leprechaun-themed purveyor
of Broccoli Bites and Queso Fundido.

New Orleans Court
Summers 1985-86
Pushed antiquated two-stroke Toro, read Joseph
Wambaugh police procedurals while concealed in
maintenance shed of Crescent City-themed apart-
ment complex.

These entries, of course, are mere appetizers to the main
course, my varied experience at the highest levels of sports
and journalism. I am counting on these entries to carry the
day with any potential employer:

Minnesota Twins
1979-1981
Liaised with thirty-five-year-old ex-carnies to

nourish patrons of condemned ballpark. Withstood extended confinement in walk-in meat freezer for entertainment of commissary manager. Learned patience and sympathy watching twenty-third-best baseball team in twenty-six-team league.

## Metropolitan Sports Center
1983
Sold popped corn to raise sodium levels of hockey and popular-music enthusiasts. Optimized beer sales to create home-ice advantage for dentally challenged members of the National Hockey League.

## Minneapolis Star
Summer 1978
Leveraged state-of-the-art technology, including Schwinn Varsity ten-speed and canvas shoulder satchel, to deliver late-breaking news to seventy-five driveways and box hedges in suburban Minneapolis.

Should my résumé prove insufficient on its own to send editors into a bidding war for my services, Marquette has established a job fair for those of us graduating in the spring. Sadly, *Sports Illustrated* is not among the employers seeking Lanche lizards for entry-level positions. The only posted job whose description I even understand—and therefore consider interviewing for—is Ricoh copier salesman. But when I fill out a card listing my qualifications—"Years of experience Xeroxing things"—the lone verb in my five-word sentence fragment disqualifies me from further consideration.

Keying into my mailbox one late winter afternoon, I find an envelope embossed in blue with the *Sports Illustrated* logo. Opening it with my index finger in the Canterbury Court vestibule, with its Chinese takeout menus and tear-off-tabbed flyers (for movers and lost dogs and guitar lessons), I find a note inside from editor Bob Brown, acknowledging receipt, several months ago, of my revised Willie Mosconi story, which he appears to have returned in the same envelope. When I unfold the enclosure, confirming his polite rejection of my manuscript, I see that it isn't my story at all. It's a contract to purchase my story for $750.

When I rode a city bus to the Northridge Mall last spring to see Willie Mosconi shoot pool at Sears, I didn't imagine this, but in my head now I'm hearing Dickey Betts sing "Ramblin' Man," the bit about being born in the back seat of a Greyhound bus rolling down Highway 41. Maybe I was born that day on the Milwaukee County Transit System, rolling up 76th Street.

At the suggestion of Alex Wolff, I've sent my résumé and writing samples to *SI* c/o Jane Wulf, whose title is chief of reporters, so that I picture her in the kind of feathered headdress we used to buy, along with rubber tomahawks and fringed moccasins, inside roadside attractions shaped like teepees on long trips in the wood-paneled Country Squire.

As Alex told me, Jane Wulf is married to *SI* writer Steve Wulf and manages a reporter named Cathy Wolf and all these lupine Wolffs and Wulfs and Wolfs contribute to my fear that the "Bullpen" (as the fact-checking department is known at the magazine) is a den of feral predation. Even after Jane Wulf calls me at Canterbury Court and introduces herself as "Bambi," a more benign woodland creature, I feel like my résumé is an alibi and she's a prosecutor poking holes in it. "Next time you find yourself in New York," she says after five minutes, "swing by the office and we can meet."

Even before I've returned the handset to its cradle, I know this will never happen. I'm not the kind of person who "finds myself" in New York as if I've woken from a deep sleep in a first-class seat to discover I'm in—ah, yes, now I remember—New York City. Nor am I likely to "swing by" Rockefeller Center on my way to someplace more important. When I confess this to Dad in our Sunday night phone call, he says: "Tell her."

"Tell her? I can't just—"

*"You have to call her back and tell her that you have no plans or any reason to be in New York."*

So I do. As with Willie Mosconi, I dial ten digits and hang up three separate times before finally dialing the eleventh digit and letting the phone ring. I tell Bambi Wulf I have no immediate *or* future plans to be in New York, as I don't really know anyone east of Cincinnati.

After a long silence and an audible sigh, Bambi says: "I'll tell you what. We'll take you on here for three months. We'll see how it goes. You'll start on June 23. Come to my office on the eighteenth floor at ten and we'll take it from there."

I stifle a scream, thank her as casually as I can, and hope

the ancient carpet in my Canterbury Court bedroom muffles the sound of my feet as I sprint in place.

"How is Steve going to survive in New York?" Mom asks Dad on the extension when I call home that night. "He can barely put his shoes on in the morning." And it's a fair point. Mom still buys my clothes, shoes, and underpants—tighty-whities with two racing stripes around the elastic waistband. It's the same style I've worn since grade school, when Tom would hoist me by that jaunty waistband until it separated from the body of the briefs, at which time he would wear it as a headband, the way fur trappers wore the pelts of their prey.

More worrisome for me: I've never rented a car, booked a hotel room, or worked any job that did not require somebody, at shift's end, to mop up. In four years at Marquette, my social circle has shrunken. It's a social triangle, really. At most a square.

But I do own a suit, for which I was fitted over Christmas break, at Joseph A. Bank at the Galleria, in the presence of Dad, who insisted I get charcoal. "It can do the work of a black or gray suit," he tells me, while I secretly hope it can also do the work of a magazine fact-checker. The tailor wears a tape measure around his neck like a python. He takes a knee, holds the tape measure to my inseam, and says, "And you'll be dressing on..."

"The twenty-second," I say. "Of May. It's my graduation."

"Yes, but you'll be dressing on which *side*," says the tailor, looking up at Dad, who sighs and says, "On which side of your fly do you hang your—you know—*genitalia*."

Dad says this in the most discreet manner possible, placing

the preposition at the start of the sentence, so it doesn't dangle, unlike my—you know—*genitalia.*

"Right," I whisper.

"He dresses on the right," Dad says.

As the tailor continues his ministrations with tape and chalk and safety pins, I become, in the trifold mirror, a single-vented, single-breasted, two-button, worsted-wool, flap-pocketed suit jacket kind of guy who prefers his pants cuffed and flat-fronted with a long rise and a crease sharp enough to slice ham.

And now it hangs in my closet in Milwaukee, awaiting graduation day beside a crisp white dress shirt, dry-cleaned for the occasion and hanging in its one-hour Martinizing bag because I prefer hangers to boxes, and light starch to heavy. Or so Dad informs me. I think of the summer Tom worked at T.G.I. Friday's as an "expediter," putting the final sprig of parsley on a plate as it hit the pass, and that's what Dad is doing now, garnishing his son before sending him into the world.

Before I leave school forever, I knock on George Reedy's open door in Johnston Hall. He bellows for me to enter. I'm holding a new edition of his 1970 book *The Twilight of the Presidency,* reissued in the dying light of the Reagan administration. It was a Christmas present from Mom and Dad, who insisted I have it signed. I can't help but notice that Professor Reedy's black-and-white author photo on the dust jacket bears some resemblance to my own, except that his head is bowed as he hammers away at his portable typewriter, a bronze bust of LBJ on his desk. At his Texas ranch, while still president, LBJ gave Reedy his Lincoln Continental to persuade him not to quit. As White House gifts go, it's better to be presented with Johnson's Lincoln than Lincoln's Johnson. It's a thought I keep to myself as Reedy produces a ballpoint pen from his shirt pocket—he has three clipped there, in real life and on his dust jacket—and signs in a shaky hand.

Out on the sidewalk, I read the inscription: "To Steve, With all good wishes for all good things in life."

Whatever those things are, they all seem possible on graduation day, sitting in my single-vented suit in Mom and Dad's room at the Holiday Inn downtown, which doesn't resemble in any way the Holiday Inns that captivated me ten or fifteen years ago, with their thrumming pop machines and their Holidome pools redolent of chlorine and industrial towel detergent. Where is the paper ribbon around the toilet seat certifying that it has been Sanitized for Your Protection? There are no crinkly bags around the drinking glasses, hermetically sealing them against airborne viruses. When I search in vain for a thrumming pop machine stocked with Tahitian Treats and RC Colas and other exotic beverages of the 1970s, Dad tells me to take his room key, which isn't a key at all. It's a card that slides into a slot in the door, not a brass key lashed to a green plastic diamond embossed in white with the hotel's address and the phrases "Drop in any mailbox. We guarantee postage."

The Holiday Inn no longer provides each room with a "guest bag"—"waterproof and dustproof"—to be used (per directions printed on the bag) "for wet bathing suits, soiled laundry, shoes, sweaters, toilet articles, as a shower cap or ice bag and for many other personal items." Most guests used the bag to steal Holiday Inn hand soaps, green-striped Holiday Inn bath towels, Holiday Inn pens, Holiday Inn stationery, Holiday Inn ashtrays, Holiday Inn shoehorns, Holiday Inn matchbooks, Holiday Inn sewing kits, and "Holiday Inn sanitary napkin disposal bags for personal hygiene and cleanliness," filling the waxen Holiday Inn ice bucket with any overspill.

None of these items are evident in the room, and not because they were stolen by the previous guest. Once upon a time, the sheer quantity and variety of items in every room at every Holiday Inn that we visited in our Country Squire wagon could—and *did*—fill a carry-on suitcase. My favorite was always the Holiday Inn flyswatter, representing as it did the *expectation* that there would be flies in the room.

Now the Holiday Inn looks like every other hotel. The great green-and-yellow sign outside has been replaced by a discreet logo above the lobby exterior. No longer does an electric star light the night sky—like the star of Bethlehem only better, because this one signified that there *was* room at the inn. No lighted arrow points cars to a parking lot or a porte cochere, as it did when Holiday Inn truly was the Nation's Innkeeper, "Your host from coast to coast."

There is no outdoor pool, nor any stewardesses sunbathing beside it, nor any ten-year-olds drinking milkshakes from frosted steel mixing cups while sunning themselves on a shuffleboard court. There are no NFL linemen signing autographs in the lobby. The Holiday Inn that I knew in the warm cocoon of childhood no longer exists, and neither will that cocoon in another hour. After receiving my diploma, by the tradition he's established with Jim and Tom before me, Dad will give me the Golden Handshake, and my legal taxpayer status will change from Dependent to Single, probably

forever, though Mom holds out hope that someday I'll be
Married, Filing Jointly.

What is comforting in this final hour in the Holiday Inn is
that the Celtics are on TV, and I'm watching them with Mom
and Dad just as I once watched them with Mike and Ope
on the Richie the C TV in the McCollows' basement. Game
7 of the Eastern Conference Finals against the Hawks, live
from Boston Garden. Larry Bird and Dominique Wilkins
are locked in an epic game of one-on-one, both scoring at
will in the fourth quarter. "It's a duel!" says Tommy Heinsohn on CBS, in his Fred Flintstone voice. "Who's going to
blink first?"

The answer is: Mom and Dad. They won't let me watch
the game play out, won't let me see how many points Larry
and 'Nique will score in the fourth quarter alone (20 and 14
respectively) or if the Celtics will advance to the finals (yes),
or witness what will instantly be called the greatest playoff
game in NBA history, a status that won't be challenged in the
coming quarter century.

Instead, halfway through this historic fourth quarter, Mom
insists we get down to MECCA—the Milwaukee Exposition
Convention Center and Arena—where I've watched Larry
play against the Bucks on that fabled court designed by pop
artist Robert Indiana. I graduated from high school on the
home ice of the Minnesota North Stars and will graduate from
college on the home court of the Milwaukee Bucks.

"Let's go," Dad says, switching the TV off and lifting me
from the chair by my lightly starched collar. "This diploma
cost us a lot of money, and you're going to pick it up."

Which is why I'm sitting in cap and gown on the hallowed

floor where Kareem Abdul-Jabbar and Oscar Robertson once dazzled crowds, listening to the chief justice of the United States Supreme Court say that life is "a great shopping mall." If so, I hope to spend my days as I once did at Southdale, when Mom would drop me at B. Dalton Bookseller while she went shopping, sometimes buying me a treat after. I'd be happy with that life—immersed in words, with an Orange Julius on the way out. But the chief justice has something else in mind. Time is currency, he says. We may use it to purchase "worldly success, love of music, enjoyment of painting, a six-handicap golf game."

Of these, only music interests me, but I see his point. "It is impossible," William Rehnquist says, "for anyone to be so rich in time that he can enjoy every single one of the things that time might buy. So there is a choice to be made."

My mind wanders. Time is money. TYME is money—Take Your Money Everywhere. It's the ATM card I got with Mom and Dad at the M & I Bank the day they dropped me here four years ago. As the sixty-three-year-old Rehnquist describes his journey from suburban Shorewood to Washington and various points in between, I think of a title for his memoir: *Have Gavel, Will Travel.*

My train of thought is a hundred cars long, coupled behind the locomotive of this commencement address, with a single epiphany at the caboose: I'm five minutes from becoming a writer, or at least an entry-level journalist, instead of (as Mom once gently suggested) going to law school, as the judge at the podium did. But if I do become a writer, the chief justice and I will have something in common. We'll both spend the better part of our days in a robe.

\*    \*    \*

When it's over, and I have my degree, and Marquette has officially become my *alma mater* ("nourishing mother," as a Latin-fluent Jesuit informs me), I walk back to the Holiday Inn with Mom and Dad to receive, at the corner of 19th and Wisconsin in front of the Holiday Inn, the Golden Handshake.

Mom solemnly takes the Instamatic from Dad, who straightens his tie and tugs his sport coat into place and shakes my hand, pumping it for a good ten seconds as if trying to get water from a well, giving Mom time to snap off ten frames, increasing the odds she has a good one. They will add this Golden Handshake portrait to the ones previously taken with Jim and Tom, preserved under cellophane in a photo album in the upstairs hall closet in South Brook.

"The Golden Handshake," Dad says, gripping and grinning. "On this twenty-second day of May, in the year of our Lord nineteen hundred and eighty-eight, I, Donald Rushin, hereby absolve myself of any future financial responsibility for you, Steven Rushin, from this day forward, in perpetuity..."

What I don't know—and Dad doesn't want me to know—is that this declaration is non-binding. He has no intention of enforcing it. The Golden Handshake is a motivational tool designed to keep me employed. For the same reason, he'll advise me someday to have a mortgage and to make car payments. "*You* need the incentive to keep working," he says, knowing the effort required to get me to mow the lawn. More than the worsted-wool suit, *this* is his graduation gift to prepare me for real life: the gift of no-more-gifts.

When Amy and John have been given Golden Handshakes of their own, Dad will frame color photocopies of all our diplomas and display them beneath the Sears studio portraits each of us had taken as children that still hang, staggered up the staircase, at 2809 West 96th Street.

That's the house we drive home to now, through Wisconsin Dells, where I slept through the Apollo 11 moon landing as a two-year-old moving from Chicago to Bloomington nineteen summers ago. Amy is eighteen, already accepted at Saint Mary's College in Notre Dame, Indiana. John is fifteen, fielding late-night phone calls from the ladies on the basement phone, on which he has written—on the plastic-covered slip of paper meant for emergency phone numbers—"Fresh J Hotline."

I have two weeks at home before moving to New York, barely enough time to prepare. I have to buy "dress socks" and close my passbook savings account and convert all of my meager assets into traveler's checks. Mike and Ope and I meet at White Castle, less for ironic laughs than for the cheap sustenance of late-night sliders. The Castle has performed many services over the years—hangout, feed bag, freak show—and will have something to offer us at any age, to judge by the old men seated at single tables nursing hot coffees and staring into the middle distance beyond Lyndale Avenue.

"It's like the Giving Tree," I say.

"It really is," Mike says.

Above all it's been the theater of dreams, a place to imagine our future selves. On Thursday, June 2, 1988, eleven days after graduating from Marquette and a week before I leave for New York for three months or more, I walk to the mailbox to see who's on the cover of *SI*. Several recently

dismissed coaches, it turns out, beneath the blunt cover slug
YOU'RE FIRED! Walking up the driveway, my head bowed to
the hymnal of the magazine, giving it the customary cursory
riffle, I'm drawn to a headline: "In Pool, the Shark Still Leaves
a Wide Wake." And beneath the title is my byline, so that my
surname has made the miraculous quarter-inch journey from
the mailing label ("The Rushins") to an inside page. On that
page is a photograph of Mosconi bowed over the emerald
baize of a pool table. I burst through the screen door and run
to the kitchen to show Mom, who wipes the Crisco off her
hands with a dish towel and holds the magazine up with both
hands, as if she's Patton studying a map.

"This is *wonderful!*" she says, kissing my cheek and wrapping her arms around me. The woman who quit teaching to
raise five kids—who brought me to the Penn Lake Library
every week, abandoned me for hours at B. Dalton Bookseller,
was my English substitute in seventh grade, fished stories out
of my bedroom wastebasket for the perusal of her bridge-club
cronies, and took an author photo for the dust jacket of a book
I haven't written—doesn't release me from her hug for five
full seconds. When she does, there are tears in her eyes.

"I can't believe it," I say.

"I can," she replies.

Reclaiming the magazine, I retreat to my room for the
weekly ritual of reading it, as I've done since I was twelve.
And there, on page 85, near the end of a story on Red Sox
"ace" Roger Clemens, is an ad for a bicycle manufacturer.
Next to a small black-and-white snapshot of two kids idling
on their muscle bikes in the 1970s is the line, "Remember
your first Schwinn?" They're contemporaries of mine, these

frozen-in-amber eight-year-olds, poised to pop wheelies on some suburban street, on some long-ago Sting-Ray afternoon. Below them is a color photograph of the same two kids, now young adults, on modern-day Schwinn ten-speeds. And the advertising copy says: "So much has changed!"

# PART III

# Stompin' on the Avenue
# by Radio City

# 14

# Into the Great Wide Open

The second time I arrive in New York, I stride purposefully past the gypsy cabdrivers trying to seize my luggage, maintain a death grip on the soft-sided suitcase that was my high school graduation gift—meant to take me around the world, or at least away from home—and join an infinite snake line at the taxi stand. I'm not standing *in* line, as I would in Minnesota. I'm standing *on* line, as we say in New York.

The city is stewing. The cabdriver's T-shirt is translucent with sweat. Every four minutes, every hour, around the clock, 1010 WINS tells us that it's 91 degrees in Central Park.

"Forty-Eighth between Second and Third," I say. "Take Crescent to the Fifty-Ninth Street Bridge."

"Triborough faster," the cabbie says.

"Fine."

The city shimmies in a heat haze. Alex Wolff has left me the use of his rent-controlled apartment while he's on various overseas assignments for the summer, along with a guide to the neighborhood he composed and dot-matrix-printed for me on three continuous fan-folded sheets of sprocket-feed paper, the kind with longitudinal holes on either side that tear off at the perforations. This is a great leap forward from the copy paper made of newsprint that I used in classes at Marquette. This is what professional writing looks like before it's published. I feel like an East Berliner seeing West Berlin for the first time.

The apartment itself is "book-lined," as they say in newspaper profiles of famous authors. Its former tenant was Alex's grandmother, a book editor, who had her own imprint at Harcourt Brace Jovanovich, one of those publishing partnership names that has always intrigued me on book spines, like "Houghton Mifflin" or "Harper & Row" or the insuperable "Funk & Wagnalls," a phrase Ed McMahon invokes when introducing Carnac the Magnificent: "These envelopes are hermetically sealed. They've been kept in a mayonnaise jar on Funk & Wagnalls' porch since noon today..."

Alex's grandmother—she was the subject of a long profile in *The New Yorker,* which he has left for me on the coffee table—brought *Doctor Zhivago* to American readers and also published Günter Grass and Amos Oz and other writers I've heard of but never read, including Umberto Eco, whose *Name of the Rose* Dad famously picked out of a twirly rack at the Minneapolis airport before a long business trip and forced himself to complete, despite hating it—finally sending it windmilling across the bedroom in triumph one night after reading the 592nd and final page. This apartment has that book and hundreds of others, along with stacks of *Spy* magazine, a satirical monthly that ridicules the rich and famous of New

York, especially the city's most famous real estate mogul, who is described in every issue as "short-fingered vulgarian Donald Trump."

All these books and magazines are an invitation to stay in. But the city beckons me out, or at least the immediate neighborhood does. According to Alex's guide, it's called Turtle Bay, despite the absence of turtles, or bays. The three-story townhouse next door, Alex writes, is the home of novelist Kurt Vonnegut. I might see him on the sidewalk. Vonnegut was hired at *Sports Illustrated* in its inaugural year of 1954. Given a photograph from a steeplechase competition, and told to write a caption for it, he shut himself in an office for hours. After he left—never to return—an editor found a single sentence on the sheet of paper rolled into the typewriter: "The fucking horse jumped over the fucking fence."

Vonnegut's wife, Alex writes, is a photographer named Jill Krementz, who specializes in black-and-white author photos for dust jackets. This sounds perfectly natural to me. When you're young, your mom takes your author photo; when you're older, your wife does. But the Vonneguts are not my only well-known neighbors.

From high above Second Avenue, in the condo tower around the corner, Mets captain Keith Hernandez presides over the East Side like a bachelor monarch. One block north, I might literally run into Katharine Hepburn, whom I last saw in tenth grade, in *On Golden Pond,* with Mom and Dad, at the Southtown Theatre.

And in this very building, with its maroon canopy and doorman, lives the eminent sportswriter and NBC Sports personality Pete Axthelm, author of *The City Game,* a classic book about New York City basketball that I took from Tim McCollow's basement bedroom in Bloomington and never returned during my brief but torrid biblio-kleptomania days.

It isn't long before I see Keith Hernandez buying eggs at Gristedes, the grocery store on Second Avenue. Soon I'll see O. J. Simpson and his blond wife walking arm in arm on Lexington Avenue. I'll fall in behind Muhammad Ali strolling along 50th between Fifth and Sixth, surrounded by strangers calling "Champ!" It's like being backstage at America.

The *Sports Illustrated* workweek is Thursday to Monday, with Saturdays off, though Sundays often require an all-nighter in the office. The workday starts at 10 a.m., three hours later than Dad arrives at Mickey Mining. Which is why I arrive outside the Time & Life Building for the first day of the rest of my life on a Thursday, at 9:30 a.m., suited, in shined shoes, dressing on the right. I walk around the building for half an hour until I've worked up a full sweat, glazed like a Christmas ham.

The city is on fire. In the absence of a single friend or acquaintance, my principal pursuit is the act of being hot. It was 97 on the 21st and 98 the next day, yesterday, the hottest June 22 on record and the most Con Edison mega-watts used in the city's history. The main story on the front page of the *Times* tomorrow will not be the Yankees' firing of manager Billy Martin. (The team has fired Martin on four previous occasions—not just the time he punched out a marshmallow salesman in the bar of L'Hotel Sofitel on the Strip in Bloomington—so that story is below the fold.) Nor will the top story be "The Crack Plague." That one, halfway down the front page, will declare that "the city's police have all but conceded the fight to abolish trafficking in the drug, saying the growth has overwhelmed traditional law enforcement tactics."

Rather, the top story in the *Times* tomorrow will be about the infernal heat on the day I arrived in journalism wearing several yards of worsted wool. Beneath the headline GLOBAL WARMING HAS BEGUN, EXPERT TELLS SENATE, the paper will note that the first five months of 1988 have been hotter than any comparable period in the 130 years that records have been kept. James E. Hansen of NASA "was 99 percent certain that the warming trend was not a natural variation but was caused by a buildup of carbon dioxide and other artificial gases in the atmosphere."

"It is time to stop waffling," Hansen told a Senate energy committee.

"If Dr. Hansen and other scientists are correct," the *Times* writer will add, "then humans, by burning of fossil fuels and other activities, have altered the global climate in a manner that will affect life on earth for centuries to come."

There will be thirty-two days this summer in New York with temperatures 90 or higher, a record, and the front page of the paper will accurately convey the New York I am already coming to know: a heat-crazed, crack-addled, baseball-frenzied cauldron.

The eighteenth floor of the Time & Life Building looks nothing like the *Sports Illustrated* offices of my fevered imagination. I had expected to see senior writer Frank Deford in a smoking jacket at the Xerox machine, George Plimpton in an ascot at the water cooler, Cheryl Tiegs in a fishnet one-piece being photographed against a false backdrop of palm trees for next February's swimsuit issue.

The place looks like Community State Bank, with softly cooing phones and carpeted hallways that muffle my footsteps. There is no newsroom, much less a clatter of typewriters, but as I near the Bullpen, the fact-checkers' bank of offices in the northeast corner of the eighteenth floor, the people in the hallway are getting younger. Bambi's office overlooks the Radio City Music Hall marquee, kitty-corner to 30 Rock, where Letterman's cue-card guy is no doubt, at this very moment, Magic-Markering onto poster board the line: "It was so hot in Central Park today I saw a squirrel fanning his nuts."

I'm given a shared office and a list of staff home phone numbers in the event that an editor—God forbid—needs to be reached out of office hours. I get a quiver of sharpened red pencils and a stack of creamy stationery embossed with the *SI* logo on which I'll write to everybody I can think of. In the event this job lasts only three months, I shall hoard a lifetime of letterhead.

The Bullpen and its immediate environs is populated by med school dropouts, law school castaways, stand-up comics, screenwriters, novelists, filmmakers, musicians, and various other moonlighters, the overqualified and the underslept, with first names—Merrell, Morin, Duncan—I have never encountered in Bloomington.

Morin Bishop is a sesquipedalian editor-in-training who can deliver an extemporaneous monologue on any topic. Speaking in perfectly composed paragraphs, he extols the virtues of knockwurst and admires Frank Sinatra's frequent insertion of the word "cuckoo" in his live performances: "The cuckoo warm

September of my years," "Baubles, bangles, and them cuckoo beads." In his verbal dexterity, wit, and baldness—to say nothing of his suit selection, from the "House of Cromwell," deep in the Garment District—Morin is almost Churchillian. His first-day invitation to lunch with other Bullpen stalwarts feels like a lifeline.

Merrell Noden was a track star at Princeton, ran the mile in 4:11.2, and eats cake for lunch dessert every day. "He's the world's fattest thin man," says another reporter, Sally Guard, by way of introduction. "Or the world's thinnest fat man." Merrell invites me to play in his Monday night pickup basketball games at 112th and Broadway, and afterward to lay waste to the neighborhood bars. There are even more Irish bars in New York than there were at Marquette, and I visit them with the other writers and comics who play basketball, including Merrell's best friend, Joe Bolster, who has appeared on *Carson* and *Letterman*. In the bar at a comedy club called Catch a Rising Star—Manhattan's answer to the Carlton Celebrity Room—Joe will introduce me to another comic I recognize from *The Tonight Show:* Jerry Seinfeld is drinking water and wearing a leather jacket. I shake the hands that shook the hands of Johnny Carson and Letterman. Already, I'm passing through the looking glass, the gray-green glass of our family-room Zenith in South Brook.

In the Bullpen, many of my new colleagues do devastating impersonations of the editors they hope to write for or replace. Because we see every story pass through the computer system—from the writer's draft through three layers of editing—a favorite parlor game is to imagine how famous first lines of literature would survive this editorial spanking machine.

"Call me Ishmael," in this exercise, becomes "Call me Ishmael—a six-foot-four-inch, 267-pound left tackle for the Buffalo Bills."

"It was the best of times—and, paradoxically—it was the worst of times."

Fact-checking queries are appended to Orwell: "It was a bright cold day in April [ed: specific date?], and the clocks were striking thirteen [ed: not possible; please fix]."

Alex Wolff will see James Brown sitting courtside at a college basketball game and describe the legend thusly: "He felt good. You knew that he would." The line will be changed to: "He felt good. You knew he would." Only in the Time & Life Building would an Ivy League editor copy-edit the Godfather of Soul.

So we spend time copy-editing classic songs. "I can't get no satisfaction" becomes "I can't get any satisfaction." "Ain't no woman like the one I got" becomes "No woman is similar to the one I have." And thus passes a paid hour in the office. The mordant humor and ear for language and voluminous knowledge of song lyrics and TV shows and advertising jingles make me feel instantly at home, despite fundamental differences over what my predominantly East Coast–raised coworkers call our childhood snack cakes. My Ding Dongs are their Ring Dings, my Ho Hos are their Yodels, my Cupcakes are their Yankee Doodles. Our primary fault line is not so much Midwest vs. Northeast but Hostess vs. Drake's.

And yet the stresses of the job are always in evidence. Slats, my new colleague across the hall, is on the phone with a sports publicist at the University of Kentucky, fact-checking a minor item in the magazine. The Kentucky official is taking

Slats to task for an alleged error that appeared in *SI* sometime in the distant past. And even though he was not responsible for this minor oversight, which may not have been an error at all, Slats apologizes abjectly on behalf of the magazine, assures the man he will take this complaint straight to his bosses, and expresses his general admiration for the good people of the Bluegrass State, and for the University of Kentucky in particular.

After hanging up, Slats keeps the phone to his mouth and shouts down the line every profane thing he had wanted to say to Mr. Kentucky, before repeatedly banging the handset of the phone onto his desktop. Every hammer blow is punctuated by an f-bomb. When he has calmed down, Slats bungs the whole phone into the metal trash can next to his desk, turns to his open door, and says, "Well, that was fun."

Sundays are more stressful still. That's when most of the stories come in and the staff labors late into the night. On Sunday mornings, en route to the office, I attend Mass at Saint Patrick's Cathedral to see if I can store some tranquility to draw upon later, like water in a camel's hump. In the marble vastness of Saint Patrick's, echoing with organ music, the horns and sirens of Fifth Avenue feel far away. The altar does too. There are three hundred pews seating nearly three thousand people. Our family's unwritten rule of attending Mass at Nativity—"Arrive early to get the good seats in back"—is made moot here. I can sit midway up the aisle and still be a mile from the priest. To behold from the sidewalk the rock-candy spires of Saint Patrick's rising toward the heavens, before walking a block to another kind of cathedral, the Time & Life Building, is to be certain that these two institutions—Mass and mass-circulation magazines, the Catholic Church and the printed word—are utterly, eternally invulnerable.

In the office, every so often, a writer files a story that has the letters "TK" in it. "TK" I'm told is a placeholder for information that is "to come." For instance: "The Seattle Mariners have lost TK night games in the Kingdome this season." It is the fact-checker's job to find this information. An editor named Sandy Padwe one night, reviewing a story littered with TKs, turns to me and says, "Rushin, if you ever become a writer at this magazine, *put in the fucking TKs!*"

We fact-checkers set about to do so. A story on Penn State coach Joe Paterno mentions his modest car, but not the model, or the color. By the time the piece is being edited, at 2 a.m. on a Monday morning, when the Bullpen is expected to be awake and at the ready, the only way to fill in this fucking TK is to call Paterno's home number, wake him up, and ask him the color of his car. This absurd task falls to the intern, Rog, and we gather around his office to watch. Predictably, Paterno assumes the call is a prank, possibly from a drunken fan at Ohio State, and hangs up. Beyond the journalism clichés I learned from *Lou Grant* and *All the President's Men*—make that extra call, details bring writing to life, the news doesn't punch a clock—the lesson is clear to me: journalists can, with impunity, wake a famous man in the middle of the night to ask him the color of his car.

For other facts, we have a warehouse of knowledge just down the hall. *Sports Illustrated* maintains the world's largest sports library, with shelves of red folders alphabetized by subject containing newspaper clippings from A (Aaron, Hank) to Z (Zalapski, Zarley). It reminds me of our old Encyclopedia

Americana in the basement, thirty volumes covering every facet of human knowledge from aardvarks to zymotic disease. This library is a walk-in encyclopedia. In these folders and books and press guides and magazines are all the known facts ever recorded about sports, all accessible in a single room, almost always after a short search (and a long session at the photocopier). I spend my *Sports Illustrated* weekends—my Tuesdays and Wednesdays—in the library in a T-shirt, jorts, and Adidas Samba indoor soccer shoes. I can't imagine a more convenient portal to human knowledge, everything I ever wanted to know at my fingertips.

The most eager reporters among us triple-check the facts. A legendary summer intern, I'm told, once called the Boston Red Sox PR man to confirm that the left-field wall at Fenway Park was indeed renowned as the Green Monster. The same intern later rang up Barbara Nicklaus to verify that her husband, Jack, really was nicknamed The Golden Bear.

On *my* first Sunday night, as I sit around developing an ulcer, wondering if I might have to wake someone at midnight, Sally Guard mentions that she's going out to get sandwiches for the Bullpen at A & K, the twenty-four-hour deli at 50th and Seventh. Sally's father, Dave Guard, was a founding member of the Kingston Trio, whose "Where Have All the Flowers Gone?" was in heavy rotation on Mom's kitchen tape deck.

"Can I get you anything?" Sally says.

"Bologna and American on white?" I say. "With mayo?"

She laughs. Everyone in earshot does. I'm not sure why. Perhaps they know it's the sandwich I've had most days since the first grade.

And yet Sally brings me the bologna and American on

white. The people in the Bullpen are kind to me and to each other and devastating to everyone else: the editors whose queries we answer, the writers we'd like to supplant, the athletes and coaches we're covering.

Like an alpinist with acrophobia, I bring a fear of talking on the telephone to a job that requires cold-calling people on the telephone. While fact-checking a story on Doug Moe, I'm told to find out what the Denver Nuggets coach majored in as a college undergraduate. I ask the Nuggets PR intern, who calls back an hour later and says, "Coach Moe told me to tell you 'nuclear physics.'"

"Hmm," I say. "That would be his BS, I presume?"

But I'm overcoming my fear, acquiring a life independent of Minnesota and Milwaukee. I open a bank account at Manufacturers Hanover and learn to call it Manny Hanny. I'm now saying "graduated high school" instead of "graduated *from* high school." The NCAAs are now a "*tore*-na-ment," not a "*turn*-a-mint."

My grocery store is now Gristedes, not Red Owl, my church is Saint Patrick's, not Captivity, my local news anchors are now WNBC's Chuck and Sue, whom I like to think of as Suck and Chew.

Mike and Ope visit from Bloomington. We drink in every Irish bar on Second Avenue and hit White Castle in Manhattan, though the visit is redundant, because so many places in Manhattan approximate White Castle: Tad's Steaks, the Blarney Stone chain of watering holes, the Port Authority Bus Terminal—each provides a constituent part of the Castle ambience.

Otherwise, what passes for leisure is reading *Bonfire of*

*the Vanities* in my shorts in front of the window AC unit on another brick-oven afternoon. Tom Wolfe's crack and Wall Street blockbuster has a black-and-white photo on the back: the author in white double-breasted suit with billowing pocket square. As jacket photos go, Wolfe's is better than mine. Without Mom here to buy them, I have no interest in clothes and remain loyal to a small rotation of khakis and golf shirts that I sniff in the morning. My graduation suit was dry-cleaned once in a joint wallpapered with eight-by-ten headshots of Broadway and soap-opera and prime-time-television stars, so that it's a small thrill to be given the same light starch once enjoyed by Hong Kong Phooey himself, the late Scatman Crothers. My suit hangs in the closet, chemically embalmed beneath its dry-cleaning bag, never again to be worn to work.

A complimentary copy of the *New York Times* is delivered to my desk every day so I supplement it by buying the *Post* off the newsstand on the walk in. A poor sap in Queens has slipped while climbing a wrought-iron fence and impaled himself through the soft tissues beneath his chin. The man was rescued by firemen after dangling there like a fish for a couple of hours. The *Post* headline — MR. LUCKY — makes me wonder out loud: "If this is Mr. Lucky, who is Mr. *Un*lucky?"

Another day a man in Turtle Bay menaces a midday crowd of pedestrians with a Gurkha sword.

One Sunday morning I emerge from Mass to see a homeless man in a raincoat squat to the ground. When he stands, there is something on the sidewalk that hadn't been there before, and I wonder if this man has just laid an egg. But it's not an egg.

When I call home on Sunday nights and report these stories back to Mom and Dad, there is a stereophonic howl from the two phones they're on, before one or both say, "You're not in Kansas anymore." And then Mom asks, "Are you eating?" and "How's your social life?"

Every evening after work I stop at Original Ray's for two plain slices on a greased paper plate and again at Smiler's Deli for two Coors Lights and thus resume my Silver Bullet Nights. I'm alone in a crowd, living with four guys who played football together at Yale and work for the same bank and go out together at night. Upon Alex Wolff's return from abroad, I've moved to a shared bedroom in a high-rise building overlooking Sparks Steak House, on East 46th, where Big Paul Castellano—head of the Gambino crime family, the "beleaguered kingpin of American organized crime," as the *Daily Snooze* called him—was whacked while getting out of a town car on a December day at 5:30 p.m., in broad twilight. Big Paul has been replaced by John Gotti, the "Dapper Don," in jocular tabloid headlines, in the daily soap opera of a city whose characters we're supposed to know by their headline epithets: Preppie Killer. Iron Mike. Doc. Darryl. The Donald.

On civilian weekends—midweek at the magazine—my roommates throw parties attended by women who prefer bankers to fact-checkers. I learn to sleep through George Michael and the B-52's. Tom visits from Chicago and takes a leak off our balcony on the thirty-first floor, despite the presumed presence of Gambino lieutenants disembarking from town cars below. More likely, the urine is only making it to the balconies on the twenty-ninth floor. Still, I'm never quite convinced that the random precipitation I feel as a pedestrian on clear days in New York is condensation from window unit air conditioners. I know it could be anything.

One September morning, as my three-month job is about to expire, I arrive in the office and am told to return to my apartment, pack a bag, and join the New York Rangers hockey team for their exhibition game tonight in Edmonton. On arrival, I'm supposed to tell the Rangers that I'm traveling with them to their next game in Denver. I'm twenty-one, don't have a credit card, don't know where Edmonton is, and have never been to Canada. The $1,000 cash advance I'm given in the Time & Life Building takes me as far as LaGuardia, where I spend $925 to retrieve my plane ticket at the American Airlines check-in counter, unaware that the ticket was prepaid and that I've now purchased it twice.

The Rangers aren't expecting me because I haven't called them, nor would anyone in their organization know who I am. I don't have a business card. I simply turn up at the Northlands Coliseum with no return plane ticket, no hotel reservations, and scarcely enough money—seventy-five bucks—to cover meals and cab fare for three days on the road. Nor do I have a press credential to enter the Northlands Coliseum. But I've worked at Met Center and sneaked into at least five dozen movies in five separate theaters, and I know that a confident stride and an air of purpose can get me in just about any place. I walk into a construction zone outside the arena, which leads me to an open door, which leads me into the empty stands for the Rangers' afternoon skate around. There is one man on the concourse, and I recognize his face as one I scissored out of *Goal!* magazine in the 1970s. Phil Esposito, now the Rangers' general manager, was then a star for the Bruins. He is not a god but something greater. Bumper stickers in Boston once read JESUS SAVES BUT ESPO SCORES ON THE REBOUND.

My fear of Espo is exceeded only by the terror of being stranded in Edmonton with no money, no plane ticket, and—far worse—no story. So I approach the great suited man, clear my throat, introduce myself, tell him I'm here to write a story on Guy Lafleur, the thirty-seven-year-old former Montreal Canadien and future Hall of Famer who has come out of retirement to play for the Rangers. And oh, by the way, may I fly to Denver with the team after tonight's game?

"Sure," Esposito says, eyes locked on the ice. "No problem."

After the game that night, I board the team bus last, as instructed by the traveling secretary, and take the only empty seat, an aisle. Next to me, staring out at the rain, his face reflected in the window, is "The Flower" himself, Guy Lafleur, whose photo graced—still graces—our basement in South Brook, cut out of *Goal!* magazine like Espo's and Bobby Clarke's and J. P. Parise's and all the hockey heroes that Jim and Tom and John and I pretended to be in our stocking-footed Saturday morning donnybrooks.

I want to tell Lafleur that I vended popcorn at his games in Bloomington, but I find myself incapable of speech. We ride in silence toward the airport for five minutes until he turns to me and says: "*Sports Illustrated* did a front-page story on me in 1977." As if I don't know! THE FLYING FRENCHMAN OF MONTREAL was the cover headline, above an action photo of Lafleur, hair swept back in the self-made breeze of the Flying Frenchman, steering the puck with his Koho around some poor sap on the Capitals.

"I know," I squeak, and we're off, Lafleur anticipating the

questions I can't bring myself to pose, asking and answering them in what the Jesuits taught me was a rhetorical device called "hypophora." As with popcorn vending and girls, I'm relying on my silence to prevail. "Ask me, ask me, ask me," as Morrissey sings. And for the first time since Willie Mosconi, silence has worked.

The Rangers' team charter doesn't take off until 1 a.m. The notion that I'm part of the traveling party of an Original Six team in the National Hockey League is absurd. We arrive at the Westin in Denver at 4:30 a.m. There will be another exhibition game tonight, against the Pittsburgh Penguins, after which I'll compose a story on my state-of-the-art Tandy TRS-80 Model 100, a computer that was handed to me, without instructions, on my way out of the Time & Life Building. It runs on four AA batteries, has a screen that displays eight lines of text, forty characters per line, and yet the whole thing is small enough to fit on my lap. To file the story, I attach two linked black cups to the Tandy, place the handset of my hotel telephone into this device, called an "acoustic coupler," and say a prayer. After three failed attempts, my story magically flies from Denver to Manhattan through the telephone lines, by way of a rubber brassiere.

I've listened to Paul Simon's "Graceland" a thousand times on a Walkman since leaving Edmonton, and can attest: these are the days of miracle and wonder.

The woman who assigned me this story, Bambi's deputy, J. E. Vader, has FedEx'd her American Express card to the front desk of the Westin, so that I might pay for my room and a plane ticket back to New York. When I return to the office from Denver, I'm told that prepaid airline tickets by their very nature don't require a second, redundant payment; that if I hope to work at *Sports Illustrated*—or anywhere else for that matter—I had better apply for an American Express card; that it's necessary to phone teams in advance to secure a press credential if I expect to cover their games; and that my reportage—rewritten by hockey writer Austin Murphy, and running under his byline, replete with the details of Lafleur riding the bus in the rain and checking into the Westin at 4:30 a.m.—received positive reviews in the office. My three-month job has been extended for six more months.

On a Saturday night in October I'm enjoying my usual dinner in front of the TV, plain slices and Silver Bullets off a coffee table found on the street, when hobbled Dodgers slugger Kirk Gibson swings at a backdoor slider with a full count and two outs in the bottom of the ninth, a runner on second, his team down 4–3 against untouchable Dennis Eckersley of the A's in Game 1 of the World Series. "High fly ball into right field," sings Vin Scully on NBC. "And she...is...*gone!*" For the next minute and fifteen seconds, as Gibson circles the bases like some evangelical churchgoer commanded to rise from his wheelchair and walk, the only sound is the levitational roar of Dodger Stadium. I'm alone in the apartment, hands on head in disbelief. I walk out to the balcony, hear the honking of the indifferent city a mile below, then return to the TV, to the televised roar, and am overwhelmed with the sensation that I want to be *there,* not here. To watch this without being able to tell anyone about it—in prose—is a kind of torture.

For now, though, I'm downwardly mobile. With the high-rise lease expiring, my roommates and I decamp to East

77th Street, where I get a single room with a single barred half window in a basement. A giant water bug crawls out of my shower drain every morning. I think I see a smoldering cigarette pincered in one of its raptorial front legs. With the other appendage he appears to be flipping me the bird. On the phone, I ask Mom to send more of my "personal effects," a phrase I've picked up from celebrity obituaries. And she does, but continues to hedge her bet, holding back the books in my bedroom because they're heavy and expensive to ship and—though she never actually says it out loud—let's see if I'm still living in New York in six months.

Or perhaps those books on the shelf above my bedroom desk—Jim's handwritten Gettysburg Address is taped to the same bookcase, near Tom's prom photos in their cardboard frames—are a happy reminder, eggshells left in an empty nest.

Sundays have become dread inducing. One Sunday morning, sitting at my desk, anticipating a long night of fact-checking, my lips begin to tingle and my fingertips go numb and I'm sent to see a nurse, who tells me it's stress and I need to walk around the block now and then. When the Calgary Flames win the Stanley Cup, and Al MacInnis is named the MVP, and I have to fact-check the magazine's instant feature on him that Sunday, I wait by the phone for twelve hours, assured by the Flames that their star defenseman will call me. Ravenous at 10 p.m., I ask my colleague Albert Kim in the office down the hall if he'll cover my phone while I run to A & K for a bologna sandwich. When I return twenty minutes later, there is a yellow "While You Were Out" slip on my chair, and a message, in Albert's hand:

*Al MacInnis*
*(403) 555-736*

"Is this a joke?" I ask Albert.

"No," he says. "He really called."

"But the phone number," I say, vein twitching in my forehead. "It's missing a digit."

Albert stares at the message slip. "I'm sorry," he says. "I don't know what happened." But the missing number, Albert's certain, is the last one.

For the next five minutes, Albert and I stand at my desk, phone on speaker, taking turns dialing the last digit: 555-7360, 555-7361, 555-7362, and so forth, asking Calgarians hungover from the weekend's Stanley Cup victory if their most celebrated citizen could come to the phone. Everyone who answers hangs up, some of them profanely. When Albert gets to 555-7367, and asks for Al MacInnis, Al MacInnis replies, "This is Al." And I am so grateful that I nearly weep.

My hair, meanwhile, has begun to fall into the shower drain, to the annoyance of its resident water bug, and I sometimes linger in Saint Patrick's after Mass, dreading the Sunday ahead. But I am eventually rewarded for surviving these Sunday nights when my employment status is made permanent. After an eternal probation, I have the fact-checking job. "First prize is two tickets," as Dad used to say when the Twins were terrible. "Second prize is four tickets."

The good news is that I'm suddenly salaried with benefits, though an *SI* writer warns me that the company's 401(k) scheme is really a scam. "You can lose two or three grand at a pop," he says. When I mention this to Jim on the phone—he's now a benefits consultant in Chicago—he laughs for a solid minute before telling me to enroll in the 401(k) and never take financial advice from a sportswriter.

With my newly minted business card, and my shiny American Express ("Member Since 88"), I am duly dispatched to Florida to write a one-page story on fifty-year-old Jack Nicklaus, who is playing in his first major golf tournament on the Senior PGA Tour. Again, I leave for the airport hours after learning of the assignment, and that evening, arriving straight from the rental car lot at twilight at PGA National in Palm Beach Gardens, I see Nicklaus walking off the driving range. He is instantly recognizable from, among everything else, the American Express commercials that aired when I was a kid. They began "Do you know me? On the golf course you might." They ended with "The American Express card—don't leave home without it." I want to say, "I do know you, and I don't leave home without it. I learned that one the hard way."

As I make my cotton-mouthed introduction, Nicklaus talks to me amiably without breaking stride. He's still talking when we approach the windowless door to the locker room. But when he steps inside, I stop at the threshold, assuming I'm not allowed in, even as a guest of the greatest golfer in history. As a result, when the door swings shut, Nicklaus is still talking to me—except that I'm no longer there. He's talking to a ghost. Through the door, I hear him stop in midsentence, evidently wondering what became of me. But my fear of going where I'm not allowed—of getting in trouble, of accruing a police record, of trespassing—has frozen me to my spot. Nicklaus must think I'm an imbecile. But he doesn't come back out.

Still, the story on the Senior PGA Championship gets filed,

on deadline, and will appear three days later in mailboxes across North America, including the one at 2809 West 96th Street in South Brook. "Golf's most junior senior," I write, "was trying to win his most minor major." Jaime Diaz of the *New York Times* sends the piece from his phone because I can't get the rubber brassiere to connect with New York through the handset of the press tent pay phone.

Two weeks later I'm sent to Milwaukee to write a deadline story on the Brewers. Nothing has changed at County Stadium since I came here in college except I'm sitting in the Brewers' dugout now instead of getting hammered in the bleachers. "I tell young players and young writers the same thing," the Brewers' batting coach tells me. "The travel isn't easy. You'll see." He is Don Baylor, who played for the Twins in 1987, when Mike and Ope and I sat in the left-field seats at the Metrodome. "You better pace yourself," Baylor says.

But I don't. I'm assigned another baseball story the following week, in Chicago. White Sox catcher Carlton Fisk—whom I pretended to be in the backyard, waving foul balls into fair territory, as he did in Game 6 of the '75 World Series—declines to speak to me because "I have a meeting today."

"I'll be here for the next four days," I say.

"I have a meeting the next four days," he replies.

Every week, Thursday to Monday, I'm on a road trip. "Trip" is the right word, for life is now an extended hallucination. Angels manager Doug Rader throws his pants at me in anger in the visiting manager's office at Fenway Park. At the Oakland Airport Hilton, near the Coliseum where the A's play, I sit at the bar with seven-foot-seven Golden State Warriors center Manute Bol, feeling as if I'm in the *Star Wars* cantina.

The job requires me every week to write two thousand words overnight in a hotel room, to be filed by 8 a.m. on Sunday morning, my panic rising with each sign that the dawn is drawing nearer: the complimentary copies of *USA Today* being dropped in the hall, the bill slipped under the door, birds chirping outside the window, the first light leaking through the blackout curtains.

And yet none of my siblings or friends wants to hear that this is work. In the visitors' clubhouse at Wrigley Field, Pirates pitcher Jerry Reuss takes hold of the credential around my neck and says, "Working press? That's an oxymoron."

Often it is. I go out drinking with Reds pitcher Jack Armstrong immediately after his Saturday night start in Cincinnati, and sneak him in my rental car into Riverfront Stadium on Sunday morning, long after he was supposed to arrive. The photographer on that feature story, with a plane to catch after the Sunday matinee, cabs to the airport, leaving his rental car in a parking garage in downtown Cincinnati. He isn't sure which one. "I'll call Hertz," he tells me. "They'll find it. I've done it before."

The expense scarcely matters. *Sports Illustrated* is minting money, chockablock with the advertising bounty of Philip Morris, General Motors, Anheuser Busch, Seagram's, and various companies clamoring to get their perfume strips up the nostrils of *SI*'s three million subscribers and twenty million weekly pass-along readers.

I've been shot out of a cannon, far past the safety net, with no idea when or where I might land. One day I fly from Chicago to Montreal to write about the Expos, check into my hotel, see the red message light on the nightstand phone, am told by the front desk to call my office, am told by my office to forget the Expos and fly to New York to write about the Mets, and then check out eight minutes later with the same clerk who checked me in: "Did you enjoy your stay, Mr. Rushin?"

I get back into the same cab, return to the airport, fly to LaGuardia, and cab next door to Shea Stadium, where a famous member of the New York Mets, naked in the clubhouse, pauses in front of a group of reporters en route to the shower and stage-farts at us from point-blank range. And I ask myself, not for the first time: What kind of job is this? Is this the real life, or is this fantasy?

There is no distinction now between work and life. I get no haircuts, make no dental appointments, eat one large daily meal like a boa constrictor, usually at 2 a.m. after night games. I get my glasses from LensCrafters "in about an hour," so that I am described by a journalist, in a hardcover history of the magazine, as looking like Funky Winkerbean from the comic strip of the same name.

It doesn't matter. The job is all there is now. This is made clear on the night that my apartment keys unknown to me fall out of my backpack in the press box in Cincinnati, so that I arrive in New York late at night and go straight to the Time & Life Building to sleep on the couch in Bambi's office, where I'm awakened in the morning by the squeegee squeak of window washers suspended eighteen stories above Sixth Avenue, looking at me through the glass like I'm a reticulated python in a herpetarium.

And perhaps they are right. I'm not doing anything fundamentally different from what I always have, writing in my bedroom on Mom's Royal. When managing editor Mark

Mulvoy calls me into his office and says, "I'm promoting you to staff writer"—staff writers can live anywhere they want, so long as they're near an airport—he immediately follows with, "Now don't tell me you want to move to Keokuk, Iowa."

"It's Minnesota," I want to say, but don't, because East Coast natives, I've discovered, make no distinction between Minnesota and Michigan, between Minneapolis and Indianapolis. The Bloomingtons—in Indiana and Illinois and Minnesota—are all the same.

There is another reward for my formal promotion to writer. In recognition of my thirty-eight weeks on the road in 1990, Mulvoy sends me to Bali, Indonesia, to write a travelogue for the annual *SI* swimsuit issue. Beyond forty-five minutes in Tijuana on a family trip to California in 1977, and my forays into Canada to cover hockey, I've never left the country. But now I get a rushed passport in Midtown and fly from JFK to Amsterdam, Amsterdam to Karachi, Karachi to Singapore, Singapore to Jakarta, and Jakarta to Bali. (Six days later, I'll fly home through Tokyo, making a complete circumnavigation of the globe in a week.) On one long leg of the outbound flight—Karachi, Pakistan, to Singapore on KLM Royal Dutch Airlines—I am the sole passenger in the upper deck of a Boeing 747, the airplane cabin that captivated me as a kid. Only now I have the upstairs berth entirely to myself, except for the Dutch flight attendant with whom I chat for most of the eight-hour journey, all the while wondering: *How did I get here, wherever I am?*

In our house in South Brook, above the fireplace, hangs a painting that Dad bought for five bucks in the Philippines. It depicts a man and his mule. In Bali, I buy a large wood carving of a man and his ducks. On my return to New York, I ship it to Mom, who gamely displays it on the mantel, under the donkey painting she never loved.

On a rare summer visit to the office to do my expenses, I read in my complimentary copy of the *Times* that a grisly discovery has been made on North 25th Street in Milwaukee. An alleged serial killer named Jeffrey Dahmer has been apprehended there, five blocks from my old apartment in a neighborhood that was—the *Times* notes—"popular as inexpensive housing for Marquette University students."

Dahmer had worked downtown at the Ambrosia Chocolate Factory, whose bewitching Wonka bouquet reached me on a westerly wind. His first Milwaukee victim was slain in the fall of my senior year, in a room at the faded art-deco Ambassador Hotel.

But there is a happier reminder of Marquette too. At Mass on a Sunday morning at Saint Patrick's, I see a heavyset rugby player I passed on campus during my freshman and sophomore years. He's walking up the aisle to receive communion in zebra-striped Zubaz sweatpants, a white T-shirt, and black Chuck Taylor high-tops, unlaced. He's three years older than I am, and I didn't know him at school, but I am pleased to see him—hours after performing on *Saturday Night Live* and presumably attending its famous after-party—finding comfort, as I have, in the ritual of Mass.

When Chris Farley stars in his own movie, *Tommy Boy,* he'll set the first ten minutes at Marquette, in off-campus housing like my own, where a young person's dreams seemed—at the same time—distant but somehow inevitable.

\*    \*    \*

The doorbell rings in a rented beach house in Malibu. I'm sitting inside, consuming the Doritos and Diet Cokes I've just retrieved from a local strip mall, at the request of the French supermodel being photographed on a rented white horse on the beach. I'm here to write a story for the *Sports Illustrated* swimsuit issue, about this photo shoot, but I'm too self-conscious to do anything but run errands and sit inside and watch TV and wait for FedEx to deliver a lens for the fashion photographer who is running the show. When the bell rings, I open the door and find the FedEx man holding a package and proffering a clipboard for my signature. He looks at me—in my Minnesota Timberwolves cap—and smirks. Only then do I notice that the French swimsuit model has joined me in the doorframe, in a bikini, to see who's at the door and what he's delivering.

And I laugh, because the FedEx guy thinks I'm the home-owner, and the model is my girlfriend, and that I'm living a fourteen-year-old boy's dream in his kid sister's Barbie Malibu Dream House.

He's wrong in every particular but this: the job is one fourteen-year-old boy's dream, though there are many weeks when I sit in a baseball press box, surveying the crowd on a Friday night in Baltimore, and wish that I was among the twenty-four-year-olds in the seats drinking beer, not up here hammering out two thousand words on the Orioles. But at this point I'm a passenger on a bullet train. It's much easier to stay on than to jump off.

On the road four weeks out of every five, I return to New York long enough to file my $15,000 in monthly expenses. To

296 • NIGHTS IN WHITE CASTLE

pay off each staggering American Express bill, I get a cash advance in the Time & Life Building and walk it three blocks up Sixth Avenue to the Amex office inside the Hilton. Every month, the ritual is the same, my pockets filled with bricks of cash as I go "stompin' on the avenue by Radio City." When Steely Dan sang those words every night on the boom box between the beds in the room Tom and I used to share in South Brook, I didn't know it was an affirmation.

I walk north, green lights all the way up Sixth Avenue to Central Park, where the city appears to end abruptly at the edge of an uncharted wilderness, the great unknown.

In the vestibule of my apartment building, where my subterranean room holds all my possessions, I collect my mail. In it, a postcard. On it, two aerial photographs of a cloverleaf freeway interchange. I recognize the image immediately as the western terminus of the Strip in Bloomington, even before I see the yellow letters: METRO AREA 494 STRIP. Quite why anyone would manufacture this postcard, or anyone would buy it, is a mystery. But I know why the sender sent it. Because she knows this was the boulevard of my adolescent dreams.

On the reverse of the postcard, a caption: "Aerial view of two of the interchanges of the Metro area's I-494 in Bloomington, Minnesota." Beneath that is a message in gorgeous cursive: "Dear Steve, Having a great time. Wish you were here. Thought you would like to keep this on your desk as a reminder of this garden spot. Love, Mom."

She knows that I'm on my way, as a writer if not quite as a grown-up. And I know that she knows this because she has added a PS:

"Books on way tomorrow."

# 15

# Nothing but Flowers

Readers of my previous book, *Sting-Ray Afternoons*, will know that Mom died on September 5, 1991, of a swift-moving disease that left the remaining six of us bereft in the driveway at 2809 West 96th Street in Bloomington. I had been awakened before dawn by a phone call in the Marriott on Michigan Avenue in Chicago, where I was staying to write about the White Sox. The next month, the Twins won the 1991 World Series, and I wrote the story for *SI* overnight, while staying in the basement of my childhood home, in front of the basement TV where I first tried to catch a split second of scrambled nudity when cable came to South Brook.

"You're the guy from Kennedy," Kent Hrbek said to me in the Twins' clubhouse.

Dad by then was a senior executive at Mickey Mining, in his fourth decade at the company. When any musical artist that recorded on Scotch brand tape achieved a significant sales milestone, their record label or engineers often sent

Dad a plaque by way of thanks. Dad had never heard of—much less listened to—any of these bands (nor any bands at all), but he occasionally brought home one of these plaques from work and asked at holidays if we were familiar with the "artists" paying tribute to him and his colleagues at Mickey Mining.

"Ever heard of..." he'd say, squinting down through his bifocals at an engraved brass plate.

"Bytches with Problems?" I'd say, reading the inscription. "You've been given an award by the Rodgers and Hammerstein of explicit female rap."

"So you *have* heard of them."

He also received a plaque, never displayed in the office, commemorating the platinum status of MC Ren's EP *Kizz My Black Azz.*

By then, Dad was living alone in the house in South Brook, though we all still gathered at holidays. That first Christmas after Mom died, all of us—except John, who was playing hockey for Notre Dame—took Dad to Hawaii, to escape Minnesota. Another Christmas, we went to Palm Desert, California, home to a strip mall called the Beer Hunter, which had hundreds of exotic beers from around the world in cans, bottles, and corked earthen jugs. Dad sat at the bar, examined the offerings, and told the bartender to bring him a succession of beers in increasingly larger containers, so that at the end of the night his empties appeared to be a lineup of Russian nesting dolls. One of the Rushin boys acted as a designated driver that night, and was urged by his brothers on the ride back to our rented house to give someone a "lawn job." He complied, driving up the curb and across a front yard. The next morning, we drove past the lawn we had violated the night before and—reflecting on the effort and resources required to grow a lush lawn in the desert—were overcome with remorse. But the larger point remained: whenever the Rushin children gather, for the rest of our lives, we will become who we were when we shared that house in South Brook—one redhead, four shitheads.

Likewise, I remained that same kid long into adulthood whenever I was around Flip Saunders, in whose backyard we contested the SHIT tournament. Flip went on to become the head coach of the Minnesota Timberwolves in the NBA, as well as the Detroit Pistons, Washington Wizards, and Timberwolves again. I met Flip for a drink one night after a Timberwolves game and he introduced me to his friend, the former Celtics forward Kevin McHale, whose games so enthralled and occasionally enraged me, Mike, and Ope on the Richie the C TV in Mike's basement. "I got Rush his job at *Sports Illustrated*," Flip said to McHale. And in a very real way he did, for if he hadn't invited us to play on his court, I never would have written to *SI* in the first place. In 2005, when his Pistons played in the NBA Finals and I received an award as National Sportswriter of the Year, Flip texted me: "We've come a long way from the SHIT." He was joking, because of course we hadn't come any distance at all: Flip was still trying to win a basketball tournament and I was still writing about it.

Flip died in 2015. On that day in 1984 when we watched Ryne Sandberg hit two home runs against the Cardinals on the NBC *Game of the Week*, Flip had vowed to name his firstborn after the Cubs' second baseman. Two years later,

Flip and Debbie Saunders had a son. Ryan Saunders—close enough—is now an NBA coach like his father.

Jane Bachman "Bambi" Wulf, who even more than Flip was responsible for getting me my job at *Sports Illustrated*—on faith, over the phone, never having met me—died in 2017. At her memorial service in Larchmont, New York, dozens of writers shared stories similar to my own, of being hired on a merit that was evident only to Bambi. Her obituary in *Sports Illustrated* stated, with a fact-checked accuracy that would have made her proud: "Perhaps no person has done more to promote the careers of sportswriters in the U.S. over the last 40 years than she did." Among her charges were my first friends at the magazine, Sally Guard and Merrell Noden, both of whom died too young. I think of them whenever I have a beer (Merrell) or bologna sandwich (Sally).

Bambi hired me largely on the word of Alex Wolff. His enthusiastic reply to a kid who wrote him a letter about a basketball tournament in a Bloomington backyard was one of hundreds of similar letters he wrote to aspiring journalists over the decades. Alex was honored by the Naismith Memorial Basketball Hall of Fame in 2011 for his "significant contribution to the game of basketball," not the least of which was his *In-Your-Face Basketball Book,* whose co-author—Chuck Wielgus—became the boss of USA Swimming, whose athletes won 156 Olympic medals during his tenure.

Alex went on to write a book about basketball around the globe. Among the many players and innovators he profiled in *Big Game, Small World* was the itinerant coach of a professional team in Poland. His name was—still is— Mike McCollow. Mike has coached college and professional basketball in North America and abroad, including with Flip Saunders in the Continental Basketball Association. One night in New York, where he was advance scouting for the Toronto Raptors of the NBA, I met him for a drink and we recalled the last time we were both in New York together: at Alex Wolff's apartment in the summer of 1988, when our nights-in-White-Castle dreams were just taking shape, and I marveled at a real writer's real computer.

Speaking of computers: despite its memorable 1984 commercial, Apple did not free the world from the tyranny of looking at a screen. On the contrary.

Fortunately, we can still look at books unmediated by a pane of glass. In 1986, the chain of B. Dalton Booksellers was sold to a company named sixty-nine years earlier for partners William Barnes and Clifford Noble. In acquiring B. Dalton, Barnes & Noble instantly became the second largest bookseller in the U.S., on its way to superstore status.

Ramshackle Renaissance Books, a superstore in my estimation, was shut down by the city of Milwaukee, which cited the building's "structural problems." Long after the humans had left, thousands of books remained inside, like the sunken treasures of a wrecked ship. Radio Doctors of Milwaukee went the way of all record stores. But the Ambassador Hotel was purchased by a Marquette alumnus and restored to its former glory as an art-deco jewel. I've stayed in it several times on visits to Marquette, whose surrounding streets are almost unrecognizable. A decades-long campaign to revitalize the nearby blocks has made the campus safer. In the process, the Avalanche bar succumbed to the wrecking ball, prompting almost all of its patrons to ask, "How could you tell?"

The same was said of McCormick Hall, torn down in 2019. It was replaced by a state-of-the-art residence hall called the Commons. I returned to Marquette in 2007 to deliver the commencement address. I told the Class of '07, nineteen years after William Rehnquist spoke to the Class of '88, just prior to my Golden Handshake, that I once ate chimichangas out of a parking lot mud puddle there.

Three years later, the Minnesota Twins moved out of the Metrodome to play home games outdoors for the first time since they left Bloomington twenty-eight years earlier. Outside gate 14 at Target Field is a bronze statue of number 14, Kent Hrbek, running the bases with his arms extended in triumph after hitting that grand slam in Game 6 of the 1987 World Series. He still lives in Bloomington, a corner of which will forever be the People's Republic of Hrbekistan.

When I go to Twins games now, or anywhere else in the Twin Cities, I have the unsettling sensation of entering my house at night to find the furniture was replaced in my absence. This is especially true of Bloomington. In the 1980s, twin calamities—bankruptcy, bulldozing—befell the Carlton Celebrity Room, where Exile will never again appear at the Backstage disco to sing, "I wanna kiss you all over."

The Carlton site was subsumed into Bloomington's next claim to national relevance: the Mall of America. Met Stadium and Met Center were also torn down to make room for the nation's largest shopping center. In 1993, the Minnesota North Stars moved to Dallas, where they dropped the "North" from their name. But if you visit the Mall of America now, you just might hear the faint echo of a seventeen-year-old boy meekly stage-whispering: "Pop-CAWN! Getcha pop-CAWN HEAH!"

Near the other end of the Strip, Wally McCarthy's Lindahl Olds has vanished, along with its free Saturday morning hot dogs, and in its stead stands the world headquarters of the Best Buy Company, itself an endangered bricks-and-mortar species, with scarcely an inch of magnetic tape—audio or video—for sale.

One night in 2018, Dad said to me on the phone, "It seems hard to believe that everything I sold—eight-track tapes, audiocassettes, videocassettes, the whole business I was in for thirty-eight years—just disappeared."

"Dad," I replied. "I'm a magazine writer. I understand."

*Sports Illustrated* moved out of the Time & Life Building in 2015, to smaller offices near the former site of the World Trade Center. The Time & Life Building is perhaps now best known as the fictional offices of Sterling Cooper & Partners, the ad agency employing Don Draper in the television series *Mad Men*.

Happily, the White Castle still stands on Lyndale Avenue in Bloomington, though it is no longer bookended by Beanie's Arcade and Lyn-Del Lanes. The Chinese restaurant and bar is still thriving across the street, however, its great red neon sign spelling out DAVID FONG's in a font familiar from a hundred strip-mall kung fu studio windows.

As for the rest of our former haunts, most are long gone, as are many of the joints that made the Strip so alluring to a teenager. Even now I can't drive down 494 without hearing the Talking Heads song "(Nothing but) Flowers," released in 1988, the year of the Golden Handshake, when David Byrne sang unhappily about a world—post-cataclysmic?—that has reverted to the so-called beauty of nature: "I miss the honky tonks, Dairy Queens, and 7-Elevens."

One honky-tonk that remains, albeit in New York, is an ancient bar called the Dublin House. Its great neon harp is a pink-and-green beacon on West 79th Street. The British writer and restaurant critic A. A. Gill extolled the virtues of the Dublin House in his memoir *Pour Me*. "It was everything I wanted from a pub: dark, old photos, red leather, cigarette smoke, purposeful, utilitarian, fit for its calling—a room to drink in," Gill wrote. "A long room, filled with generations of solitary thoughts. There was an old jukebox, and I'd sit at one end of the bar and drink glasses of dark Beck's with Wild Turkey chasers and smoke Lucky Strikes, a combination that has never been bettered in all drunkenness. I'd read the *New York Times* and the *Post* and the *New York Review of Books*. The barman, a third-generation Irish New Yorker who still nursed a discernible Dublin Northside brogue, was friendly but taciturn...That was probably the best—just there, that time."

I thought it was the best too. It was in the Dublin House on a May night in 2001 that I was introduced by chance to a woman at the end of the bar. She recognized my name and asked, "Didn't you write a column in *Sports Illustrated* making fun of women's basketball?"

Indeed, I had. My armpits ignited, because this woman, as I knew, was herself a famous basketball player. When she asked me how many women's basketball games I'd ever attended, I told her none. So Rebecca Lobo invited me to watch her play for the New York Liberty against the Los Angeles Sparks at Madison Square Garden. Silence—my default strategy in popcorn vending, and interviewing, and most other aspects of life—had once again paid off. With scarcely a spoken word, I had met my future wife.

We have four children now, and fly with them every summer to Minnesota, where I'm afforded an aerial view of Bloomington before landing. That vista always reminds me of the postcard Mom sent, just ahead of my books, of that bird's-eye view of the Strip. "Thought you would like to keep this on your desk," she wrote, all those years ago. And through every move, on every desk, the card has remained within arm's reach: "a reminder," as Mom wrote, "of this garden spot."

# Acknowledgments

When I wrote about a Minnesota boy who moved to New York and immersed himself in words, that proposal found its way to Phil Marino, a Minnesota boy who moved to New York and immersed himself in words. What luck. He edited the manuscript with grace and humor (and perhaps a touch of homesickness: he asked me to add more snow).

Many others at Little, Brown helped to make this book, including Karen Landry and Dianna Stirpe, who worked on its predecessor, *Sting-Ray Afternoons*. I am grateful again to Michael Pietsch and Reagan Arthur, as well as Elizabeth Gassman, Jessica Chun, and Juliana Horbachevsky. John Parsley, who edited *Sting-Ray*, now stands back, like a father, and watches that bicycle wobble on its further journeys.

Esther Newberg's enthusiasm for this idea and all the other ones I've ever had persuaded me that I could complete it. Esther said what every author wants to hear from his or her agent when writing against a deadline: "I'm sure they'll give you another month."

The Rushin family of South Brook—Jim Rushin, Tom Rushin, Dr. Amy Kolar, John Rushin, and our parents, Don and Jane Rushin—provided me with source material and permission to write about it. The residents of South Brook and the people of Bloomington have been exceptionally kind. My Minnesota friends, particularly Mike McCollow, Keith Opatz, and Dan Olson, shared their recollections.

I'm indebted for life to the teachers and faculty of Nativity of Mary, Bloomington Lincoln High School, Bloomington Kennedy High School, and Marquette University. Ring out ahoya to Mike Hodan, Mike Villafana, and Todd Larson. Dan DeWeerdt bears partial responsibility for the Smiths appearing in the preceding pages.

In addition to those mentioned in the book, I wish to thank colleagues past and present at *Sports Illustrated,* including Steve Cannella, Chris Stone, Greg Kelly, and Michael Jaffe.

My wife, Rebecca, and our children—Siobhan, Maeve, Thomas, and Rose—provide, among everything else in my life, a daily invitation to procrastinate. Without these five, my writing would be twice as fast and half as fun. I have told them that whatever my next book is about, the title should be *Enough About Me.*

# About the Author

Steve Rushin is the author of *Sting-Ray Afternoons,* which was named one of the Best Books of 2017 by Amazon. As a writer for *Sports Illustrated,* he is a four-time finalist for the National Magazine Award. His work has been anthologized in *The Best American Sports Writing, The Best American Travel Writing,* and *The Best American Magazine Writing* collections. His essays have appeared in *Time* magazine and the *New York Times.* He lives in Connecticut.

# Also by Steve Rushin

*Sting-Ray Afternoons: A Memoir*

"Magnificent...You will not read a better book this summer—and maybe well into the fall and winter, too."
—Mike Vaccaro, *New York Post*

"A fiercely funny memoir about family, sports, music, food, and fads."
—Priscilla Kipp, *BookPage*

*The 34-Ton Bat: The Story of Baseball as Told Through Bobbleheads, Cracker Jacks, Jockstraps, Eye Black, and 375 Other Strange and Unforgettable Objects*

"*The 34-Ton Bat* is full of bits of information that will give even the most knowledgeable fan a new understanding of baseball...Certain elements of the game will never seem quite the same after you read Rushin's book."
—Paul Dickson, *Wall Street Journal*